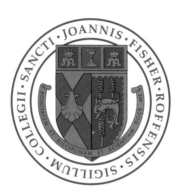

Lavery Library

St. John Fisher College
Rochester, New York

D1116626

The Shi'a of Lebanon

The Shi'a of Lebanon

Clans, Parties and Clerics

RODGER SHANAHAN

TAURIS ACADEMIC STUDIES
LONDON • NEW YORK

Published in 2005 by Tauris Academic Studies, an imprint of
I.B.Tauris & Co Ltd
6 Salem Road, London W2 4BU
175 Fifth Avenue, New York NY 10010
www.ibtauris.com

In the United States of America and Canada distributed by
Palgrave Macmillan a division of St. Martin's Press
175 Fifth Avenue, New York NY 10010

Copyright © 2005 Rodger Shanahan

The right of Rodger Shanahan to be identified as the author of this work
has been asserted by the author in accordance with the Copyright,
Designs and Patent Act 1988.

All rights reserved. Except for brief quotations in a review, this book, or
any part thereof, may not be reproduced, stored in or introduced into a
retrieval system, or transmitted, in any form or by any means, electronic,
mechanical, photocopying, recording or otherwise, without the prior
written permission of the publisher.

Library of Modern Middle East Studies 49
ISBN 1 85043 766 1
EAN 978 1 85043 766 6

A full CIP record for this book is available from the British Library
A full CIP record for this book is available from the Library of Congress

Library of Congress catalog card: available

Printed and bound in Great Britain by TJ International Ltd, Padstow,
Cornwall
Camera-ready copy edited and supplied by the author

Contents

List of Maps, Figures and Tables

Note on Transliteration

English transliteration of Arabic words follows the system used in the *International Journal of Middle East Studies*, which does not, due to technical limitations, include dots and microns. The only time I do *not* follow the system is when I quote directly from a written source, in which case I adopt the author's original spelling.

In general, my guiding principle has been to maintain consistency. This means, for example, that I use Hizbullah throughout, in preference to derivations such as *Hezbollah*, *Hizb'allah* and the like. In the case of family names, I have also tried to stay as close as possible to the original Arabic; so for example I use *Himadeh* rather than the better known *Hamadeh*, and *'Usayran* instead of the more common *Osseiran*. Where a family name begins with the definite article (Arabic: *al*; English: *the*), I retain only the Arabic, hence *al-As'ad* clan rather than the tautological *the al-As'ad* clan.

Acknowledgements

Many people assisted me during the production of this book. In particular I wish to thank Professor Ahmad Shboul, Chair of the Department of Arabic and Islamic Studies at the University of Sydney, for his guidance and advice, and Professor Stephanie Fahey Director of the Research Institute for Asia and the Pacific, for the use of the Institute's facilities and for its financial support. In Beirut the staff of the Australian Embassy was outstanding in arranging interviews for me during my field trip in June 2001. Finally, the support of my wife Louise was invaluable, particularly as the writing of this book coincided with the birth of our second child.

Figure 1. The Shi'a Imams

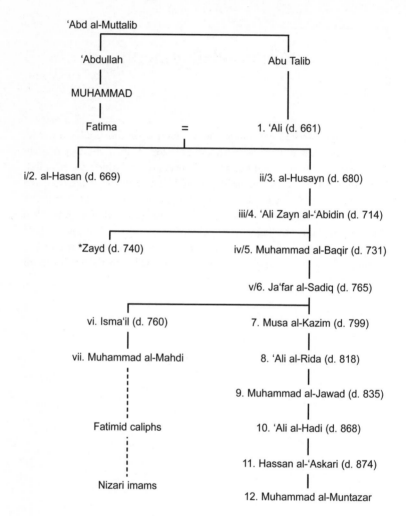

*Recognised as *imam* by the Zaydis.

Arabic numerals indicate the line of succession recognised by the 'Twelver' Shi'a.

Roman numerals indicate the line recognised by the Isma'ilis.

Source: Hourani, *History of the Arab Peoples*, London, Faber & Faber, p486.

Map 1. Traditional Districts of Mount Lebanon and their Relationship to Land Formations

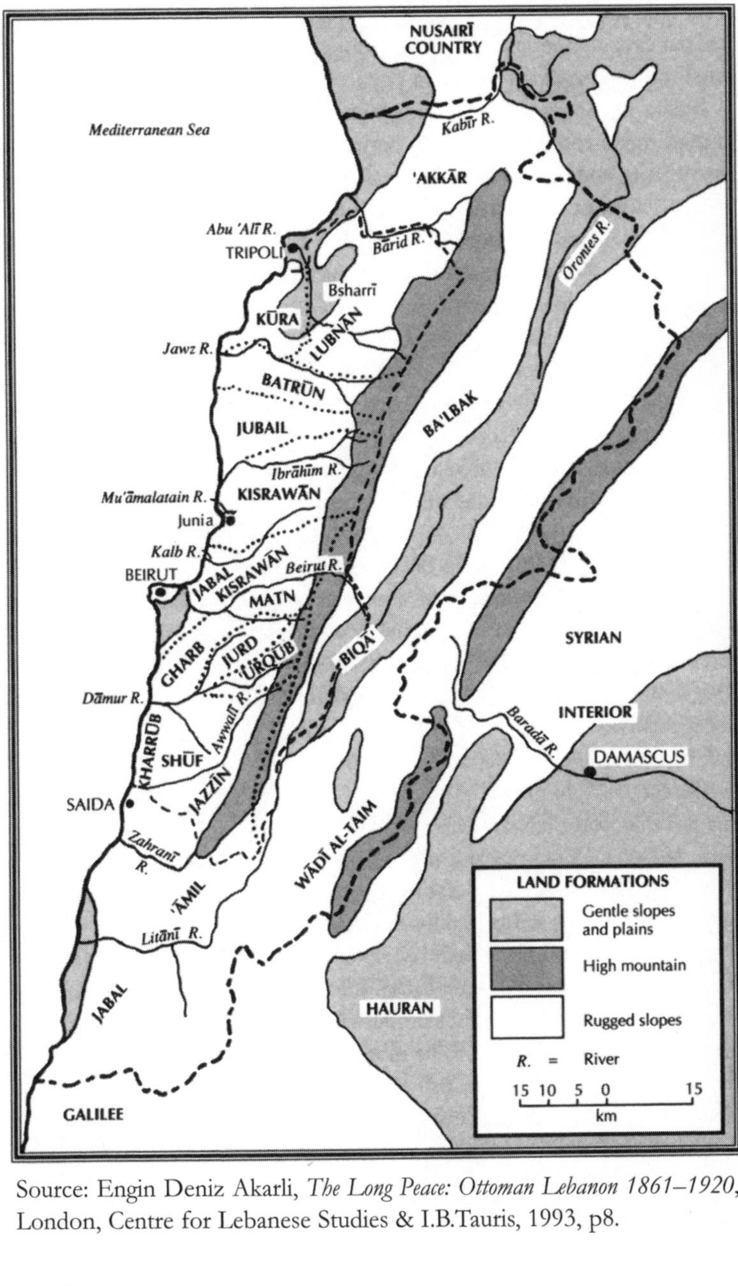

NUSAIRĪ
COUNTRY

Mediterranean Sea

Kabīr R.

'AKKĀR

Abu 'Alī R.

TRIPOLI

Bārid R.

Orontes R.

Bsharrī

KŪRA

LUBNĀN

Jawz R.

BATRŪN

JUBAIL

BA'LBAK

Ibrāhīm R.

Mu'āmalatain R.

KISRAWĀN

Junia

Kalb R.

BEIRUT

Beirut R.

JABAL KISRAWĀN

MATN

SYRIAN

GHARB

JURD

'URQŪB

BIQĀ'

Dāmur R.

INTERIOR

Awwalī R.

Baradā R.

DAMASCUS

KHARRŪB

SHŪF

JAZZĪN

SAIDA

Zahranī R.

'ĀMIL

WĀDĪ AL-TAIM

Litānī R.

JABAL

HAURAN

GALILEE

LAND FORMATIONS

Gentle slopes and plains

High mountain

Rugged slopes

R. = River

15 10 5 0   15

km

Source: Engin Deniz Akarli, *The Long Peace: Ottoman Lebanon 1861–1920*, London, Centre for Lebanese Studies & I.B.Tauris, 1993, p8.

Introduction

The struggle for political empowerment by ethnic and religious communities is a recurring theme in the history of the Middle East. The creation of states whose political boundaries, drawn up after the end of the First World War, are largely artificial, has led to the situation in which societal elements with varying degrees of affinity for the state they inhabit have struggled for equal recognition in its political system. This is illustrated by the situation confronting the Kurds in Turkey, Iraq, Iran and Syria, and the Shi'a Muslims in Iraq, Bahrain and other countries. The question of political participation by ethnic or religious communities in Middle Eastern states is of critical importance in determining the region's future direction. At the moment, and increasingly in the years to come, demographic realities will pressure governments to give these communities greater political representation. At the same time, entrenched political systems perpetuated by the ruling elite will present considerable obstacles to accomplishing this. Nowhere is this more the case than in Lebanon, a country whose borders are amongst the most artificial of all the Middle Eastern states' and which accommodates communities from many of the region's religious groupings. The political accommodation of these communities is such a fundamental issue in Lebanon that parliamentary representation is allocated on the basis of religious affiliation. Although this system was established to meet the demands of a multi-confessional population, its inability to take into account changing demographics (particularly the expanding Shi'a population) has made the state inherently weak. Added to this is Lebanon's dual burden of being host to hundreds of thousands of Palestinian refugees and having the southern part of the country under Israeli occupation for nearly twenty years. For the purposes of examining how political consciousness develops amongst communal groups, we find in Lebanon, with its combination of a unique political system and the experience of a major crisis in the absence of civil society during the 1975–90 civil war, a case study worthy of further attention.

Of all the aspects of Lebanese politics, perhaps the most interesting is that of the political development of the Shi'a. Historically the Shi'a, as a branch of Islam, have been politically marginalised amongst the Arabs of Iraq, Lebanon, Kuwait, Saudi Arabia and Bahrain. It is only in Persian Iran that they find themselves the dominant group, although this is beginning to change in post-invasion Iraq. The manner in which the Shi'a have adapted to these straitened circumstances, and continue to do so, is important to the future stability of the countries in which they live as well as to the region as a whole.

The question of Shi'a political development first gained widespread attention during the events surrounding Ayatollah Khumayni's rise to power in Iran in 1979. The nature of the Iranian revolution, as well as the prominent political positions held by the clerics, served to stereotype the Shi'a in the eyes of many. The popular view of Shi'a political activism became one of confrontation, with the participation of members of the clergy a central feature. This view has been further reinforced by the political and military successes of Hizbullah in Lebanon and more recently of some Shi'a political groups in Iraq. But the reality of Shi'a political development is more complex than this simple view of cleric-led confrontation, and it needs to be examined in the context of each country's unique societal makeup.

The political development of the Shi'a is not an issue that has traditionally captured much scholarly attention, although in the aftermath of the Iranian revolution there was significant academic interest in Iran's Shi'a community. Currently, however, Shi'a political development has once again caught the interest of a wider audience. The US-led invasion of Iraq has given the Iraqi Shi'a an opportunity to turn their numerical superiority into political power. And in the Kingdom of Saudi Arabia, where the Shi'a, estimated at ten per cent of the population, are concentrated in the oil-rich Eastern province, their potential political influence has been demonstrated in recent municipal elections.

In the case of Lebanon there has been an upsurge of academic interest since the 1980s, although this has focused nearly exclusively on Hizbullah and, to a lesser extent, Amal. There has been a number of reasons for this narrow focus: the dominance of a few leading political families; a concentration on the chaotic civil war, making research on a single community a peripheral and somewhat dangerous affair; and the relatively recent establishment of the Lebanese Republic, which has made it difficult to undertake any long-term study of the community's political development.

Until recently, the Shi'a have been the most politically quiescent of Lebanon's religious communities. Under-represented politically throughout their history, they have struggled to make an impression against the dominance of their Sunni Muslim and Christian countrymen; and although they have been included in the makeup of Lebanon's political institutions, it has normally been in such small numbers as to be of little more than symbolic utility. The political representation that the economically and socially disadvantaged Shi'a population did achieve resulted in little, if any, improvement in their living standards, nor did it result in the building of state infrastructure in those areas of Lebanon most heavily populated by the Shi'a. Instead, the Shi'a have been very much subordinated to the traditional power brokers in Lebanese society – the powerful familial heads, or *zu'ama*. This small number of families virtually monopolised formal political power and, within their own territory, acted as a *de facto* government authority.

That is not to say there was *no* political activity outside the traditional patron-client relationships the *zu'ama* controlled. Large-scale politicisation independent of these traditional Lebanese powerbrokers began in the 1960s with the emergence amongst elements of the Shi'a of a more politically militant attitude. Leftist political parties, active since the 1930s, began to attract the Shi'a, who saw in them a way of changing the existing, discriminatory political order. Others found inspiration from a group of activist clergy who had been heavily influenced during their religious studies at Najaf (in Iraq) by the teachings of leading Shi'a scholars such as Muhammad Baqir as-Sadr and others. These clerics advocated the view that Islamic jurists should provide temporal leadership to the community of believers, and they were willing to put this view into action. The emergence of these alternative centres of political leadership, combined with socio-economic forces that led many Shi'a to move to Beirut from their traditional homes, meant that there was a gradual shift away from the traditional patron-client relationship that had for so long consigned them to a life of political subservience.

The beginning of large-scale politicisation of Lebanese Shi'a in the 1960s highlights, against a backdrop of continued dominance by the traditional clan leadership group (*zu'ama*), the Shi'a's relatively diverse approach to the notion of political advancement. Of particular note in the Shi'a experience is the degree to which their political empowerment owed its beginnings to events that began outside the country. External influences were so significant due largely to the proximity of Syria, as a result of which branches of political parties formed initially in Syria were then established in Lebanon, and because traditional political structures were so much a part of the Lebanese consciousness that indigenous political groupings found it difficult to develop independently. Amal,[1] for instance, was founded by Musa al-Sadr, a scholar who, though of

Lebanese heritage, was Iranian by birth. The Islamic Da'wa party had its origins amongst the intellectual elite of the Iraqi clergy. And Hizbullah continues to owe considerable practical and ideological allegiance to its Iranian sponsor. Of the secular groups, both leftist and pan-Arab parties such as the Lebanese Communist Party or the Ba'th Party are offshoots of Syrian parent organisations. Yet despite the fact that these organisations are of external origin, they have nevertheless served as effective vehicles for advancing the Shi'a political cause in Lebanon.

This study focuses on the political development of the Shi'a from the creation of *Le Grand Liban* in 1920 until the last national elections in 2000. But to understand this development fully we must also devote some attention to the activities of the Shi'a prior to 1920. The first chapter of this study therefore provides some historical background to the evolution of a Shi'a political culture in Lebanon: how the community became established in what is now Lebanon, how the indigenous leadership and later institutions of governance developed, and what role the Shi'a had within them. Brief mention is also made of the 1932 census and the population movements of the 1960s – two events that had, and continue to have, a significant impact on the Lebanese Shi'a's political development. The next three chapters examine the main drivers in this development and the degree to which their influence has been maintained or degraded over the period in question. Chapter Two looks at the role of the the *zu'ama*, who were the established powerbrokers within Lebanon's Shi'a community. Since they were the mainstay of Shi'a political power for so long, it is essential, if we are to understand the manner in which competing centres of power within the community subsequently developed, to ascertain the extent to which the *zu'ama* maintained or lost their influence and power in this period. The next two chapters examine the roles that two alternative loci of power played in developing a Shi'a political consciousness: the political parties (Chapter Three) and the clerics (Chapter Four). Chapter Three discusses Shi'a participation in the early manifestations of political parties prior to and during independence, as well as the Shi'a's subsequent attraction to Syrian and Arab nationalist parties and later the radical leftist parties. It was not until the civil war of 1975 that identifiably Shi'a-based parties such as Amal and then Hizbullah emerged, first as militias and later as fully-fledged political parties. Chapter Four deals with the role of the Shi'a clerics in the community's political development. In Hizbullah the high profile that the clergy enjoys in the Iranian political system has been replicated in certain ways. But the clergy's contribution overall has been, and remains, much more substantial than a presence in a single political party. The unique relationship in the Shi'a tradition between the *'ulama* and the community of believers (*umma*) has meant there has always been the (largely unrealised) potential for the clergy to play a significant leadership role. Chapter Four looks at the types of political role the *'ulama* have played and that have subsequently shaped their political contributions. It also examines the historical background to Shi'a Muslim scholarship and Lebanon's place within it. Particular emphasis is given to the manner in which external stimuli shaped how the clergy saw themselves as being either part of, or separate from, the political process.

Literature – particularly in English – about the historical development of the Lebanese Shi'a can best be described as patchy. A paucity of written records, and the relatively minor political role played by the Shi'a until recently, has meant that the community generally rates only a passing mention as one of the less relevant players on the Lebanese political scene. What literature there is on the politicisation of the Lebanese Shi'a focuses mainly on the contributions made by Amal and Hizbullah rather than on the political activities of Shi'a outside these groups. This perhaps reflects the high profile of Hizbullah in particular, and the fact that Western audiences are more interested in their activities. Whilst significant work has been done on the history and organisation of Hizbullah (less so for Amal), there has been no examination of its performance within the formal Lebanese political system. Similar difficulties arise in the treatment of Shi'a involvement in secular political parties and the political activities of Shi'a *zu'ama*. Arnold Hottinger has written the only dedicated English language work on the Lebanese *zu'ama*, although his article deals with *zu'ama* from all communities. While it is a good study of the concept of the *za'im* in Lebanese society, a coherent examination of the development of the Shi'a *zu'ama* must nevertheless rely on information from a variety of other primary and secondary sources. As for the role played by the Shi'a of Lebanon in secular political organisations, precious little work has been done. This is in contrast with studies of Shi'a political participation in other countries, which do provide such data; for example, Hanna Batatu's 1978 work *The Old Social Classes and the Revolutionary Movements of Iraq* provides a valuable breakdown by religious affiliation of members of the Iraqi Ba'th and Communist parties.

Extant studies of Lebanese Shi'a political development can be divided into three broad categories: general works on Lebanese political history that include references to the Shi'a; works on activist Shi'a Islam in general (often with a section on Lebanon); and works about particular elements of Lebanese Shi'a political activism, be they studies of Hizbullah or the development of Amal. Of English language material on these subjects, a larger collection exists than may at first be realised; there are also some studies and journal articles in French. Whilst I have not directly quoted Arabic language material in this study, I have used translations of the source material where appropriate. Much contemporary primary source material is available in English. Some of the material, such as interviews, has been translated from its original Arabic. Additional material was acquired through interviews conducted with the aid of an interpreter.

Primary source material for this study came from three main areas. For some of the early (pre-independence) political personalities, Walter L. Browne's excellent collection of United States consular dispatches from the 1920s to the 1950s provides an external source of information largely devoid of the communal subjectivity that may colour the views of local authors. This is not to say that the dispatches are without their own, foreign bias. More contemporary insights into the thinking of leading Shi'a political figures were sourced from interviews that had either been translated from their original Arabic or published in English-language newspapers, magazines or journals. Muhammad Fadlallah and Hassan Nasrallah, in particular, are two significant Shi'a figures who have been willing to give interviews to a wide range of media over many years. Similarly, speeches from some political figures are often available on the website of the organisation they represent. The accounts of parliamentary speeches given by Hizbullah deputies that are referred to in this book have been translated from their original Arabic (from the 1992-1996 volumes of the *mahadir majlis al-nuwwab*) into French and then into English. Perhaps the most worthwhile primary source is the series of interviews I conducted with several Shi'a political figures during field research in June 2002. These interviews provided information that could never have been obtained from existing published sources in either Arabic or English.

A criticism of the general historical studies of modern Lebanon is that they generally neglect to examine in any depth the political activities of the Shi'a. This is principally because the Shi'a were marginalised for much of the republic's history. But there is another reason: many historical studies of modern-day Lebanon have been written to reinforce the idea, prevalent amongst Western scholars, that Lebanon is essentially Christian. Consequently, accounts of Mount Lebanon focus on the region's Maronite history at the expense of its Muslim. A good example of this pro-Maronite bias can be found in a comment by Iliya Harik in his 1968 book *Politics and Change in a Traditional Society: Lebanon 1711-1845*. He notes that when Shi'a rule in the north was replaced by that of the Shihabs, 'the *Matawilah* [a derogatory name for the Shi'a] there were crushed and the industrious and law-abiding Maronites were encouraged to replace them in Kisrwan.'[2]

One of the benefits of a study such as this is that it provides a much-needed update on the state of Shi'a political development. Many of the major works on Lebanese history and politics such as Kamal Salibi's *Crossroads to Civil War* (1976) and Michael Hudson's *The Precarious Republic* (1968) were written more than a quarter of a century ago. Even the more recent works by Augustus Richard Norton and Fouad Ajami were both written in 1987, well before the end of the civil war. Much has happened since that time, both to the Lebanese Shi'a and to Shi'a in other countries in the region. This study presents a more contemporary picture of the Shi'a, a picture of an increasingly complex political phenomenon. This is important to our understanding of where the community is now. It is also necessary if, for a region very likely to experience considerable political change, we are to have any chance of predicting where that community will be in the future.

1

The Shi'a and Lebanon

The Emergence of a Shi'a Identity: Historical Background

That the Islamic community has developed along two closely related yet distinct paths – Sunni and Shi'a – is well known if not well understood. The causes of the split and the conflicts that ensued bestowed upon the followers of each branch of the religion distinctive characteristics that have set them apart until the present day. Given that the disagreement concerned the relative strengths of the claims of those who sought to be the successor (*caliph*) to Muhammad, and that this successor would be leader of the nascent Muslim community (*umma*), the disagreement was as much about temporal power as it was about spiritual leadership.

The man elected to the position of caliph was the Prophet's uncle and close companion, Abu Bakr. His rival, 'Ali, Muhammad's cousin and son-in-law, did nevertheless receive considerable support from the *Banu* Hashim (Muhammad's immediate clan) and from other Muslims. Those who believed that 'Ali and his descendants were the legitimate successors came to be referred to as 'partisans of 'Ali' (*Shi'at 'Ali*). As for 'Ali himself, although he did eventually give his allegiance to Abu Bakr and to the second caliph, 'Umar, – there is no evidence that he did so to the third caliph, 'Uthman – he did not, however, recognise any of the precedents set by these first three caliphs on matters of jurisprudence.[1] This was to influence greatly the development of separate Shi'a and Sunni schools of law. Whilst 'Ali must have believed that he was the Prophet's rightful successor, there is no evidence that he actively agitated against the early caliphs. Rather, he is regarded largely as a quietist opposition leader, a stance adopted also by some of his own successors, and one which helped define Shi'a political attitudes for many centuries.

At this point in Islam's development it would be inaccurate to speak of Shi'a and Sunni Muslims. Neither group had developed to any degree the features of their separate traditions, such as juridical institutions or adherence to the familial chain of succession from the Prophet. They became more differentiated, however, under the leadership of the third caliph, 'Uthman. 'Uthman was of the *Banu* Umayya who, as traditional rivals of the Hashim, sought to dominate the rapidly expanding Muslim empire. The emergence of the Umayyad dynasty and of the opposition it provoked within parts of the empire, served to crystallise Shi'a attitudes and led to the martyrdom of Husayn (680 CE), the most emotive event in Shi'a history.

'Ali was eventually to become the fourth caliph, after 'Uthman died violently at the hands of aggrieved members of the Arab army in Egypt. Of more importance to Shi'a history, however, was the belief amongst 'Ali's supporters that he was the *first* caliph to combine both the spiritual and dynastic principles of succession. This distinction is critical: it is the basis of the Shi'a notion of the *Imamate*, with 'Ali being the first *Imam*. Although in general the term *imam* denotes a prayer leader, it has a special meaning for the Shi'a which includes the idea of the Imam as a spiritual and political authority. This belief in the Imam as sole legitimate authority, 'by virtue of his being an infallible leader and authoritative interpreter of Islamic revelation, and therefore qualified to establish the Islamic state',[2] was not enunciated until the Imamate of Ja'far as-Sadiq (731–765 CE). As-Sadiq is credited with articulating the principle of divine designation (*nass*), according to which a new Imam would be 'divinely designated' by his predecessor, so long as this chain could be traced back to the first Imam, 'Ali; in addition, the Imam would be the exclusive authoritative source of religious knowledge and the sole diviner of the correct path for people to follow in their lives. According to the Twelver Shi'a tradition, 'Ali was the first imam and was followed by eleven more, ending with the Twelfth Imam Muhammad al-Muntazar (the Awaited One), who went into occultation (*ghayba*) in the ninth century CE.[3] There are also Isma'ili and Zaydi Shi'a traditions. These are distinguished largely by the different paths of succession they follow (see the diagram on page xi).

Another central feature in the development of a Shi'a politico-religious consciousness was the celebration of martyrdom (*shahada*) in the pursuit of a just Islamic order when the community was faced with political oppression. This is exemplified by the death at Karbala of 'Ali's second son, Husayn (the Third Imam in the Shi'a tradition). When the Umayyad caliph denied Husayn the temporal authority which the Shi'a considered to be the Imam's by divine right,[4] his death at the hands of the Umayyad 'usurpers' was seen as a noble act of direct political action against an illegitimate head of the Muslim community. For the nascent followers of 'Ali, the death of Husayn and his supporters at Karbala resulted in, as Jafri puts it, the 'consolidation of the Shi'i identity.' Jafri explains:

> The fate of Husayn was destined to become the most effective agent in the propagation and comparatively rapid spread of Shi'ism. It is also undoubtedly true that the tragedy added to Shi'i Islam an element of 'passion'...[that] becomes a feature of the Shi'is.[5]

Husayn's one surviving son, 'Ali Zayn al-'Abidin adopted a quietist approach to political leadership, most likely as a result of his father's martyrdom in battle against a caliph he believed illegitimate. Yet many supporters of 'Ali's family were attracted to Shi'a leaders who actively opposed the Umayyads – Muhammad Ibn al-Hanafiya, for example, another of 'Ali's sons (to a wife other than Fatima). Such splintering was to occur periodically throughout the Shi'a community's development until a 'mainstream' philosophy had evolved. This philosophy was to be the Twelver Shi'a model, based on the succession of 'Ali Zayn al-'Abidin. It became Shi'a Islam's dominant branch, and it forms the subject of this study. One of its characteristics is that Zayn al-'Abidin's successors continued to adopt his relatively quiescent approach to political issues, in contrast to that of the other claimants to the leadership of the 'Alid followers. Eventually the more activist Shi'a claimants were displaced by the *Banu* al-'Abbas, who in turn led the agitation that brought about the Umayyad rulers' downfall. The *Banu* al-'Abbas established the 'Abbasid caliphate (750–1258 CE), whose caliphs eventually assimilated many of the other factional Islamic communities into what became a state-sanctioned view of Islam. As Jafri notes:

> the very policy of quiescence caused them [Zayn al-'Abidin's followers] to be overshadowed by other activist members of the family; at the same time, through this very policy, they in the long run survived as the Imams and

emerged as the recognised leaders of the future majority group of the Shi'a.[6]

Successive Imams, who effectively advocated that activism should await the most propitious conditions before seeking to establish the legitimate and just leadership that had been divinely ordained, continued this policy of political quiescence. This made sense inasmuch as activist struggles against 'illegitimate' rulers had not to date advanced the Shi'a cause. In this context the occultation (*ghayba*) of the Twelfth Imam functions as a divine act designed to save the Shi'a Imamate by, as it were, removing the Imam from the temporal sphere. The belief in *ghayba* and the awaited return of the Twelfth Imam to establish the rule of justice, is therefore often understood as justification for the Shi'a's continued political quietism, but equally it can be interpreted as justification for their activism. As Sachedina writes:

> It [*ghayba*] has been the guiding doctrine both behind an activist political posture, calling upon believers to remain alert and be prepared at all times to launch the revolution with the Mahdi who might appear at any time, and a quietist posture waiting for God's decree, in almost fatalistic resignation, in the matter of the return of the Imam at the End of Time.[7]

This contradiction has been a central feature of theological disagreement among Shi'a clerics, and it has significantly influenced Shi'a political development.

The 'Abbasids consolidated their rule from the eighth century CE, ensuring that their claims to both spiritual and temporal leadership of the community were recognised. Yet the Shi'a's different interpretation of the path of succession from the Prophet stood as a threat to the 'Abbasid caliphate's legitimacy. To counter this threat, the ninth century 'Abbasid caliph, al-Mutawakkil (847-61 CE), formally established what have become the tenets of orthodox Islam. The followers of this orthodoxy came to be known as Sunni.[8] All those now regarded as heterodox Muslims (including Shi'a) came to be considered dissenters and were subject to varying degrees of persecution by their orthodox rulers. If the concept of *ghayba* was ambiguous and could be understood to promote activism *or* quietism, al-Mutawakkil's actions unequivocally gave the Shi‘a a compelling reason to refrain from overt political action.

Mindful of the relatively weak position of minority Shi‘a populations in largely Sunni Muslim communities, some Shi‘a jurists strove to ensure their community's survival by advocating a form of political, and even spiritual, quietism through what is known as 'precautionary dissimulation' (*taqiyya*). Taqiyya sought to 'shield the true intent of the faithful community from non-believers and outsiders'.[9] In its most extreme form, it permitted Shi‘a to hide the fact that they were followers of a heterodox branch of Islam; so during times when heterodox sects were being persecuted, the practice of *taqiyya* ensured that the Shi‘a communities survived. This in turn enabled the conditions that would allow the Shi‘a to establish their ideal Islamic polity when the Twelfth Imam reappeared. *Taqiyya*, then, provided a juridical caveat against the premature development and promotion of a distinctly Shi‘a political agenda.

Establishment of the Shi‘a in Lebanon

The paucity of written records means the exact date when Twelver Shi‘a Islam was established in modern-day Lebanon remains open to conjecture. Albert Hourani notes that, according to the oral tradition of Shi‘a scholars of South Lebanon, their community was founded by Abu Dharr, a Companion of the Prophet and a strong supporter of ‘Ali's claim to the caliphate;[10] Abu Dharr, after travelling from Medina to Damascus, was exiled to the rural districts of *Bilad ash-Sham* (Syria).[11] From this we may infer that Abu Dharr was instrumental in spreading the Shi‘a faith, although whether he did this alone or with the assistance of other Shi‘a immigrants who may have arrived with him is unclear. The motivation for such claims that link the establishment of the Shi‘a with someone as noteworthy as one of the Companions is not difficult to decipher: they are designed to substantiate the Lebanese Shi‘a community's religious authenticity. Early twentieth-century scholars, on the other hand, such as Phillip Hitti and Henri Lammens, claim that the Shi‘a's antecedents were Persian. But most Lebanese Shi‘a reject such claims, believing that they are designed to diminish the Arabic roots of their sect. More recent studies postulate that Shi‘a families in Lebanon today are descended from Yemenite tribes which migrated to the area sometime before the tenth century.[12] Rula Abisaab claims that South Arabian (Yemenite) tribes, such as the Twelver Shi‘a *Banu* Hamdan, were present in Jabal ‘Amil during the early centuries of Islam, and that the term *'Amil* was itself the name of a Yemenite tribe.[13] Clear evidence for this can be found in early Islamic historical and literary records; furthermore, the 'Amila tribes are known to have been politically active in the region during the Umayyad period (seventh and eighth centuries CE).

However Shi'a Islam was established, it is apparent from written records that by the tenth century Shi'a groups were widespread throughout Syria (including Lebanon, Palestine and East Jordan).[14] This happened in a period when the Shi'a temporarily dominated the region, although not as a unified community. The Isma'ili Shi'a Fatimid caliphate (908–1171 CE)[15] based in Cairo and the Persian Twelver Shi'a Buyids (932–1055 CE)[16] in Baghdad represent between them the apex of Shi'a political power. And in the same period, the Arab Emirate of the Hamdanids in northern Syria and upper Mesopotamia was known for its Shi'a sympathies. However, the rivalry between the Isma'ili and Twelver groups destroyed whatever hope there was for a unified Shi'a ruling dynasty. Interestingly, during the tenth and eleventh centuries Fatimid rule extended into much of what is now modern-day Lebanon.[17] It should be noted, however, that the Isma'ili caliphate of the Fatimids did not systematically impose its Shi'a beliefs on its subjects in Egypt.[18] It is fair to assume, then, that this also applied to the empire's other subjects, meaning that the presence of the Syrian Twelver Shi'a pre-dated the imposition of Fatimid rule.

The Shi'a were also present in large numbers in what is now Christian and Sunni northern Lebanon. Nasir i-Khusraw, a Persian philosopher-poet with Isma'ili-Fatimid sympathies, noted during his travels circa 1088 that Tripoli was mostly inhabited by Shi'a.[19] The sect's local dominance was also reflected in the fact that the Shi'a clan of *Banu 'Ammar* were governors of areas within the northern Levant (under Fatimid or Seljuk suzerainty) and were, it is claimed, pivotal in repelling attacks on Tripoli by the Crusaders in the early twelfth century.[20] It is also interesting to note the possibly sectarian tensions apparent during this resistance. The local sultan sought assistance from the Seljuk sultan in Baghdad, who declined to provide any support, and Tripoli eventually fell to the Crusaders. At the same time, the inhabitants of Tripoli petitioned the Fatimid rulers in Cairo for assistance. The Fatimids dispatched a fleet to assist, but by the time it reached Tyre, Tripoli had fallen.[21] It is difficult to blame the fall of Tripoli on the failure of the Sunni Seljuk leader to send help, but the lack of response may indicate that tensions between the sects were already sufficient to override notions of Islamic unity.

The coming of the Crusaders spelt an end to the widespread Shi'a presence in Syria. There is no evidence that the *Banu* 'Ammar, for example, retained any influence in the region after Tripoli fell. The losses suffered by the Shi'a at the hands of the Crusaders, as well as the fact that the Muslim resurgence and eventual expulsion of the Crusaders was led by Sunni Muslims (notably Saladin and later the Mamluk sultans), meant that the Shi'a of Syria declined in power and influence. This in turn exposed them to the domination of the orthodox Sunni Muslim dynasties that were to rule the region for the next 700 years. Salibi notes that by the end of the thirteenth century the Sunni Mamluk dynasty had begun a process, virtually amounting to a pogrom, that would see the contraction of the Shi'a presence within the region. In the north, the Shi'a of Jabal 'Akkar and Jabal al-Dinniya were overrun by the Mamluks from 1292 onwards and their populations either forcibly converted to Sunni Islam or dispersed and replaced by Sunnis.[22] The Kisrawan region of Mount Lebanon (also the former site of a large concentration of Shi'a) was conquered by the Mamluks in 1305;[23] the remaining Shi'a population dispersed, their place taken by Maronite settlers and Sunni Turkoman clans both of which the Mamluks brought in to settle and guard strategically important areas of the Syrian (Lebanese) hinterland.[24]

Despite this history of persecution, conversion and eviction by the Sunni Muslim majority, the Shi'a continued to dwell in significant numbers in two areas in particular, and they do so to this day: Jabal 'Amil, generally defined as the area bounded by the Awwali River to the north and Galilee to the south (see map on page xi); and the northern part of the Biqa' valley, particularly around the towns of Hermel and Ba'albak. These areas are not contiguous, and the Shi'a within each developed their own distinctive characteristics. A more sedentary life was lived by the Shi'a of Jabal 'Amil, most working the fields for the benefit of landowning families who in turn gave them protection and arbitrated their disputes: a feudal type of system. The Shi'a of the Biqa', on the other hand, were for hundreds of years a more nomadic and less rigidly defined society. They were not so dominated by a few landowning families but existed more as a series of clans, some of whom were considered more powerful than others and were paid allegiance accordingly.

Development of Leadership Systems in Lebanon

Any examination of the political history of modern Lebanon must take into account two key factors. First, the mandated borders that define the Lebanese Republic are highly artificial. Second, *traditional* cultures have had more political influence than *imported*.

The borders of modern-day Lebanon did not exist until the 1920s, when the French authorities, in consultation with the British, decided to create a new territory separate from Syria and Palestine. This new territory included Jabal 'Amil and the Biqa', the two areas with large Shi'a populations. Both these areas were for much of their histories administered separately. Under the *ajnad* system of the seventh to tenth centuries CE, the Biqa' lay in the *jund* of Damascus. It was again administered by Damascus in the Mamluk period, as part of the northern administrative division (*safaqa*).[25] Sur (Tyre), in the south, was governed from Acre during the Mamluk period;[26] it formed part of the mountain and coastal *safaqa* that comprised Palestine.[27] During the Crusades (1099–1291 CE), the Biqa' and Jabal 'Amil belonged to the County of Tripoli and the Kingdom of Jerusalem respectively. During the Ottoman era they were ruled, with differing degrees of authority, by the governors firstly of Damascus and then of Saida.[28] At the end of the eighteenth century the Biqa' came under the control of the *amirate* of Mount Lebanon. Mount Lebanon, also known simply as 'the Mountain', was regarded traditionally as the heart of Lebanon. The Shi'a's presence in the Mountain has already been noted; yet by the 1860s, due to emigration arising from persecution, displacement and their desire to settle in larger confessional groupings, they constituted less than six per cent of the Mountain's population.[29]

Arguably the most influential feature of the area that was to become modern Lebanon was the strength of traditional Arab ties of tribal loyalty. What Ibn Khaldun has referred to as *'asabiyya*, or 'kinship loyalty', has continued virtually unabated from its historical genesis in pre-Islamic times and has strongly influenced the political and social development of Lebanese from all communities. This means that families and clans are the units to which allegiance has traditionally been shown. Michael Hudson, writing in the 1960s, noted that '[t]he extended family is the basic political, as well as social, unit in Lebanon. This structure – patrilineal, patrilocal, patriarchal, and endogamous – comprises the power base of nearly all the important politicians in modern Lebanon.'[30] An even more complex web of power relationships dictates relations *between* families.

Incorporating 'an elaborate hierarchical code of obligations and inter-
woven into the larger social units of clan, village and tribe,' the family,
Hudson wrote, 'is the primary bulwark of the notable's local autonomy.'[31]
When these 'notables' combined their family power bases, they could
bring significant force to bear either to support or oppose forces seeking
to impose their will on the region. In Lebanese society today, despite the
development of a multi-party parliamentary political system and the
emergence of ideologically-based political groups, a number of families
still wield significant *informal* political power, although this is no longer as
strong as it was in its heyday.

Traditionally, dominant families derived power from their ownership
of land or from their social and political influence. In the Seljuk, Mamluk
and Ottoman eras, however, when external rule was imposed, more
formal systems of power came into place; and although there was no one
single system, all hinged upon economic control, whether through
owning land or by being given tax-raising responsibilities by the caliph's
representative. In this way, a form of feudal loyalty developed, particularly
between those who owned land and those who worked it; and this supple-
mented the influence of purely familial loyalties.

The system that evolved in Mount Lebanon is often referred to as the
iqta'. This has best been described as a system 'in which authority is
distributed among a number of autonomous hereditary aristocratic chiefs
subordinate in certain political respects to a common overlord.'[32] The
term *iqta'* was used widely, especially by the Buyids and the Seljuks, to
mean a grant of land for a limited tenure, either in lieu of a wage or sometimes in addition to it. These grants grew in size and in length of tenure
– some becoming hereditary – until they were indistinguishable from
provincial governorates, so that the term *iqta'* came to apply equally to the
land and to the political authority vested in it.[33] By Ottoman times,
someone who possessed an *iqta'* was referred to as a *muqata'ji*. The *iqta'*
system was dominant in the Mountain, but the Ottoman empire as a
whole had no such dominant organisational structure, so it is not possible
to identify a common system of land ownership and local political
authority in modern-day Lebanon. Nevertheless, for our purposes the
iqta' system will be referred to as the norm.

Another financial consideration that influenced areas of modern-day
Lebanon was the raising of taxes, a main concern of the Ottoman sultan.
The central feature of Ottoman tax collection was the basic annual tax,

the *miri*, collected by the Porte (Ottoman central government). Essential to this tax-collection procedure was the *iltizam*, in essence a tax-farming scheme where the responsibility for raising taxes within a province (*wilayat*) was sub-contracted out to a person known as a *multazim*. Although some sources refer only to the *multazim's* tax-raising authority,[34] some scholars argue that it was also a method of governance because the *multazim* was empowered to execute the law on behalf of the governor (*wali*).[35] The power and influence of such a position is obvious, and ambitious outsiders as well as local notables vied for it. Naturally, a *multazim* who lived amongst the people he was taxing tended to treat them better than did an outsider. As the *iltizam* could be a very short-term proposition, the *multazim* responsible for it tended to influence the locals far less than did a *muqata'ji*. Of particular relevance to the societal position of the Shi'a is the fact that, whereas the Mount Lebanon *iqta'* system was non-confessional, the *iltizam* system, which represented foreign (i.e. Ottoman) rather than indigenous interests, allowed only Sunni Muslims to bid for the position of *multazim*.[36]

The *multazim* ruled his region as a representative of the *wali* who had appointed him. The *wali* controlled the means of tax enforcement through his levy of troops. In contrast, the *muqata'ji* 'was a hereditary noble chief who enjoyed political authority over a *muqata'a*, the region over which his governmental rights extended.'[37] He was responsible for collecting the *miri*, for arming his subjects and leading them into battle, and for administering government in his *muqata'a*. As a result, he was also the one whom people expected to safeguard their rights. The reciprocal obligations inherent in this *iqta'* system suited the traditional social order of the Mountain, where differences in rank and status were normally established at one's birth and observed throughout one's life.

The *iqta'* system was hierarchical both vertically and horizontally. Patron-client relationships could be established between landowners and agricultural workers, whilst families had different degrees of influence depending on their wealth, history or the number of clients beholden to them. While all those eligible to be landowners or tax collectors were considered *muqata'jis* by dint of their regional responsibilities, there existed gradations in influence and title. The highest position was that of *amir*, the next that of *muqaddam*, and the lowest that of *shaykh*. The prince-governor (*al-Amir al-Hakim*) had the power to raise commoners to the nobility. He could not, however, officially strip *muqata'jis* of their power, although this was done in rare cases where the *muqata'ji* had become enfeebled politically or socially or had engaged in insurrection against the *amir*.

The Role of the Shi'a within the Indigenous Leadership

The area of Lebanon referred to as the Mountain developed a formalised local leadership culture based on the supremacy of *al-Amir al-Hakim*, which became known simply as the *amirate*. The *amirate* came to be dominated by the Druze (an offshoot of the Isma'ili community), who had a reputation both for the secrecy of their religious teachings and for their physical courage. Their skill as fighters enabled them to resist the imposition of Ottoman rule over the region of Mount Lebanon for a number of years. In 1593 CE, after they had maintained a protracted resistance, the Ottoman governor of Damascus recognised their independence by appointing a Druze chieftain, Fakhr al-Din bin Kormaz Ma'n, as *amir* (prince commander) of Saida.[38] Fakhr al-Din was the first person able to initiate in a formal sense the primacy of indigenous Lebanese leadership over a group of similarly powerful local families, and in the process began the Ma'ni leadership dynasty. As Albert Hourani noted of his legacy:

> 'he first created a close and permanent union of a number of hitherto separate lordships, and gave them a leadership that most of them recognised...[H]e created the political institutions around which Lebanon would eventually crystallise...the princedom.'[39]

The *amirate* system created by Fakhr al-Din relied on being able to reach internal agreements on issues as well as the ability to appease the governors of those Ottoman provinces such as Tripoli, Saida and Damascus who still possessed sufficient power to influence events in the *amir's* domain. Thus, whilst they were autonomous in one sense, ultimately 'it was the governors who invested in the *amir*, in the name of the Sultan...the authority to oversee the affairs of the Mountain.'[40] The relative disparity in power between the Mountain's local *amir* and the Ottoman governors was amply demonstrated when the Porte, on receiving complaints from Syrian and other local merchants regarding the manner of Fakhr al-Din's control of the main Mediterranean ports, ordered his arrest and execution. Fakhr al-Din was executed in 1635, and the Ma'ni dynasty lasted until 1697 when the last Ma'ni *amir* died. The Shihabis, another prominent regional family, subsequently provided the Mountain with its new *amirs*.

It was during the rule of Fakhr al-Din that the Shi'a of the Biqa' and the *amirs* of the Mountain first became connected politically. There had already been economic links between the two regions. The Biqa' had long provided the bulk of its grain and many of its animal products to the Mountain; and, with its rich agricultural output, the Biqa' was also a prize much sought after by *walis*. In a region with a large Shi'a population, the most influential of the Biqa'i community was the Harfoush family,[41] and it was they who would feature most prominently in the political relations with the *amirate* of the Mountain. As early as 1497 an Ibn Harfoush was the governor of Ba'albak,[42] and his family provided at least three more governors of Ba'albak over the next century. The proximity and importance of the Biqa' to the Ma'ni *amirate* meant that contact between the Harfoush and the Ma'nis was inevitable. Indeed the Harfoush clan and Fakhr al-Din became linked by marriage: Fakhr al-Din's daughter was married to the son of Yunus al-Harfoush. Relations between the two influential families were not, however, harmonious. They became rivals for power: a struggle in which Fakhr al-Din overcame Yunus al-Harfoush.[43] Formal political connections between the *amirate* and the Biqa' then followed, and control of Ba'albak was eventually granted to Fakhr al-Din by the Ottoman governor of Damascus in 1625.

Even after the governor of Damascus ceded control of the Biqa' to the Ma'ni *amir* of the Mountain, the Harfoush clan continued to play a prominent leadership role in the Biqa' for nearly 200 years. Given that Fakhr al-Din was executed by the Ottomans in 1635 and the Ma'ni dynasty ended in 1697, the Harfoush clan were able to re-establish control within the Biqa' in the absence of rivals. Relations between the Harfoush and their Ottoman governors were frequently strained, and Ottoman tolerance for the various Harfoush *amirs* was largely dependent on the latter's ability to collect and remit the requisite taxes. On the occasions when this did not occur, direct Turkish rule was established, and this frequently led to revolts instigated by the Harfoush. In 1859 the final Harfoush revolt was quelled and their leader, Amir Salman Harfoush, was arrested. After this, the clan's power went into terminal decline.[44]

The degree to which the sectarian identity of notable families influenced how their Ottoman governors treated them is hard to determine.

There is evidence to suggest that some families were willing to change their sectarian allegiances. There is the contention, for example, that by the end of the sixteenth century Musa al-Harfoush, a governor of Ba'albak, was already developing leanings towards Sunni Islamic beliefs.[45] Why he did so is difficult to ascertain, although it was not unknown for prominent families to change their sectarian beliefs for non-political reasons. It may also have had something to do with the Ottoman rulers constantly playing elements of influential clans against each other to divide them and hence make them easier to control. Ma'oz, for example, recounts the conspiracies that the Sunni Ottoman provincial council in Damascus hatched in an effort to defeat the Shi'a Harfoush *amirs*.[46] Whatever the case with Musa, the Harfoush clan was still predominantly Shi'a as late as the nineteenth century; yet as the family's prominence declined, the links with its Shi'a roots faded, and later the clan converted to Christianity. In all likelihood this conversion was designed to resurrect the family's political fortunes, and it is indicative of the increasing political dominance of the Christian Lebanese as well as the increasing political liability of being Shi'a.

As well as the Harfoush, there was another Biqa' Shi'a family that became a prominent political force. The Himadah clan, who continued to feature prominently in Lebanese politics until late in the twentieth century, played a leadership role for hundreds of years. Their origins remain a mystery, although they themselves contend that their lineage dates back to the fifteenth century.[47] What we do know is that after the death of Fakhr al-Din in 1635, the Shi'a Himadah clan was given the north of Lebanon as an *iqta'* by the Ottoman governor of Tripoli.[48] This meant the Ba'albak-centred Himadahs had taxation powers over the Maronite-dominated districts of Bsharri, Batrun and Jubayl, the Orthodox district of Kura, and the Sunni-dominated regions of al-Dinniya and 'Akkar. Not only does this illustrate the relatively weak position of Christians in this area at the time, it also highlights the fact that, contrary to popular perceptions of their historical role in the country, there were periods when Shi'a commanded a significant degree of authority over non-Shi'a (including Sunni Muslims) within certain regions of Lebanon. Even so, the power accorded the Himadahs was to last for less than 150 years. In 1759 their subjects began to revolt, and in 1773 they were defeated by Druze and Maronite forces under Amir Yusuf Shihab.[49]

The influence of the Ma'n and Shihab *amirates* on the population of the Biqa' is undeniable. Their formal political influence meant there was significant interaction between the Shi'a of the Biqa' and the population of the Mountain hundreds of years before the creation of the Lebanese Republic. In 1748 the Biqa' Valley was brought under the control of the Shihabi dynasty after the Shihabi *amir* defeated the forces of the *wali* of Damascus. The Ottoman rulers were placated because the financial levies were maintained – taxes from the residents of the Biqa' were henceforth collected by the *wali* of Saida – whilst the region itself became subject to the same rules of local governance that applied in the Mountain.[50] This arrangement was formalised in 1799 when the Grand Vizier, operating at the head of his Turkish forces in the region, was supplied with wheat from the Biqa' by the Shihab *amir*, Bashir. In return, the Grand Vizier recognised Bashir as governor of Ba'albak and the Biqa' and removed him from subordination to the Pasha of Saida.[51] In 1808 the Governor of Damascus, Yusuf Pasha Kenj, confiscated the Biqa', but the Shihabis once again gained control over it (along with Mount Hermon and parts of Ba'albak) when Amir Bashir II's forces under the command of Shaykh Bashir Jumblatt successfully attacked Damascus in 1810.[52]

In the south, Jabal 'Amil had been under Ottoman rule since the early sixteenth century, initially forming part of the *wilayat* of Damascus. The Shi'a inhabitants of Jabal 'Amil inhabited well-fortified villages in mountainous regions and had a history of being rebellious and difficult to control.[53] Due to their physical isolation from the provincial capital, they were also left largely to their own devices. By 1661, however, a new *wilayat* that took in the Jabal 'Amil region was established with its capital at Saida. Yet the authority of the *wali* of Saida did not remain unchallenged: between 1698 and 1699 the Shi'a shaykhs rose in revolt.[54] The military weakness of the Saida *wali* is evident from the fact that he required support from Amir Bashir Shihab to quell the revolt.

The *wali* subsequently placed most of the Shi'a areas in his *wilayat* under the control of Bashir Shihab,[55] which indicates that there was a political connection between Jabal 'Amil and the Mountain well before the creation of the Republic. A *wali* of Saida's relative weakness was not unusual during Ottoman times. Throughout the empire *walis* were in a somewhat invidious position: having limited tenure (the *wilayat* of Saida had more than 40 successive *walis* in the first half of the eighteenth century[56]), their success at administering their *wilayat* was measured by their ability to raise the requisite taxes for the Porte. Consequently *walis* spent little time improving their *wilayats* and most of their time ensuring that the *multazims* were successfully collecting and remitting their *miri* contributions.

In the case of the *wilayat* of Saida, there were significant internal pressures on an already weak institution. Dahir al-'Umar, a strong indigenous tribal chief from Palestine (who had also been appointed a *multazim*) was able to build up great wealth for himself and his followers by monopolising the cotton market.[57] European demand for Palestinian cotton had presented Dahir with the opportunity to establish *de facto* control over much of the *wilayat* of Saida and to seek official sanction for his actions from the *wali*[58] (which indicates that the Mountain's control over Jabal 'Amil had lapsed by this stage). Such was the power of Dahir that by the mid-eighteenth century, it is claimed, the authority of the *wali* was limited to Saida itself.[59] Despite this, the *wali* continued to perform his most important function: collecting and remitting taxes to the Porte. In this he was of course dependent on the goodwill of his *multazims*, and in most cases the *multazims* continued to forward him the tax revenues because they did not wish to provoke military intervention by the Porte.

The *wali's* influence outside Saida was minimal, and Dahir himself had only limited control over the Shi'a within Jabal 'Amil. Dahir's relations with them were, however, generally good. He underwrote their *miri* obligations and kept order within their territories if required, but he left them to maintain their traditional system of tribal and clan allegiances.[60] Indeed, many of the Shi'a *shaykhs* benefited economically (hence politically) from Dahir's monopoly in the growing and selling of cotton, as their increase in wealth was directly attributable to Dahir's free reign.[61] The bond forged between Dahir and the *shaykhs* is illustrated by the fact that, when the Porte eventually challenged his authority, the Shi'a provided Dahir with highly capable military forces. Together Dahir and his Shi'a allies defeated the *wali* of Damascus in 1771[62] and again in the following year. Dahir was eventually killed in 1775 while defending his capital Acre against forces sent to restore Ottoman authority in the *wilayat*.

From the time of Dahir's death, the Ottomans sought to re-establish control over their Levantine provinces and to restore to the central government the taxes that had not been forthcoming for some years. Ahmad Pasha al-Jazzar was dispatched with the task of reimposing Ottoman control over Jabal 'Amil, a task he eventually undertook with zeal. As a champion of centralised Ottoman rule, his concept of governance was the antithesis of the Shi'a's, most of whom retained their independence by remaining in their well-fortified mountain villages. Shi'a in the more vulnerable coastal regions around Tyre were more inclined to cooperate with al-Jazzar. At first, al-Jazzar treated the Shi'a with equanimity, requesting their assistance to put down a local Druze rebellion. The Shi'a, despite their lack of affinity with the Druze, refused the request.[63] They continued to maintain their autonomy throughout the early years of al-Jazzar's reign, when he was busy consolidating his rule in the more accessible areas of the *wilayat*.

Once he had accomplished this, al-Jazzar moved to assert his authority over the Shi'a of the region. In 1781, he undertook a punitive expedition against the Shi'a, defeating them on the battlefield (at great cost to his forces), razing their fortified villages, and appointing governors in the region.[64] In retaliation the Shi'a launched periodic uprisings against al-Jazzar's forces – in 1782, 1784 and 1785[65] – some of which successfully took back territory, but only temporarily, for after each uprising al-Jazzar brutally re-established his authority. The effect of this constant warfare on the region was twofold. Firstly, the ruthlessness of al-Jazzar's forces meant that many villages and crops were destroyed, which increased the economic pressure on those who were left to produce taxable goods. Secondly, while al-Jazzar continued to collect the *miri* from the population as a whole, traditional leaders were also collecting taxes from their respective villages: a double taxation that impoverished many Shi'a who were already finding economic conditions difficult. This, combined with the casualties the Shi'a suffered during the rebellions, must have devastated Jabal 'Amil. Indeed, a French traveller in the late-eighteenth century noted, with some exaggeration, al-Jazzar's impact on the region when he wrote:

> Since the year 1777, Djazzar, master of Acre and Saide has incessantly laboured to destroy them [the Jabal 'Amil Shi'a]...It is probable they will be totally annihilated, and even their name become extinct.[66]

The effects of al-Jazzar's punitive rule were still being felt by the Shi'a into the middle of the nineteenth century. British travellers to the region, amongst them the well-known David Urquhart, observed the relatively

under-developed state of the Shi'a areas as well as the Shi'a's propensity
for blaming al-Jazzar's rule – decades earlier – for their current predicament. Urquhart noted that the Shi'a

> have been prevented by their religious schism from being
> included in the administrative order of the empire. Their
> position in the Lebanon was neither that of princes called
> upon to govern nor...that of a tribe which has displaced the
> original population and occupied the soil.[67]

This was obviously written with no knowledge of the leadership role the
Shi'a had played in the past in certain regions of the Levant.

There is one final point to make about the actions of al-Jazzar. Many
of the survivors of the last battle in al-Jazzar's 1781 expedition to Jabal
'Amil fled to Ba'albak and the Biqa'.[68] This indicates some communal
affinity between the two dispersed Shi'a groups well before the establishment of the republic.

Institutional Political Development in Lebanon during the Late Ottoman Period

The *amirate* and the *iqta'* system were the two formalised leadership structures that operated within the area that was to constitute the future
Lebanese republic. It was not until the middle of the nineteenth century
that an institutionalised political system emerged. In 1841 the Ottoman
governor of Beirut introduced the first formal political organisation with
the creation of the Council for the Mountain.[69] This was followed by the
division of Lebanon into two districts (*qa'im maqamiyat*) in 1842 and by the
imposition of the Statute of 1845. This administrative organisation and
its resultant political structure were limited in role and did not apply
uniformly across all parts of what would eventually become Lebanon.
Consequently the impact of this bureaucratisation was felt not by the
complete body of Lebanese Shi'a but only by the Shi'a in the Mountain.

The Council for the Mountain was established purely for the purpose
of hearing complaints about, and creating a new schedule for, the levying
of taxes. It therefore represents the first attempt to gain consensus about
a significantly political issue from all the major confessional groupings.
The Council membership consisted of three Druze, three Maronites, one
Sunni, one Shi'a, one Greek Catholic and one Greek Orthodox. As

communal population broadly determined the makeup of the Council, the relatively small numbers of Shi'a in the Mountain dictated the single representative. It is noteworthy that the Shi'a were not represented by a Sunni member but were treated as a community in their own right. The Council was short-lived, however. Sectarian troubles between the Druze and the Christian Amir Bashir al-Qasim led to the latter's recall to Beirut and the Council's dissolution.

At the same time, European powers in the Levant began to exert an increasing influence, ostensibly to protect the interests of their co-religionists. The strength of their influence was evident in the first formal political arrangement implemented by the Ottomans following violence between Maronites and Druze in 1841. Such was the intensity of the fighting that it effectively ended the autonomy the *amir* had enjoyed under the Ottomans. The Porte reasserted Ottoman control, abolishing the Shihab *amirate* and briefly appointing Omer Pasha as Ottoman governor. Under pressure from the Great Powers – France, Britain, Russia and Austria – the Porte later abandoned direct rule, and Mount Lebanon was, at the request of the Great Powers, subsequently divided into two districts (*qa'im maqamiyat*, also spelt in some texts as *kaymakamate*). The Ottoman government believed that this 'solution' merely sowed the seeds of future troubles because the populations were too mixed to be partitioned effectively.[70] European pressure triumphed, however, and Mount Lebanon was divided into northern and southern districts, with the northern under the control of a Maronite governor (*qa'im maqam*), and the southern under a Druze *qa'im maqam*.

These governors were to be inhabitants of their respective districts and were to be appointed by the Ottoman governor of Saida. They would not only bring to Lebanon its first taste of political bureaucratisation, they would set the precedent for the introduction of confessional representation as a basic element of Lebanese public life.[71] Within the districts themselves tensions continued, because neither district was confessionally homogeneous and there did not exist any effective method of conflict resolution. In response to this situation, the Statute of 1845 was enacted. This Statute, also known as the *Reglement Shakib Effendi* after the Ottoman foreign minister, sought to achieve effective regional governance by peacefully resolving internal conflict in a religiously heterogenous area. Most importantly, the *Reglement* created an advisory council (*majlis*) in each district, essentially for the resolution of disputes. These councils comprised a judge (*qadi*) and an adviser from each of the six main confessional groupings.[72] It is interesting to note that, whilst a Shi'a adviser was allowed on the council, a Shi'a *qadi* was not. This was because religious disputes were resolved according to Sunni jurisprudence. When it came to institutionalising political processes in Mount Lebanon, then, the Sunni Ottoman leadership continued to treat the Shi'a as dissenters.[73]

Following the outbreak of sectarian violence in 1860 which resulted in the massacre of over 15,000 Christians in Mount Lebanon and Damascus, the Great Powers together with the Ottoman government imposed what became known as the *Reglement Organique* in 1861. Under this Statute, Mount Lebanon was to become a single governorate (*mutasarrifiyat*); the governor (*mutasarrif*) was to be a non-Lebanese Christian, selected by the Sultan and approved by the Great Powers;[74] and Lebanon was to be sub-divided into six *qa'im maqamiyat*, each further divided into districts and sub-districts. Only the *shaykh* or *mukhtar* at village or neighbourhood level was to be elected by the people. Wherever possible, those who drafted the Statute sought to learn from the shortfalls of the *Reglement Shakib Effendi*, with the result that the administrative divisions were made as religiously homogeneous as possible.[75] It was this system that was to remain in force, with relatively minor changes, until 1915.

The *Reglement Organique* appeared to be somewhat contradictory in what it set out to achieve. On the one hand, it used the communal notables to reinforce the primacy of Ottoman rule. On the other, it appeared to dismantle their powers. Hence the desire to move away from a privileged class is apparent in the wording of the sixth article of the *Reglement*, which pronounced that 'all are equal before the law, and all privileges, including those of the *muqata'jis*, are abolished.'[76] At the same time, the realities of the traditional leadership structure, with its inherent disparities in power, are in evidence in the eleventh article where it stipulates that 'all members of the courts and administrative assemblies will be chosen and appointed by the leaders of their sect in agreement with the notables of the sect.'[77]

The *mutasarrifiyat* system also introduced a more robust political structure. Based on proportional representation, it was in some ways a precursor to later organisational structures of the Lebanese state. Its Central Administrative Council (CAC) comprised councillors from each administrative district who were elected by that district's leading *shaykhs*. The CAC had twelve members in total: four Maronites, three Druze, two

Greek Orthodox, one Shi'a and one Sunni Muslim. The Shi'a member, according to population estimates of the day, came from the Matn district of the Mount Lebanon governorate. A census taken in 1868 resulted in the district from which the Shi'a councillor was appointed changing from Matn to Kisrawan.[78]

Little is known of the history of these Shi'a councillors. It may be that the lack of Shi'a notable families[79] meant their appointment was more open to competition from a larger Shi'a group here than in the Biqa' or the South. Support for this view can be found in a dispute over the results of the March 1909 elections involving the incumbent Muhammad Muhsin and his rival al-Hajj 'Ali Kazim.[80] The dispute concerned how much influence one of Muhsin's Maronite co-councillors brought to bear to ensure Muhsin's re-election. Neither family appears to have retained any political standing after the League of Nations mandate, which may lead one to conclude that the Shi'a's relatively small numbers must have forced them to make tactical alliances for political gain rather than rely on a client base as they did in the South or the Biqa'.

There is other evidence to support the view that the Shi'a of the Mountain led an existence far less subservient to the Shi'a notable families than did their co-religionists elsewhere in Lebanon. Although generally-speaking the numbers of Shi'a in the Mountain were relatively small and therefore little about their development is known, Fuad Khuri's study of local political processes in two Lebanese villages sheds some light on this question.[81] One of the villages in Khuri's study, Shiyah, had been owned by the Shihabi *amirs*. Over time, some of the Shi'a peasants in the village made money from silk production and were able to purchase land as a result. As Shihabi rule declined and land prices consequently fell, other Shi'a from the neighbouring village of Burj al-Barajnih (now part of Beirut) also began to buy land.[82] This indicates that the Shi'a of the Mountain possessed a degree of social mobility rarely if ever available to their co-religionists in other parts of Lebanon. Their ability to advance themselves economically through land ownership could go some way to explaining why the Shi'a of the Mountain were less tied to the traditional sectarian patron-client system and were more likely to adopt an independent course of political action.

Mandatory Power and the Creation of the Republic

Partly as a result of their long-standing links with the Maronites, the French sought a mandate at the end of the First World War over Syrian territories that had been part of the Ottoman Empire. The San Remo conference of 1920 conferred on France the right to assume mandatory rule over the former Ottoman *sanjak* of Mount Lebanon; and in fulfilment of a plan urged on France by prominent Maronites, the State of Greater Lebanon (*Le Grand Liban*) was established on 30 August 1920 by the French High Commissioner and Commander-in-Chief in Syria, General Gouraud.[83] The inclusion of Jabal 'Amil and the Biqa' in *Le Grand Liban* (it was not declared a republic until 1926) brought with it significant numbers of Shi'a whose historical links with the Mountain had been patchy at best. As a result, many Shi'a had greater affinity with areas outside the new state than, say, with its new capital of Beirut. Many 'Amili Shi'a, for example, considered the port of Haifa their main town[84] because of its economic importance to them. Similarly, many in the Biqa' considered themselves closely aligned economically and politically to Damascus.

The creation of *Le Grand Liban* was not supported by many people outside the Maronite community. In fact the largely Sunni-dominated Arab nationalist movement in the region vigorously opposed the move. These nationalists viewed the area of modern-day Lebanon as a legitimate part of Syria, and from the time of the Ottomans' defeat to the entry of Faisal into Damascus on 1 October 1918[85] they had tried to create an independent Syrian Arab state. The nationalists established a Syrian Congress in Damascus, built up an army and bureaucracy, and in July 1919 declared independence. Although the Shi'a community as a whole is not associated with the Arab nationalist movement, some Shi'a from the newly-mandated state played a prominent part in the movement and in the Syrian Congress in particular. This will be discussed later.

The French understood well enough why the Sunni Muslims were reluctant to become part of *Le Grand Liban*, so they sought to make the Arab nationalist movement less attractive to Muslims in general by cultivating the loyalty of the Shi'a minority (this 'divide and rule' method of colonial administration was standard practice amongst the French and other ruling European powers). The French made the creation of Lebanon attractive to the Shi'a by recognising them as an independent sect – a status denied them during Ottoman rule. Previously, their only

legal recourse for so-called 'personal status' issues had been through
Sunni jurists acting under Hanafi law. Now, at the behest of Shi'a deputies
elected by the Representative Council in 1923, a motion was put forward
requesting that their right to exist as a separate religious community be
recognised. In January 1926, the French High Commissioner approved a
law allowing Shi'a to use the Ja'fari school of jurisprudence under the
jurisdiction of a Shi'a *qadi* for personal status legal actions. The French
timed this formal recognition of the Shi'a well, for Syrian nationalists
were working hard to enlist the Shi'a to their cause. As Pierre Rondot
observed, the impact of this recognition in the late 1920s 'brings to the
Lebanese Chiites [*sic*] an appreciative satisfaction [of *Le Grand Liban*] at
the time when they are influenced by the separatist propaganda.'[86] French
willingness to recognise the separate identity of the Shi'a enabled the
French to secure their support, particularly amongst the prominent 'Amili
and Biqa' Shi'a families.[87]

The most enduring legacy of French rule was the introduction of a
Lebanese national parliamentary system of political representation which,
although significantly flawed, was robust enough to be carried over into
the post mandatory period. Barely two years after mandatory control was
granted, France allowed the newly formed state to elect a Representative
Council. The Lebanese who participated in the political process manifested their political affiliations in a variety of ways. Some formed political parties of a type recognisable in the West. Others continued to
support the traditional leadership, as they had for centuries. Still others
ran as independents intent on representing their region or community.
One form of political organisation favoured in the new republic was that
of the political 'bloc': a group united by a common aim (often pure self-
interest) but without the formality or internal discipline of a political
party *per se*.

The 1932 Census and the National Pact

Whilst parliamentary rule was a key legacy of the mandatory period, the
events with the most enduring political impact were the French census of
1932 and the subsequent Lebanese National Pact. The first French census
was carried out in 1921, to gauge the demographic makeup of the newly
mandated territory. The people recorded in this census were recognised
then for the first time as Lebanese, and were granted the right to vote in
elections.[88] The next (and last) census taken in 1932 was purportedly for

administrative statistical purposes only, although it was to have far more
enduring consequences. According to this census, out of a total resident
population of approximately 793,000 the resident Shi'a numbered just
over 155,000.[89] Just prior to the census, moreover, legislation was passed
that allowed for the inclusion of emigrants, and this strongly favoured the
Christians who represented the vast majority (85 per cent) of emigrants
at this time. As a result, the Shi'a proportion of the population dropped
from 19.5 per cent based on residency figures alone, to 16 per cent once
emigrants were included.[90] Even the higher figure, it has been suggested,
may underestimate the actual proportion of Shi'a.

Whilst the 1932 census provided the baseline for apportioning political power in the Republic, the establishment of the unwritten National
Pact (al-Mithaq al-Watani) provided the means to do it. Yet to achieve the
Pact's aim of formalising the state of Lebanon, a compromise had to be
reached so that 'in return for Christian rejection of French mandatory
rule, Muslim leaders would acquiesce to a Christian-advocated independent Greater Lebanon'.[91] This required a respected Sunni leader of
sufficient Arab nationalist persuasion to influence his co-religionists, as
well as a Maronite leader who could ensure the primacy of Christian
power in negotiations with the Arab nationalists. These roles fell respectively to Riad al-Sulh and Bishara al-Khoury.

Within the newly constructed mandate of Lebanon, powerful political
leaders juggled the roles of representing the majority of the population
while at the same time advocating what was in the best interests of their
own particular community. It was in just such an environment that the
Shi'a were most likely to be at a disadvantage. Having already accepted the
existence of Le Grand Liban as a result of French moves to garner their
support, they were not seen by the architects of the Pact as a minority
worth courting. Consequently Shi'a participation in the negotiations was
limited to the presence of the deputy 'Adil 'Usayran. The tangible result
of the Pact – the distribution of parliamentary representation based on
the relative numerical strengths of the sects – was reached after negotiations between Lebanese leaders, Egyptian leaders (who acted as intermediaries), the French High Commissioner General Catroux, and the British
Minister to the Syrian and Lebanese governments Major-General Edward
Spears.[92]

The final distribution of parliamentary seats was set at a
Christian:Muslim ratio of 6:5 (meaning all parliament sizes were multiples

of 11), based on the results of the 1932 census. There was little outcry over the disadvantage this posed for the Shi'a, because the powerful Shi'a families with their virtual monopoly on the community's parliamentary representation understood that their leadership aspirations could be fulfilled with the number of seats allocated to the community. Political representation for non-notable Shi'a was scarcely a consideration among the decision-makers. The Shi'a's lack of influence during negotiations is evident not only in the fact that they were allocated the relatively minor position of Speaker of the Chamber of Deputies, but that this was not automatically accepted by other minorities such as the Greek Orthodox and the Greek Catholics, who continued to contest the position after the Pact was established. Indeed in 1946 the Greek Orthodox Habib Abu Chahla was elected to the position at the expense of Sabri Himadah[93] – the first and only time a non-Shi'a has occupied it.

The Population Movements of the 1960s

Whilst the political impact of the National Pact was felt by all communities, other issues affected the Shi'a disproportionately. One of these was the extensive Shi'a migrations from Jabal 'Amil and the Biqa' – internally to Beirut and externally to West Africa in particular. These migrations, as will be discussed in detail later, played a significant role in the community's future political development.

The Shi'a diaspora actually began in the 1800s when Shi'a from southern Lebanon, seeking work after the collapse of the silk-worm industry, emigrated to the Ivory Coast.[94] These emigrants, poor agricultural workers, were not like the traditional Lebanese commercial *emigré* who sought undeveloped markets in which to prosper. Rather, they were seen as the 'linkage' class – those who would take trading work considered 'beneath' the colonial merchants but not done by the local population. Because of this work they were able to develop niche capabilities and could afford to bring out other members of their clan, thus establishing a cohesion to the diaspora that was regional and familial as much as religious. This kind of family-based immigration was evident in the influx of Shi'a from the 1930s onwards.

Significant numbers of (mainly Shi'a) Lebanese migrated to other African countries, and became wealthy as a result. Of these, the first Shi'a emigrated to Sierra Leone in 1903 because of poor agricultural harvests and subsequent overcrowding at home.[95] Unlike the Lebanese who went to western countries, these emigrants were not permanently lost to Lebanon's Shi'a population. According to Augustus Richard Norton, this was because 'the Shi'a found themselves in societies in which barriers of colour or nationality ensured that they would eventually return to Lebanon.'[96] The remittances they sent home, as well as their political aspirations to reform the traditional Lebanese Shi'a political landscape when they returned, ensured that they pursued a more activist agenda.

The onset of civil war in Lebanon of course accelerated Shi'a migration to other countries, particularly to the west. It is important to remember, however, that significant numbers of Shi'a had been emigrating to the United States since the beginning of the twentieth century. Many of them went to Detroit, where they had moved to work as unskilled labourers in the Ford factory.[97] A product of both these threads of the Lebanese Shi'a diaspora was Nabih Berri, a future leader of the Lebanese Shi'a Amal political movement, who was born in Sierra Leone and undertook part of his secondary school education in Detroit.

In addition to those who went overseas, tens or even hundreds of thousands of Shi'a abandoned their traditional farming villages for life in the southern suburbs of Beirut. It is estimated that between 1952 and 1964 the residential population of Beirut tripled,[98] due in part to the influx of Lebanese Shi'a. Most of the newcomers settled in the suburbs of Nab'a, Burj al-Barajnih and 'Ayn Rummanah. This influx, which commenced in the late 1950s, is attributed by most scholars to the depression in the agriculture sector.[99] Michael Johnson, however, contends that there had been a steady stream of Shi'a from Jabal 'Amil and the Biqa' to Beirut from the time *Le Grand Liban* was established.[100] This view is supported by Leila Fawaz, who notes that the insignificant Beiruti Shi'a population of 1895, only 80 in number, had grown to some 1,500 by 1920.[101] Similarly, sociologist Fuad Khuri, who studied Shi'a migration from the village of Aramti (prior to the civil war), found that internal migration occurred largely during the 1920s and resulted in a move on the part of the Shi'a to live in particular Beirut districts.[102] The attraction Beirut held for the Shi'a of Aramti (which would have been largely the same for other Shi'a) lay in the wages available to unskilled workers. This centralisation was the result of the emigrant Shi'a sharing the same socio-economic status and of their tendency towards religiously-sanctioned endogamous marriage that created an expectation of close familial living conditions.

Regardless of exactly when the large-scale Shi'a migration to Beirut occurred, the motivation is clear: prices for staple commodities were stagnant, state investment in the Shi'a-dominated agricultural sector was miniscule, and there was a shift towards capital-intensive (rather than labour-intensive) citrus farming.[103] Those who moved to Beirut tended to be the less-well-educated: typically farm workers in search of labouring jobs in Beirut's building industry. The Palestinian-Israeli conflict, as well as later Israeli incursions into southern Lebanon, exacerbated the movement of Shi'a from the south to the Beirut suburbs. This internal migration proved a key element in Shi'a politicisation for it gave rise to a large, discontented and marginalised minority ripe for political leadership. Excluded from Beirut's (largely Sunni) patron-client relationships, and their links to their traditional rural *zu'ama* (leaders)[104] of diminishing importance in the face of rapid social change and increasing governmental activity,[105] these migrant Shi'a were politically adrift and open to influence.

An Overview of Early Shi'a Political Development

In examining the political development of the Lebanese Shi'a, a number of general observations need to be made. Firstly, they have never constituted a unified sectarian bloc. Rather they have developed as regional communities, principally in the two separate strongholds of the Jabal 'Amil and the Biqa' (and more recently in southern Beirut) and also, in smaller numbers, in the Mountain. The differences in the political characteristics of these groups are a result of their experiences in these different environments. The Shi'a of Jabal 'Amil were dominated by a small number of landowning families who wielded great power. They also experienced harsh persecution at times from their Ottoman rulers and were denied an equal share in the development of infrastructure. The 'Amili Shi'a, although having an enviable history of religious scholarship and to a lesser degree martial prowess, have tended to be seen as subservient, both to political institutions and to a small number of largely unchallenged *zu'ama*. The Biqa' Shi'a, on the other hand, have generally been considered more independent, less subject to the influence of external authority, and having *zu'ama* whose power bases were more evenly distributed.

Unlike many other religious communities, the Shi'a could not count on external protection to guarantee their interests. In contrast, the

Maronites relied on political protection from France (having been well serviced by French Jesuit missionaries for hundreds of years), and the Druze were courted by the British in the nineteenth century as a counter to French interests; similarly, Orthodox Christians had an affinity with Eastern European nations such as Russia. For the Shi'a, the Safavid rulers of sixteenth- and seventeenth-century Persia were their most powerful co-religionists, although in no position to provide much support. Indeed, given that the Ottoman and Safavid states were in conflict for protracted periods, the Shi'a were, to varying degrees, alienated within the Ottoman empire. Consequently they relied on their geographical isolation and a policy of quietism to avoid being dragged into conflicts in which they could only suffer. Avoidance was not always possible, however, and merely illustrated the degree to which the Shi'a were not traditionally the masters of their own destiny.

The tendency towards quietism should not, however, be confused with total silence. Some Shi'a became involved in the few formal political opportunities open to them during Ottoman rule, although it was often the *zu'ama* or their allies who filled these positions in order to reinforce their traditional dominance in Lebanese society. During the final stages of the Ottoman Empire some Shi'a adopted an activist political stance to further the cause of Arab nationalism. Although few in number, they do represent the beginnings of a political consciousness that addressed issues beyond the immediate purview of traditional Shi'a familial leadership. This secular Shi'a activism is an aspect of Lebanese political history that has been little explored.

The principal difficulty in examining Shi'a political activism, particularly in pre-mandate Lebanon, is that a notion of Lebanese identity did not exist. The experiences of the Shi'a in the Biqa', Jabal 'Amil and to a lesser extent the Mountain are different and render invalid any attempt to conflate the Shi'a of this period into a single entity. Furthermore, documentary evidence of Shi'a political activism in the pre-mandate period is scarce, which makes it even more difficult to establish a complete picture of their political behaviour. Nevertheless it is fair to conclude that amidst the turbulence of Lebanon's Ottoman history the Shi'a were at best marginal political players. Their position as a largely rural people, the suspicion with which they were viewed by the Ottoman rulers and the Sunni majority due to their heterodox beliefs, and their traditional political quiescence (abetted by a clergy that avoided political involvement), all combined to ensure that they did not feature prominently in the governance of any of those parts of modern-day Lebanon where concentrations of Shi'a lived.

Much of this also holds true for the experience of Shi'a in the mandatory and early post-mandatory periods. The traditional leadership continued to dominate the Shi'a political landscape, and it was largely the impact of external events that triggered the rapid development of a Lebanese Shi'a political consciousness. These events included the influx of remittances from emigrants, the urbanisation of many Shi'a, and the success of the Iranian Shi'a in establishing an Islamic state. Despite all of this, it is sometimes easy to overlook the fact that an undercurrent of Lebanese Shi'a political activism has always existed alongside the traditional quietism. Whilst these activists were usually small in number, they too are important if we are to understand the various paths that Shi'a political development has taken.

2

The Rise and Fall
of the Traditional Zu'ama

The Nature of the *Za'im*

The oldest form of political organisation amongst the Lebanese Shi'a was the traditional leadership of the clan, itself a feature of the wider Arab world. In Lebanon the development of a clan-based society, with its emphasis on familial loyalty and its preference for clientilism as the means of social ordering, brought with it the beginnings of a phenomenon that was to typify the Lebanese polity: the *za'im* (plur. *zu'ama*).[1] The *za'im*, in simple terms, is the leader. What he leads is a regional group of supporters, many of whom act as his client group. The *zu'ama* are hierarchical, a *za'im's* status depending largely upon the degree of influence he wields. A lesser *za'im*, for example, may be beholden to a greater *za'im* to facilitate the interests of his (the lesser's) client base. In such circumstances, where the lesser *za'im* cannot himself grant the wishes of his client group, he may yet act as a conduit for securing the intervention of a more powerful *za'im* who can do this for him.

There is a temptation, in discussions of this kind, to label as a *za'im* anyone with any political influence at all. This chapter, however, will examine in detail only those *zu'ama* who had sufficient standing to play a major role in Shi'a politics and who managed to preserve this influence through hereditary succession. Consequently there is little mention of those individual members elected to parliament who influenced Lebanese Shi'a politics in their own right but who lacked the traditional authority to make an impact past their own term in office. Indeed, since continued electoral success depended on their ability to maintain a position on their political patron's electoral ticket, their tenure in parliament was itself often dependent on the relationship they had with the dominant regional *za'im*. Thus political status represented by a seat in parliament was not in itself sufficient to make the incumbent a *za'im* because it did not automatically confer the degree of permanency that a true *za'im* needed to possess. That having been said, new *zu'ama* could be created, and they often emerged as a result of connections established with prominent political figures such as the *walis* of the Ottoman period.

The traditional *za'im* normally established the conditions for his influence by creating a support base through one of two means: by owning and leasing land (as was mostly the case with the largely rural Shi'a), or by operating commercial ventures in the cities or towns such that the employees constituted part of his client base. The first of these methods evolved largely through the traditional *iqta'* system, discussed in Chapter One. Whilst the *iqta'* system was the traditional families' source of power, it was not static: new families were able to gain sufficient status as patrons, largely by buying land as an investment, to become *zu'ama* in their own right. Land ownership in this context was important not only for the income it generated but also for the client base it created, since rural workers were beholden to the owner for their livelihood.

With the exception of the work of Arnold Hottinger and more recently Nizar Hamzeh, little has been done in the way of examining the *zu'ama* as discreet political players. Yet even these scholars have not concentrated on the Shi'a *zu'ama*. As a result, the reason for the rise and subsequent decline of the Shi'a *zu'ama* as a political force is not well understood. Their decline stands in contrast to many *zu'ama* from other communities, who continue to play an influential role in Lebanese politics. Certainly *zu'ama* from all communities faced similar challenges as internal societal and external political forces transformed the existing order within which they operated. But the pressure of these forces on Shi'a society was more acute, and the traditional Shi'a *zu'ama* proved unable to adapt. More particularly, it appears that whilst they were able to translate their societal and financial strength into the political realm for some time after the creation of Lebanon, they were ultimately unable to modify their method of political operation to accommodate the various forces that led to an emerging Shi'a radicalism from the 1960s.

The emergence of competing centres of political allegiance, be they secular parties such as the Ba'thists and Communists or avowedly Shi'a parties such as Amal and Hizbullah, certainly provided the Shi'a with alternative outlets for political activism. The emergence of these parties, along with other fundamental changes in Shi'a society, combined to weaken the strength of the traditional *zu'ama*. Yet although modern political and societal forces have largely overwhelmed the traditional Shi'a *za'im* class, the question as to whether their political power has been completely erased or, in the age-old tradition of Lebanon, merely supplanted by a new class of *za'im*, has still to be fully answered.

Background to the Lebanese *Zu'ama*

The modern-day Republic of Lebanon is an amalgam of several former Ottoman *wilayat* or parts thereof, joined together to form a state. Hence the power of the *zu'ama* must be viewed, initially at least, in regional rather than national terms. The *za'im's* power stemmed from the traditional influence he gained from owning significant tracts of land. In the early days of Ottoman rule this informal system of control often emerged as a more formal system as a consequence of the *za'im's* role as a *muqata'ji*. This was particularly, although not exclusively, true of the Shi'a *zu'ama* who dominated the rural regions of the Biqa' and Jabal 'Amil. Although their support base was essentially regional that is not to say that these *zu'ama* were incapable of influencing events outside their immediate area or even outside their own community. Indeed, one of the defining elements of the power of the *zu'ama* was the size of the extended area – hence the size of the client base – they could influence.

There were, however, some geographical limits. In the Shi'a context, a definite delineation existed between the influence exercised by the *zu'ama* of Jabal 'Amil and those of the Biqa'. Historically there had been limited contact between the Shi'a of these areas, so that the familial leadership of each of these regions had largely operated independently of each other. But as we shall see, occasional tactical alliances were formed between the two leading regional Shi'a *zu'ama* – the Himadahs and al-As'ads – during the mandatory period. This regional autonomy was reinforced by the establishment of electoral districts in post-mandatory Lebanon, which meant that Shi'a *zu'ama* from the Biqa' and Jabal 'Amil would never pose an electoral threat to each other – an arrangement that was also formalised through marriage ties, as will be discussed later. Political rivalries between Shi'a from each of these areas were, as a result, played out indirectly through manoeuvrings within parliament rather than as a direct political contest during elections.

The image of the Shi'a as an historically underprivileged group belies the influence that a number of traditional Shi'a families actually had. Some of these families could trace their lineage back for hundreds of years; and indeed the degree of influence of their 'feudal' leadership in part depended on this lineage. Samir Khalaf summarises the key elements of the *zu'ama's* authority during the Shihabi period as being 'the power they wielded over an area, their relationship with the ruling Shihabs, as well as the vintage of their kinship genealogy.'[2] Given the historical antecedents of the Biqa' and Jabal 'Amil, Khalaf's second point is less applicable to the Shi'a, although a *za'im's* relationship with the dominant regional leadership was always an important determinant of his authority; influence with government, and the ability this gave a notable to reward his supporters, was always the real prize. Having said that, economic strength alone was also enough to give a family political influence. In practice this came about with the Ottoman land reforms of 1858. Designed to allow private ownership of agricultural land (ostensibly to encourage private production[3]), these reforms gave families who were able to purchase land, and in some cases become tax agents (*multazim*), for the Ottoman government the opportunity for socio-economic advancement to the ranks of the *zu'ama*. The land reforms did not only benefit outsiders. Existing *zu'ama* could also advance their economic standing: clan leaders in many instances simply 'registered what had been communal lands in their own name'.[4]

For successful business families who could for the first time afford to buy substantial plots of land, the opportunity arose to elevate themselves to the level of neo-*zu'ama*. These neo-*zu'ama* were sometimes referred to as *wujaha*',[5] with the *wajaha'* itself transforming into a hereditary status. The important *wujaha'* were often tied to a *za'im* by marriage and would act as his agent of influence in areas where they had more authority than the *za'im*.[6] From this arrangement we may infer that the neo-*zu'ama* had less influence than the established *zu'ama*. Although this was generally the case, there were instances in which a neo-*za'im* could build up a great degree of political influence over a short period of time. A case in point is the Shi'a Baydoun family, which will be discussed later.

Of the two main regions inhabited by the Shi'a, the *zu'ama* of the Biqa' Valley were generally considered to have a more established lineage than their co-religionists from the South, possibly due to the fact that notables from the South had been largely wiped out during al-Jazzar's brutal rule. Certainly, bonds between Shi'a clans were noticeably stronger in the Biqa' than in Jabal 'Amil. The pre-eminent Shi'a clan was the Himadiyya, who had moved to the rugged northern region of the Biqa' following the Maronite uprising against them in the North in the second half of the eighteenth century, and had then begun to populate the Ba'albak-Hirmil area.[7] This was despite, or even perhaps because of, the fact that there were already Shi'a clans in the Biqa' Valley, such as al-Haydar, al-Husayni and al-Yaghi (although these three clans were strongest around Ba'albak itself).

The interactions between some of the Biqa' Shi'a clans illustrate the strong family loyalties that existed in the region.[8] Their interrelationship has been described as one based on the Arab concept of *'asabiyya*, or solidarity.[9] The clan groups (plur. *'ashair*; sing. *'ashira*) themselves are subdivided into smaller family groups, and this provides a good insight into the complex relationships that began to develop in these regions. The overarching *'asabiyya* is referred to as the *'ashira* al-Himadiyya, after the dominant *'ashira*. Underneath the al-Himadah clan were two sub-strata, known as the *'ashira* Shamasiyya and *'ashira* Zouaitiriyya, after the al-Shamas and al-Zouaitir families.[10] The relationship that developed between them was one of mutual benefit. As Nizar Hamzeh from the American University of Beirut has explained: 'The Himadiyyah's *'asabiyyah* [*sic*] is not necessarily an expression of common genealogy, but more of a unified political formula which connects these clans to al-Himadah's clan.'[11]

By contrast the Shi'a of Jabal 'Amil were less cohesive. During the eighteenth century, the area of Jabal 'Amil played host to three major groups: the *Banu* Sa'b in the *muqata'a* of Shaqif, the *Banu* Munkir in the *muqata'a* of Shomar and al-Tuffah, and the *Banu* 'Ali al-Saghir in Bilad Bishara.[12] By the end of the nineteenth century two pre-eminent *'ashair* from these major groups dominated the Jabal 'Amil region: al-As'ad and al-Fadl clans.[13] Al-As'ad clan, who were descendants of the *Banu* 'Ali al-Saghir,[14] had emerged initially as minor *iqta'* holders from at-Tayyiba. At some stage during the nineteenth century, al-As'ad clan were able to expand their fief holdings into large tracts of freehold land, which consequently increased the size of their rural client base.[15] Whilst these two families could be considered the 'landed aristocracy' of Jabal 'Amil, other *wujaha'* also emerged after the introduction of the Ottoman land reforms led to an increase in the number of owners of significant land holdings. Many of these came from Saida, Sur (Tyre), Nabatiyya and Bint Jubayl.

Tarif Khalidi claims it was the 'Amili grain merchant families such as the 'Usayrans, al-Khalils and al-Zayns who were eventually to benefit most from this method of political advancement.[16] The timing of the 'Usayrans rise to power according to Khalidi is, however, doubtful. The family had been prominent around Saida for many years. Having arrived some time in the sixteenth or seventeenth century and built up significant wealth from mercantile activities, they were eventually appointed consuls for Iran. As consuls they, and their employees, were exempt from Ottoman military service and were levied a lower tax on their goods. This allowed them to build their wealth more rapidly and to gather a greater supporter base in Saida and Zahrani (where they owned land) due to the privileges accorded their employees.[17] Such was the success of these leading families that during the early 1950s, it is claimed, the patriarchs of the 'Usayran, al-Khalil and al-Zayn families as well as Ahmad al-As'ad each owned approximately 3,700 acres in Jabal 'Amil.[18]

Not all new *zu'ama* were from Jabal 'Amil or the Biqa', however, nor were they all agricultural landowners. Indeed the new political institutions made it possible for families without agricultural land holdings to establish client bases through political activity alone. One notable case is that of the Baydoun family. The Baydouns were relative newcomers to Lebanon, settling in Beirut around 1910 after leaving Damascus where they had been successful merchants. Following the move, they became wealthier. Whilst the family had not been directly politically active during the Ottoman or early mandatory periods,[19] they did, however, become prominent in founding and running the 'Amiliyya Society, a charitable organisation set up largely to provide educational services to Shi'a youth. Initially catering to Beiruti Shi'a, it established many schools in the South that were financed either directly by the Baydoun family or through donations from emigrant Shi'a. Rashid Baydoun, the Society's President, built a great deal of support across a wide section of the Shi'a community as a result of his philanthropic work. The use of philanthropic organisations as a basis for establishing popular political support was to prove a common theme in Lebanese politics. For aspiring political leaders and political parties, these welfare organisations would provide an essential and valued service. Loyalty to an institution, be it a school or medical facility, was quickly transferred to those whose funds had established it. Just as the traditional notables had built political support using their agricultural assets, newer Shi'a patrons established their political clientele through more modern means.

The question of traditional leadership links between families has already been touched upon. These links, it should be understood, were not exclusive to Shi'a notable families from the same region, nor to Shi'a in general. The use of intermarriage as a form of alliance building or status advancement has a long history in Lebanon.[20] In the post-mandatory period, there are many examples of it amongst all communal groups, and the political alliances necessary to operate in the new parliamentary system of government were readily discernible from the relationships established through marriage (see Figure 1 below). For example, three of the large landowning families of the South (al-'Arabs, al-Khalils and the 'Usayrans) were connected by marriage, and the 'Usayrans were connected by marriage to the very influential Haydar clan of the Biqa'.[21]

Figure 2. Intermarriage amongst Prominent Lebanese Families

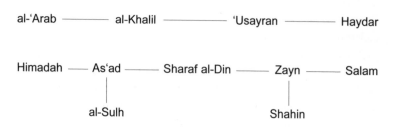

(from Dekmejian, *Patterns of Political Leadership: Egypt, Israel, Lebanon*, p. 20)

The other notable families of the South were linked by a more intricate web of intermarriage: members of the Shi'a al-As'ad, Sharaf al-Din, al-Zayn and Shahin clans all intermarried. At the same time, al-As'ad clan also had marital linkages with the Shi'a Himadah clan from the Biqa' and the powerful Sunni al-Sulh family from the South. Al-Zayns were, in turn, linked by marriage to the Salams, a rich Sunni landowning family from the

South (but whose patriarch Sa'ib resided in Beirut). What this ensured, in theory at least, was that electoral and parliamentary alliances existed between some Shi'a families from the Biqa' and Jabal 'Amil, as well as between families of different Muslim communal groups in the South. Given that the electoral laws ensured that only those from the same region became electoral rivals, the Biqa'–'Amili marriage alliances were more likely to have been undertaken for parliamentary rather than electoral alliance purposes. Notably, Sunni–Shi'a marriage alliances existed only in Jabal 'Amil; consequently it is more likely that they were politically advantageous for the Sunni families because these families would have required support to be included on the electoral ticket of a dominant Shi'a notable family such as al-As'ad.

Political Motivation of the *Zu'ama*

The political ideology of the *zu'ama*, inasmuch as one existed, centred on their maintaining traditional power by monopolising access to the formal political structure in place at the time. Whilst a *za'im's* client base gave him relative independence and great influence, it was not sufficient on its own to allow him to operate without the support of other *zu'ama*. This type of extended support base was not necessarily a new development, as there had existed a tradition of co-operation between many of the families, particularly in the Biqa'. The marriage ties referred to previously indicate that such alliances also existed *between* families from Jabal 'Amil and the Biqa'. These links were to become critical when the regions became more closely intertwined in the new Lebanese Republic. Establishing inter-regional alliances between Shi'a *zu'ama* to facilitate the creation of parliamentary voting blocs, was essential to operating effectively within the new representative institutions that were created under French rule.

Prior to the mandate, a *za'im's* credentials had generally been established by the possession of large landholdings and/or financial strength: both brought access to a client base whose needs could be satisfied by the informal powers that the *iqta'* system had bestowed upon the *za'im*. With the advent of the mandate, it was apparent to most *zu'ama* that participation in the political process through the acquisition of some form of official office would be a necessary element of the *za'im's* continued claims for leadership of his client group. There were a number of reasons for this. Firstly, he was most likely to be able to reward his clients through the allocation of state resources and to stymie his rivals through the denial of the same resources. Meir Zamir notes the potential for state financial resources to become the currency of *wasta*[22] with the explosion of government positions allocated along sectarian lines during the early mandatory period.[23] Secondly, the political marginalisation of the Shi'a by their Ottoman rulers meant that the mandatory system of government, potentially more representative of the sectarian balance, required the *zu'ama* to dominate it, hence securing their traditional leadership function. Thirdly, the prestige that high office bestowed was in keeping with the dignity of the family's position. The immature political system of the early mandatory era meant that it was still possible for a powerful *za'im* to be the most influential political figure in his region whether he was the parliamentary representative or not. Personal pride, then, was not insignificant in motivating the *zu'ama* to seek political office.

During the periods of Ottoman and mandatory rule and from independence until the 1960s, political participation in Lebanon was nearly exclusively the preserve of the *zu'ama*. In the Ottoman era, non-*zu'ama* were virtually excluded from the political process; they lacked financial resources and/or formalised official authority (largely because the allocation of a *muqata'a* dictated this). During the mandatory and early independence periods they were normally without a sufficient client base to gain entry to an elected parliament. This was particularly the case in the Shi'a context, because the masses were largely confined to traditional agrarian activities, were poorly educated, and were consequently beholden to the traditional leaders for dealings with the government of the day. The inequity in the relationship between the patron and his client group meant that the client group was effectively barred from seeking political office as it would have involved challenging the pre-eminence of their patron. Without an external motivating factor or a change in the socio-economic dynamics within the country, the political *status quo* was always likely to go unchallenged.

Ottoman-Era Political Involvement in Formal Institutions

The historical dominance of Shi'a notables within various *muqata'as* during the early Ottoman period was discussed in the previous chapter. Political power at that stage was synonymous with the authority to raise and remit taxes. But once the introduction of the *Reglement Organique* in 1861 had led to the creation of the autonomous province of Mount Lebanon, membership of the resultant formal political structure, the

Central Administrative Council, became an attractive prize for the strong families. As Bishara al-Khoury recalled:

> The great offices formed nearly without exception a *waqf*
> for the great families of the country. This came from the
> *de facto* influence of feudalism after feudalism had been
> officially ended. Office in those days was everything. It was
> the aim of all eyes and the source of all influence and
> dignity. Sons of one family or close friends would jump at
> each other's throats in order to attain it.[24]

The attraction of the Council demonstrated how formal political office would have to be contested, as there were fewer representative places than candidates from amongst the notables vying for them. This lesson was certainly well understood in the South, where the pre-eminent Shi'a *za'im*, Kamil al-As'ad, sought every opportunity to convert his family's historical pre-eminence amongst the 'Amili Shi'a into contemporary political power. This was evident from the manner in which he strove to become the leading influence in the formal political institutions established within his region. These representational bodies did not involve the Shi'a from the South until the beginning of the twentieth century when the Ottoman Parliament (*Majlis al-Mab'uthan*) was created as a result of the agitation of the Young Turks in 1908. Representatives from different provinces of the Ottoman Empire were elected to the parliament in Constantinople. Such was the view that Kamil al-As'ad had of his position in Jabal 'Amil that he took it as a personal slight when a member of al-Khalil family competed against him for election to the *Majlis*. Given the relatively recent (to al-As'ad) rise to *za'im*-status of al-Khalil family, there may well have been a degree of effrontery felt by al-As'ad clan at the comparative newcomer's temerity. It was said of him:

> Kamil Bek was of the opinion that representing the Shi'is
> of Jabal 'Amil was his prerogative [and was] precluded to
> anybody else whatever his personality and his capacities
> might have been.[25]

As it was, al-As'ad went on to represent the *sanjak* of Beirut in the *Majlis al-Mab'uthan*.[26] The political rivalry between al-Khalils and al-As'ads that manifested itself in this instance was to be a feature of Lebanese Shi'a politics for the next sixty years.

Arab and Lebanese Nationalism and the *Zu'ama*

The political participation of the Shi'a *zu'ama* was not, however, tied exclusively to existing Ottoman or mandatory political institutions. An often-unreported element of Shi'a political activity was the role played by Shi'a outside the normal patterns of political participation ascribed to them. This was the case with the emergent Arab nationalist movement of the early twentieth century. In contrast to the view that Arab nationalism was a Sunni Muslim creation,[27] there is ample evidence that the Shi'a were also involved in these nascent Arab nationalist movements. As with all political activity of the time, members of the notable families were also the most prominent members of such movements.

Whilst the Shi'a were active locally, their role must nevertheless be put into perspective. It would be rather too generous to credit the Shi'a with the presence ascribed to them by an unnamed Shi'a writer from Nabatiyya, who claimed:

> No Syrian congress was convened, no Arab meeting was held without the Shi'a representatives being there in the vanguard, protesting the conditions of their world, demanding being part of Syrian unity.[28]

In the early days of opposition to the despotic Ottoman Sultan 'Abd al-Hamid, the Arab nationalists and the Young Turks[29] co-existed peacefully, as both sought to change the *status quo*. Once the Young Turks had effectively taken control of the empire, and the Arab nationalists had realised that the demise of 'Abd al-Hamid had not given them their cultural freedom, relations between the two deteriorated and much of the Arab nationalist movement went underground.[30]

There is evidence that members of the notable Shi'a families who resided outside modern-day Lebanon (mainly as students) were active in the genesis of some of these secretive Arab nationalist movements. For example, amongst the Arab deputies, academics and officials who founded the Literary Club (*al-Muntada al-Adabi*) in Constantinople in 1909 were Salih Haydar and 'Abd al-Karim al-Khalil.[31] Although the Club was a forum for Arabs to meet in the Ottoman capital, its ideals were not avowedly political and thus it was tolerated by the Turkish authorities.[32] Initially, Arab nationalist organisations developed outside Lebanon, but later they began to emerge in Jabal 'Amil. By 1915, a Saida branch of the Society of Arab Revolution (*Jami'yyat ath-Thawra al-'Arabiyya*) had been founded under the direction of 'Abd al-Karim al-Khalil. Even though the Society was still in its infancy, it was opposed by the Ottoman authorities because it was avowedly nationalist and activist: in 1915, al-Khalil and Haydar were arrested, tried and hanged. This action by the Ottoman authorities was part of a wider crackdown; a number of Arab nationalists were also hanged at the same time in other parts of Syria as well as in Palestine. In the case of al-Khalil and Haydar, internal rivalries between Shi'a *zu'ama* may also have contributed to their demise. It was believed in some quarters at the time that al-Khalil's name was given to the Ottoman authorities by Kamil al-As'ad,[33] their two families being traditional political rivals.

After the success of the British-sponsored Arab revolt, Faysal, son of Husayn the *sharif* of Mecca, led moves to establish an independent Syria. The Second Syrian National Congress in Damascus crowned him King Faysal I of Syria on 8 March 1920. The Congress also drafted a constitution for a parliamentary monarchy. The monarchy itself was short-lived, abolished in July 1920 by the French mandatory forces.[34] Regardless, after the end of Ottoman rule the general mood of the Lebanese population was very pro-Arab nationalist, so it is difficult to determine to what degree the nationalist tendencies of political actors were driven by ideology or motivated by their desire to appeal to popular sentiment. The latter motivation can probably be seen, for example, in the fact that Kamil al-As'ad quickly identified himself with the nationalist cause once the war's direction became clear. He established contact with Faysal and was accorded the role of 'emissary for ordering the affairs of the Jabal 'Amil'.[35] It is also claimed that he raised the first Arab flag in Syria at Marjayoun in 1918.[36] These actions, whilst indicative of support for Syrian independence, are also likely to have been motivated by self-preservation, as one of his political rivals Hajj 'Abdullah Yahya al-Khalil (an uncle of the future *za'im* Kazim[37]) had already been appointed head of the provisional Arab government of Tyre on the departure of the Turkish troops.[38]

Not all the *zu'ama*, however, could be described as opportunistic nationalists. A more ideologically-motivated clan were the Haydars of

Ba'albak, who were active in another nationalist movement, the Young Arab Society (*Jam'iyyat al-'Arabiyya al-Fatat*, or simply *al-Fatat*).[39] Formed in Paris in 1911 by Arab students, it moved to Beirut some time in 1913. This Society was the first Arab political organisation to call for the complete independence of Arab provinces under Ottoman rule.[40] Sa'id Haydar was a member of the most radical faction of *al-Fatat*, a group that rejected both Britain and France as mandatory powers. A later development in the Arab nationalist movement involving the Haydars was the Arab Club of Damascus,[41] a semi-political organisation not dissimilar in aims to the Literary Club, and formed late in 1918 after the entry of Arab and Allied troops into the city. Yusuf Haydar was a founding member of the Arab Club and, shortly thereafter, a member of *al-Fatat* too.[42] Whilst it is not well known that members of the Shi'a *zu'ama* played such a significant role in Arab nationalism, it stands to reason that this was the case. Members of notable families were the ones most likely to be able to afford the opportunity to study abroad, where Arab nationalist ideas were developing. The fact that the Literary Club and *al-Fatat* were formed by both Arab students and government officials while they were studying in Paris and Constantinople is evidence of the likelihood of participation by notable families.

The Haydars continued to play a significant part in the Arab nationalist movement throughout the war years and even after. As'ad Haydar led Faysal's provisional Arab government in Ba'albak-Hirmil.[43] 'Ali Haydar played a role in the Arab nationalist movement of the 1920s; this, and his personal friendship with King Faysal, have been touched on by Farid al-Khazen.[44] The Biqa' proved to be as indisposed to the prospect of French mandatory authority as did Jabal 'Amil, although the lack of a single dominant authority, such as al-As'ad in the South, meant that there was a less unified response from the families. That having been said, on some issues a good degree of unanimity was achieved. For example, *all* the families from the Biqa' boycotted the King-Crane Commission.[45] This was probably a protest against even discussing the issue of formalised European dominance over the region.

The participation of members of the *zu'ama* in the Arab nationalist movement is noteworthy for the fact that it demonstrates their ability to understand, harness and sometimes adapt to the prevailing mood of the people – which stands in contrast to their inability to do so from the 1960s onwards. Such a pro-active approach may have resulted from the fact that Arab nationalism in the early days was largely a single-issue movement focused on political change, whereas later in the century the challenges it faced were far more complex. The impact of the political forces that sought to change the status of the *zu'ama*, as well as the more fundamental societal changes the Shi'a as a whole were undergoing by the 1960s, were to prove too difficult for the notables to address.

Lebanese versus Syrian Nationalism

The defeat of Faysal's forces by the French at Maysalun in July 1920 spelt the end of the short-lived Arab government. The imposition of mandatory rule also brought with it a modification of nationalist aspirations. In the main, the emphasis on pan-Arab nationalism shifted to Syrian unionism in response to France's creation of Greater Lebanon. Yet not all non-Christians were dismissive of *Le Grand Liban*, and whilst they were still opposed to French mandatory rule, many were inclined to support Lebanese rather than Syrian nationalism. The split between Lebanese and Syrian nationalist positions regarding the newly created state was reflected in the actions of some Shi'a *zu'ama*. During the early years of the mandate, in particular, it was not uncommon for them to switch allegiance from one position to the other, often for personal political gain.

It is difficult to ascertain a *general* attitude amongst Shi'a towards the creation of Lebanon, as their responses to it appear at times to be contradictory. This is reflected in the writings of some authors who on the one hand posited that the Shi'a had 'an attachment to a religio-cultural heritage which an independent Lebanon threatened to sentence to oblivion', yet on the other noted the 'deep-seated ambivalence with which the majority of the Shi'a *zu'ama* regarded Syrian unity'.[46] The available evidence indicates that most Lebanese Shi'a notables were opposed to the creation of the mandatory state but were later persuaded by the French to accept the reality of the new situation. Once they had, the *zu'ama* turned their attention to controlling access to the Lebanese representative bodies that were subsequently created.

The pre-eminent Shi'a *za'im* of Jabal 'Amil, Kamil al-As'ad, was vocal in opposing French rule and supporting Syrian nationalism. This is particularly evident in his actions after the Allied victory in World War I. Appearing before the King-Crane commission in 1919 as representative of all 'Amili Muslims, he publicly advocated the cause of Syrian unity and argued against the imposition of French rule.[47] He continued to adopt this stance in April the following year at a meeting of 'Amili *'ulama* and notables (*a'yan*) at Nahar al-Hujar, a meeting he himself had organised to discuss the issue.[48] Al-As'ad was also active in the insurrections against the French in 1920: he was reputed to have led a large band of Shi'a supporters in an attack on the pro-French Christian village of 'Ayn Ibl in Jabal 'Amil.[49]

The extent to which al-As'ad's stance reflected an ideological attachment to Syrian nationalism is questionable. The fact that Faysal had made him emissary to order the affairs of Jabal 'Amil would certainly have motivated al-As'ad to support Faysal and, by extension the goal of Syrian unity. The idea that the 'Ayn Ibl action was motivated by nationalism should be tempered by the knowledge that government control in the countryside was very limited and consequently allowed traditional methods of settling old scores to be adopted. The looting that was carried out during the 'Ayn Ibl action supports the view that the attack was opportunistic rather than nationalistic.[50]

Other *zu'ama* were also actively associated with the Syrian nationalist movement until the last few years before Lebanese independence. The Haydar family from the Biqa', prominent in the Arab nationalist movement and supporters of Faysal, were actively opposed to the French mandate and in favour of Syrian unity. After the failure of the Syrian revolt of 1925, Syrian nationalists met in 1928 to air their views on the question of Lebanon in a summit known as the Conference of the Coast.[51] Subhi Haydar (cousin of Ibrahim the parliamentarian) represented the Shi'a at this conference, which, in its closing communiqué, called for union with Syria. In the same year, Subhi Haydar was a prominent member of the parliamentary Opposition, and in June he attended a Congress for Syrian Unity held in Damascus.[52]

Not all Shi'a *zu'ama* were Syrian unionists. The 'Usayran family, for example, the majority of whom opposed mandatory rule, were supporters of *Le Grand Liban* and became closely identified with the Lebanese nationalist movement. 'Adil 'Usayran's father, 'Abdullah, had been the Iranian consul to Jabal 'Amil and, along with his nephew Rashid, had strongly opposed the imposition of French rule. At the Conference of the Coast in 1936, 'Adil 'Usayran refused to sign the conference's resolution calling for the four *qadas* that had been appended to Mount Lebanon to create *Le Grand Liban*, to be transferred to Syria.[53] This was a very public example of the fact that at least some influential Shi'a believed in

Lebanon's right to exist as an independent state. Famously, in 1943, the French gaoled 'Adil 'Usayran and other parliamentarians who were attempting to exercise Lebanese political independence in the face of intransigence from the French mandatory authorities.

The Arab nationalist cause held obvious attractions for the Shi'a while they were still under Sunni Ottoman rule; but in the mandatory period, the French worked assiduously to co-opt them into supporting their idea of *Le Grand Liban*. This was particularly important to the French because it let them create a rift between the Shi'a and the largely pro-Syrian Sunnis. In return for the support they received from some Shi'a notables during the Syrian revolt of 1925, the French mandatory authorities recognised the Shi'a as a separate sect in 1926 (see Chapter One). It would have been increasingly apparent to the Shi'a at this time that they could benefit more from becoming a large minority in a small state of Lebanon than by remaining a small minority in a larger, Sunni-dominated Syria. Consequently, widespread support from notables for the idea of Syrian union began to dissipate by the end of the 1920s. That is not to say that it disappeared entirely: clans such as the Haydars continued to support the goal of Syrian unity both for ideological reasons and for their own domestic political utility.

Nationalist issues, both Lebanese and Syrian, remained a feature of Lebanese politics up until the granting of independence, but their importance decreased markedly after France signed treaties in September and November 1936 assuring Syria and Lebanon respectively of their independence (although the treaties were never ratified by the French parliament). By contrast, as late as July 1936 the Syrian National Bloc leader Shukri Quwatly publicly urged pro-Syrian Shi'a in Jabal 'Amil to agitate for integration into Syria.[54] Some Shi'a from notable families heeded his call: following anti-French demonstrations in Bint Jbail, 'Arif al-Zayn and 'Ali Bazzi were arrested for signing a telegram calling for Syrian unity. The al-Zayns were a notable Shi'a family of long standing. 'Ali Bazzi was a member of a wealthy landowning family (a relative, Sleiman Bazzi, had been appointed Governor of South Lebanon by Jamal Pasha) and was later to become a Member of Parliament and a Cabinet Minister. For his anti-French activities – he was imprisoned for three months in 1936 and 20 months in 1941 – he gained great political *kudos*.[55] The concept of Syrian nationalism did not disappear altogether but maintained a profile through political groups such as the Syrian Social Nationalist Party (discussed later); yet by this stage the Shi'a *zu'ama* had ceased to play a major role in the Syrian nationalist movement.

Adoption of Formal Political Institutions during the Mandatory Period

The attitude of the traditional *zu'amas* to institutional political power in Lebanon was the same under mandatory rule as it was under the Ottomans. The families vied for positions of power and influence that would reflect their status in Lebanese society; in mandatory Lebanon, this invariably meant parliamentary representation. The French maintained a degree of control over this process, appointing some of the positions in the Lebanese parliament. But most parliamentary representatives were elected; as a result, the Shi'a *zu'ama* were in a position to use their significant client bases to garner support for their electoral campaigns. Attaining a seat in Lebanon's new parliament was of vital importance to the *zu'ama*. As the motivation for securing a position as parliamentary deputy was once described:

> To be a deputy gives the *za'im* the consecration of modernity. It also gives him many and manifold material advantages. It puts the *za'im* on the level of a privileged person in all negotiations with the state. By becoming a deputy his role as one of the leaders is recognised by the state and the administrative machine.[56]

Put simply, without political power the *za'im's* standing as a mediator (*wasita*) was diminished. The position of parliamentary deputy gave the *za'im* formal access to government funds for the development of projects he supported, as well as a greater capacity to seek government jobs for his supporters.

Given the power that parliamentary seats conferred on their holder, elections became hotly contested issues between the traditional leaders, whose large client bases meant that that politically aspiring Shi'a from non-notable families were effectively excluded. The Lebanese electoral system, in which representatives from each community were elected from particular districts, forced *zu'ama* into competition with other *zu'ama* from the same region. As a result, formal alliance-building between Shi'a *zu'ama* became necessary so that they could share client bases and exclude polit-

ical rivals from office. This was not confined to the Shi'a: notables from
all communities needed to build alliances with other powerful families in
order to access their client bases to succeed at the polls. In many cases,
families divided up the appointed and elected positions between themselves prior to election day, using the electoral process merely as an affir-
mation of the political deals already done.

The first representative organ of the mandatory period was the
Representative Council of Greater Lebanon, established in 1922. It was a
thirty-strong body elected by universal suffrage, and its role was largely
consultative. The election of the first Council was boycotted by a large
part of the population. There were two reasons for this: an election was
formal recognition of the establishment of the French mandate (which
was not universally accepted); and the powers accorded the Council were
limited. The French administration sought to influence the election's
outcome – to ensure a compliant Council – by supporting pro-French
candidates.[57] Amongst the Shi'a, this tactic proved successful: of the five
Shi'a councillors elected,[58] the United States Consulate noted at the time
that all of them were pro-French, that 'Usayran was 'a favourite of the
Administration', and that al-Zayn was 'supported by the Government in
his election.'[59]

Whilst it is clear at this early stage of modern Lebanon's political
development that members of the traditional families had begun to establish their position within the formal political system, it should not be
forgotten that amongst these Shi'a families there was anything but
universal support for the Council. The support for Arab nationalism, and
the manifestation of this in the emergence of Faysal's short-lived provisional Arab government, showed just how weak backing was for foreign
rule (hardly surprising given the recent demise of Ottoman rule).
Consequently, the results of the election did not accurately reflect how
little influence the Council had in the Shi'a regions. No member of the
dominant al-As'ad family was on Council, for example, nor were either of
the Shi'a representatives from Faysal's former provisional Arab government – As'ad Haydar and 'Abdullah al-Khalil. The reason for As'ad's
absence from the Council is not recorded, but it may have been that his
agitation against mandatory rule prompted the French authorities to
oppose his candidature; alternatively, like some of the Sunni notables in
Beirut, he may have refused to stand as a protest against the French
administration.

Even within families there was dissension as to what kind of relations to develop with the French. The 'Usayrans are a case in point. Whilst one branch of the family – 'Abdullah and his avowedly anti-French, Lebanese nationalist son 'Adil – remained opposed to the mandate and its institutions, 'Abdullah's brother Najib was successfully courted by the French and ran in the mandatory-period elections. Such was the tension surrounding the political differences between these family members that when 'Adil was arrested after demonstrating against the French in Nabatiyya in 1936, he refused his uncle Najib's offers of assistance for his release.[60] Similar differences in political orientation may also account for Ibrahim Haydar's appearance on the Council when his family were noted Syrian nationalists.

Whilst the mandatory power was certainly not accepted by the *zu'ama* universally, the Shi'a *zu'ama* realised the benefits of participating in the mandatory political system, and the risks of remaining outside it. A significant consideration was the opportunity that participation in these political processes gave the *za'im* to be an influential player on a national, rather than local, stage. After only a short period of time, the utility of seeking political office proved overwhelmingly attractive. The *zu'ama* were soon able to dominate the mandate's political institutions, and this is illustrated by the results of the first parliamentary elections held in 1929 (as distinct from the earlier Council elections). In fact the elections demonstrate not only that a small number of Shi'a *zu'ama* had complete political dominance over their community, but that they were able to mobilise their traditional support base to ensure their electoral success. The election was in two stages: the male population elected delegates, then the delegates elected deputies from a list of candidates.

In the Biqa', there were only enough candidates to fill the available seats, so all were approved. South Lebanon was little different, with five Shi'a vying for three seats. Of the 107 delegates eligible to vote, the successful candidates ('Abdulatif al-As'ad, Najib 'Usayran and Yusuf al-Zayn) received 102, 105 and 106 votes respectively. Despite the fact that the main representatives of the al-As'ad and 'Usayran clans did not field candidates, the ability of the families to mobilise support from amongst the Shi'a was still evident. Whilst the Maronite-dominated, pro-mandate Mount Lebanon electoral district achieved the highest first-round voter participation of 52%, the Shi'a-dominated, recently-appended districts of South Lebanon and the Biqa' both achieved the next best turnouts of

Table 1. Mandatory Period Shi'a Electoral Representation

1929 Election	1934 Election	1937 Election
Biqa' Ibrahim Haydar Sabri Himadah	**Biqa'** Sabri Himadah	**Biqa'** Sabri Himadah Ibrahim Haydar Rashid Harfoush (appointed)
South Lebanon Yusuf al-Zayn 'Abdulatif al-As'ad Najib 'Usayran	**South Lebanon** Fadl al-Fadl Najib 'Usayran	**South Lebanon** Ahmad al-As'ad Rashid Baydoun Kazim al-Khalil Najib 'Usayran Yusuf al-Zayn 'Ali 'Abdullah (appointed) Bahij al-Fadl (appointed)
Appointed Ahmad Al-Husayni Fadl al-Fadl 'Ali Nasrat al-As'ad	**Appointed** Ibrahim Haydar	
		Mount Lebanon Ahmad al-Husayni

48% and 37% respectively. It is likely that the relatively large participation rate in these latter two areas was due more to the ability of the *zu'ama* to mobilise their clients than to any popular enthusiasm for the new Lebanese parliament.

The *zu'ama* continued to dominate the political scene in subsequent elections. Table 1 (opposite page) illustrates the ascendancy of a few Shi'a families. The 1934 election was the first to allow for direct popular vote, although some Members of Parliament were still appointed. Candidates in the Biqa' and South Lebanon were elected without opposition. In the Biqa', all three candidates (Shi'a, Greek Catholic, and Sunni) were elected unopposed, undoubtedly running on a list endorsed by Sabri Himadah, the dominant *za'im* of the region and a candidate himself. The situation in 1937 was only slightly less controlled than in 1934. The third candidate (a non-*za'im*) for the two Shi'a seats in the Biqa' withdrew prior to the election, leaving the other two candidates to run unopposed. In South Lebanon, only six candidates ran for the five seats on offer. The unsuccessful candidate was 'Adil 'Usayran, the anti-French nephew of sitting member Najib 'Usayran. 'Adil had been arrested by the French the year before, yet he was beaten decisively in the election. This suggests several possibilities: that Najib's control of the electoral process was strong enough to deny the accession of his nephew; that the mandatory administration interfered in the electoral process; or that the type of Lebanese nationalist stance 'Adil adopted held little appeal for most Shi'a after the French-Lebanese Treaty of the previous year. The 1937 election was also the first time that two of the most powerful *zu'ama* from Jabal 'Amil chose to run for a place in the mandatory government. Neither Kazim al-Khalil nor Ahmad al-As'ad (son of the venerable Kamil) had sought a place on the electoral ticket before, but when they did, they were successful in attracting a large percentage of the vote and entering Parliament. It would appear that their lack of access to formal political power up to this point had not weakened their local influence. Such was the power of al-As'ad, in fact, that he had far more influence in his local area than did the mandatory government. He had, however, maintained some family contact with the mandatory institutions, for his cousin 'Ali Nasrat al-As'ad was an appointee to both the 1923 Representative Council and the 1929 Mandatory Parliament.

The fact that al-As'ad, al-Khalil and 'Adil 'Usayran all chose to contest the 1937 election marks a turning point in the 'Amili *zu'ama's* acceptance of the mandatory parliament. As‘ad's decision to run for election came after Shukri Quwatly had failed to gain his, and others', support for his campaign in Jabal ‘Amil in 1936 in favour of Syrian union. This could indicate that As‘ad had changed his mind about participating in the mandatory parliament earlier than 1937 – probably because he became aware that the treaty with France was likely to be concluded and that it would consign Syrian nationalism to the political margins. The influence Ahmad al-As‘ad had in the community is reflected in the fact that the mandatory authorities urged him and other Shi‘a leaders, in the face of opposition from Quwatly and the pro-Syrian National Bloc, to support publicly the creation of a separate Lebanese state.

Even the Shi‘a *zu‘ama* who actively participated in mandatory politics were not necessarily enthusiastic supporters of French rule; some remained opposed to the creation of *Le Grand Liban*. The Haydar clan are a good example of this: while taking part in the formal mandatory government, they nevertheless continued to use their profile as Syrian unionists to advance their private political interests. Their history of involvement in Arab and then Syrian nationalist causes allowed the Haydars to exploit France's unease with Lebanese expressions of Syrian unionist sentiment by attempting to obtain favourable political outcomes for their constituency. This was illustrated during a French-initiated campaign against corruption in Lebanese government departments. Leaders of both the Christian and Muslim communities accused the authorities of singling out their communities for attention, and consequently they tried through political agitation to minimise the punishments meted out to their constituents. When the corruption investigation centred upon the Ministry of Finance, which was headed by Subhi Haydar, members of the Haydar family launched a new campaign to incorporate the Biqa‘ into Syria[61] that was perhaps designed to distract the French from pursuing legal action. Whilst the Haydar family's loyalty to Arab (or Syrian) nationalist causes was a matter of historical record, they were certainly able to use it to their advantage in their political dealings with the mandatory authorities. During the 1934 parliamentary election, for example, Sabri Himadah outmanoeuvred the Haydar family for the single Shi‘a seat in the Biqa‘ province by forming an unbeatable electoral ticket. In response, the Haydars began openly dealing with the pro-Syrian National Bloc and publicly supporting moves for the Biqa‘ to become part of Syria. Whether these actions were sufficient by themselves to influence subsequent French political actions is unclear, although it is not unreasonable to see a causal link between the increased support given by the Haydars to Syrian nationalism, and the subsequent political appointments given to the Haydars. Ibrahim Haydar became the only Shiʿa deputy appointed by the French mandatory authorities, and his cousin Subhi (formerly under investigation for corruption) became a director in the Lebanese administration of the French mandate.[62]

Zuʿama, Political Parties and Alliance Building

Parliamentary democracy brought with it the requirement to interact with political parties within parliament. In the Lebanese context, particularly during the early years of the Republic, parliamentary political parties were little more than names given to loose coalitions of like-minded individuals. The *zuʿama*, whilst happy to deal with these groups on occasion, rarely saw the need to belong to a party structure unless it facilitated the formation of a short-term political alliance. The manner in which a *zaʿim* exerted his influence was such that membership of political parties was not necessary for electoral success. It was not until the 1960s when secular, and later Shiʿa, political parties came to dominate the allegiance of the Shiʿa masses that political parties came to rival the *zuʿama's* political influence. During the early period of the mandate, however, some of the *zuʿama* were active members of so-called parliamentary blocs, although these were normally alliances of like-minded politicians who strove to advance their own interests, as well as those of their communal clients, rather than the interests of their constituents in general. Membership of these blocs did not alter the voting allegiances of client groups; it was also somewhat transitory. Given that the blocs were not underpinned by a binding ideology, they represented temporary political, rather than strong ideological alliances. As such, their membership was in constant flux.

That is not to say that the existence of a rather fluid system of parliamentary alliances was altogether a bad thing, nor that it is unique to the Lebanese system. Indeed, it was an important feature of Lebanese political life because it encouraged cross-communal dialogue and compromise to achieve political outcomes. On a more personal level, cross-communal parliamentary alliance-building was essential to the Shiʿa *zaʿim* because his elevation to the cabinet depended on the support he was able to muster from amongst the non-Shiʿa deputies. This was particularly the case in his relations with the Maronite presidential candidates as well as the Sunni

parliamentarians from amongst whose ranks came the future prime ministers who would in turn form their own cabinets. Accession to the cabinet
was an important means to achieve power for every parliamentarian. It
not only added to his prestige, it also gave him access to policy-making
bodies and, more importantly, to decisions about the distribution of
government funds and the appointment of top public officials. In these
ways the *za'im* could bestow patronage, thus confirming his authority. The
parliamentary blocs played an important role in enabling their members
to gain access to these privileges: they became powerful tools for
promoting candidates to Cabinet posts, and they became vehicles through
which groups of parliamentarians could oppose governments so as to
replace the incumbent ministers.

The two most important parliamentary blocs of the mandatory period
were undoubtedly Bishara al-Khoury's Constitutional Bloc (sometimes
referred to simply as *Destour*) and Emile Edde's National Bloc. The
Constitutional Bloc, which sought the restitution by France of the 1926
constitution (discussed further in the next chapter), represented one
element of the Lebanese nationalist movement. The National Bloc advocated the continuation of Lebanon's special relationship with France even
after independence. The exact date when the Constitutional Bloc formally
emerged remains in contention, but there is some evidence that the
prominent Shi'a *za'im* Sabri Himadah was present at its foundation and
continued to be involved throughout the 1930s.[63] As late as 1964,
Himadah was successfully campaigning under the banner of the
Constitutionalist Union Party; however, given his status as a *za'im*, it
would have been by choice rather than by necessity. Given that the
Constitutionalists by this stage emphasised the state's Arabic character
and favoured the gradual abolition of confessionalism and of the requirement that only resident Lebanese be able to vote or run for political
office[64] (which favoured the Muslim Lebanese), it is relatively easy to
understand Himadah's sympathy for their cause.

The power of these parliamentary blocs to attract cross-communal
loyalty for immediate political gain was evident in the defeat of Sabri
Himadah's bid to be Speaker in 1946 (discussed in more detail later). The
move to deny Himadah the position of Speaker was supported by a
number of Shi'a members of parliament, and this indicates that parliamentary allegiances amongst the Shi'a were directed to the leader of their
cross-communal bloc, at the expense of sectarian loyalties. This is hardly

surprising given the electoral system. If, to be elected, a Shi'a parliamentarian had to rely on being included on the electoral list of a prominent political figure, his first loyalty would be to him, not to a *za'im* from his own community.

Some Shi'a *zu'ama* attempted to establish their own political parties. Both Rashid Baydoun and Ahmad al-As'ad used their influence and power to create political parties and thereby formalise their political standing. Baydoun's Vanguard Party (*Hizb al-Tala'i*) had begun life as a paramilitary youth group known simply as al-Tala'i, while Ahmad al-As'ad formed the Renaissance Party (*Hizb al-Nahda*) in 1947. Neither group had an independent political platform *per se*. As one scholar has noted, such parties were simply 'leadership groups made and unmade by coalitions and quarrels of the *zu'ama* or by the wish of one such *za'im* to be "modern" and "up-to-date".'[65] These groups never reached a large audience and consequently did not enjoy the degree of permanence that leadership groups from other communities enjoyed, such as the Maronite *Kata'ib*. Some claim that *Hizb al-Nahda* later formed the basis of al-As'ad's Democratic Socialist Party (DSP) (discussed later in this chapter); others believe that it dissolved in 1951, and that the DSP evolved from the Awareness Movement (*Harakat al-Taw'iyya*) formed in 1969.[66] *Hizb al-Tala'i*, on the other hand, dissolved after Baydoun joined forces with fellow Beiruti Sa'ib Salam's Movement of Reform Pioneers (*Harakat Ruwwad al-Islah*).[67]

Political Threats to the *Zu'ama*

This emphasis on the power and influence of the Shi'a *zu'ama* should not be misconstrued as implying that their position was impervious to threat. Throughout their history, the influence of these notable families had risen and fallen. The Shi'a's informal system of power had always exhibited a degree of fluidity. With the exception of the few leading *zu'ama* (in particular al-As'ads) whose prominence and/or large supporter base kept them stable in power for a long time, the power and stature of the average *za'im* fluctuated with his various alliances. The emergence of 'national' political institutions under the mandate served to formalise the competition for power and influence within the Shi'a community.

This type of competition largely replaced the more physical competition for power and influence that had characterised political life before the mandate. When the mandate ended and Lebanon emerged as an independent state, the political players were freed from their opposition to the French authorities and could then concentrate on manoeuvring for power in the post-mandatory environment. With this change in focus, there emerged a range of threats to the pre-eminent position enjoyed by the *zu'ama*. These threats manifested themselves in three main ways: from traditional intra-sectarian rivalries within the Shi'a community; from other powerbrokers within the Lebanese political system; and finally from the emergence of new (non-*za'im*) political candidates. As the Lebanese parliament matured, the number of parliamentary seats increased, which meant that rather than just catering for the few main traditional notables, it became open to more Shi'a from a wider range of families. In such an environment, political alliance-making that was aimed at advancing individual interests reigned supreme.

The most devastating political blow that could be dealt a *za'im* was the threat to his prestige through the loss of his parliamentary seat as a result of factional, rather than sectarian, political manoeuvring. The fact that parliamentary seats were based on regional proportional allocation by community, meant that it was inevitable that political rivalries would develop within the communities, and that alliance-building would be an integral part of Lebanese parliamentary politics. Rival electoral lists could pit notable Shi'a families against each other, and candidates jockeyed for favouritism with the most influential notables whose list was likely to succeed. Richard Dekmejian has referred to this aspect of Shi'a political activity as 'vertical elite bifurcation',[68] where the conflict between the *zu'ama* was matched by conflict with lower-order Shi'a political players who resented the stranglehold on political power that the notables possessed. At least until the 1960s, there was little change to this situation.

Some of these rivalries were a result of the post-mandatory electoral system itself, which pitted *zu'ama* against each other in electoral contests; others dated back to pre-mandatory rule, most notably those between al-As'ad and al-Khalil clans. An earlier manifestation of this rivalry (outlined previously in this chapter) was the reaction of Kamil al-As'ad to the news that a member of the al-Khalil family was running for the seat in the Ottoman parliamentary elections of 1908. This rivalry was to continue throughout the mandatory period and into independence. In some cases though, political pragmatism overrode traditional rivalries. This was particularly so in the 1943 elections that served to shape the direction of the newly-independent state. Despite the French urging Ahmad al-As'ad to run on a pro-French electoral ticket against the avowedly Lebanese nationalist 'Adil 'Usayran, al-As'ad chose instead to form a single electoral ticket that included his two most significant traditional rivals, 'Adil 'Usayran and Kazim al-Khalil.[69] Their history of opposition to the French mandate was in all likelihood the main reason why they decided to run on a joint ticket. All three were elected against minimal opposition.

Decisions such as this illustrate how many factors the *zu'ama* took into account when making political decisions. In the example just given, the decision to run on a single ticket was motivated in part by national interest – i.e. Lebanese opposition to the French mandate – but also by self-interest. It was self-interest that allowed these *zu'ama*, formerly opposed to each other, to act in unison when their collective influence was under threat or when advantage lay in collective action for immediate gain. That same self-interest also meant that these alliances were quickly dispensed with once the short-term goal of electoral success was achieved. For example, less than twelve months after running on the same electoral ticket, Ahmad al-As'ad became publicly opposed to 'Adil 'Usayran's presence in the Cabinet. As a consequence, the Prime Minister Riad al-Solh dumped 'Usayran to gain al-As'ad's support in an upcoming vote of confidence in the government.[70] The primacy of self-interest, as well as the continuation of old political rivalries, was clearly in evidence on this occasion.

Electoral lists were the key formal element for gauging the interaction between Shi'a *zu'ama* and their clients. The lists were to become the modern method by which power and the wielding of influence manifest themselves. The difficulties in establishing coherent electoral lists in the face of shifting inter-*zu'ama* alliances and self-interest cannot be over stated. If a candidate could not get a place on an influential *za'im's* electoral list, his chances of being elected were severely compromised. A good example of this comes from the 1957 election – when parliament was expanded from 44 to 66 seats – and it illustrates the degree to which inter-*za'im* allegiances were hostage to the allure of political office. For the 1957 elections, the district of Nabatiyya in South Lebanon had a second seat allocated to it. A correspondent from *L'Orient* at the time noted:

> This second seat considerably affects the position of Yusuf al-Zayn. He is said, in fact, to have chosen as colleague on his list Muhammad al-Fadl, who was formerly on Ahmad

al-As'ad's list. This choice is said to have aroused the wrath
of Yusuf al-Zayn's supporters among the Shahin family,
who had always supported the 'Usayran/al-Zayn group
and had hoped that the second seat would be reserved for
one of themselves, Rafiq Shahin. This family is said, consequently, to have decided to campaign against Muhammad
al-Fadl and, in that case, against Yusuf al-Zayn's clan.[71]

In the end, Yusuf al-Zayn was re-elected easily, and Muhammad al-Fadl
narrowly defeated Rafiq Shahin.

Whilst individual seats in parliament were always an expression of the
influence a *za'im* was able to exert within his region, another political prize
was particularly sought after by the Shi'a. The position of President of the
Chamber of Deputies – more commonly referred to, in the Westminster
system, as the Speaker – is always strongly contested amongst the Shi'a
deputies. The fact that the position of Speaker is filled by a Shi'a Muslim
was not dictated by the constitution but was agreed to during deliberations concerning the 1943 National Pact. The President of the Chamber
had a much more significant political role than that of the Speaker in the
Westminster system. Whereas the Westminster Speaker has an internal
procedural function within parliament, the President of the Chamber has
much more extensive powers and is generally considered to be the next
most powerful political position after that of the President of the
Republic. It was number two in the leadership troika that included the
President of the Republic and the Prime Minister. As such, the position
represents a degree of political power and prestige well above that of an
ordinary parliamentary seat. In addition, outside the Cabinet, it is the only
position for which Shi'a from different electoral districts competed against
each other for political advancement. As a result, it sometimes provided a
forum in which the *zu'ama's* traditional political rivalries could be played
out.

The degree to which the position of Speaker became the preserve of
a few of the prominent *zu'ama* is evident from Table 2 (below). During
the first forty years after independence, only al-As'ad, 'Usayran and
Himadah families filled the role (except for Abu Shahla's 1946 interlude);
Husayn Husayni also came from what is considered a notable Shi'a family.
It is not until 1992, therefore, that the Shi'a *zu'ama's* stranglehold on the
position came to an end. Given both the practical and symbolic impor-

**Table 2. Presidents of the Lebanese Chamber of Deputies
since Independence**

Period	Speaker
1943–1946	Sabri Himadah
1946–1947	Habib Abu Shahla (Greek Orthodox)
1947–1951	Sabri Himadah
1951–1953	Ahmad al-As'ad
1953–1959	'Adil 'Usayran
1959–1963	Sabri Himadah
1964	Kamil al-As'ad
1965–1967	Sabri Himadah
1968	Kamil al-As'ad
1968–1971	Sabri Himadah
1971–1984	Kamil al-As'ad (including one session in 1970)
1984–1992	Husayn Husayni
1992–present	Nabih Berri

(From Baaklini, *Legislative and Political Development: Lebanon*, p. 200)

tance of the position to the Shi'a, the way it was allocated could be used to punish parliamentary enemies or reward parliamentary allies.

It should be noted, however, that in the period immediately after the emergence of the National Pact of 1943, it was not guaranteed that the position of Speaker would automatically go to a Shi'a – a further indication, if it was needed, that the institutional political strength of the Shi'a was not considered as great as that of the other communities. An example of this was the defeat of Sabri Himadah by the Lebanese Greek

Orthodox, Habib Abu Shahla, for the position of parliamentary Speaker by 29 votes to 22.

The defeat was instigated by Riad al-Solh, who wished to punish Himadah for aligning himself with al-Solh's Sunni rival ʿAbd al-Hamid Karami.[72] Whilst this action elicited protests from the Shiʿa parliamentarians, it must also be noted that self-interest failed to ensure unity of purpose amongst the Shiʿa *zuʿama*. The United States Legation noted that, amongst the Shiʿa leaders, '[p]articular animus has been manifest against three Shiʿa deputies who failed to vote for their co-religionist.'[73] The defeat was not the first time that the position's communal allocation had been disputed. Sabri Himadah had also faced competition for the position of Speaker in 1944 when he was opposed by a Lebanese Greek Catholic, Yusuf Salim. Himadah was successful by 35 votes to 15, yet ʿAdil ʿUsayran had opposed his election. ʿUsayran's stance was largely in revenge for Riad al-Solh's dumping of him from his Cabinet the previous year (Himadah was, at this stage, a close ally of al-Solh).[74] These instances of internal political rivalry were a constant feature of national politics amongst all communal groups. Whilst it was certainly a threat to whichever *zaʿim* group was dominant at the time, the fact that it was an internalised threat meant that it was manageable within the larger group of notables. What it did highlight, however, was the lack of unity amongst the Shiʿa *zuʿama* that would eventually contribute to their demise.

The second of the threats to the *zuʿama*, that from other powerbrokers within the Lebanese political system, was impossible to avoid and probably of most concern. Given that other communal groups, particularly the Christians, were politically over-represented for the size of their communities, the Shiʿa *zuʿama* were sometimes at the mercy of political power plays initiated by leading Maronite or Sunni parliamentarians. This was particularly the case with issues involving political legislative matters that were fought over between members of opposing parliamentary blocs. Of more concern to the *zuʿama* of all communal persuasions were the actions undertaken during the Chamun and more especially during the Shihab presidencies, where efforts were made to weaken their traditional powers. These efforts, to reform the *zuʿama's* formal and informal powers, would serve as a precedent for later attempts at reform generated from within the Shiʿa community, and illustrate the fact that the power of the *zuʿama* did not go unchallenged.

The realisation that the Shi'a *zu'ama* were politically vulnerable should not disguise the fact that within their regions they still wielded significant power. It is true that in later years those determined to reduce, if not destroy, the *zu'ama's* dominance were quite successful. It is also apparent in the early years of the Republic that some Shi'a *zu'ama*, despite their inability to secure either the Presidency or the Prime Ministership, were more powerful locally than some nationally-influential Maronite or Sunni parliamentarians. This was certainly true in the case of Ahmad al-As'ad and Riad al-Solh. Al-Solh was the first Prime Minister of the independent Republic. He was also a Sunni from Saida in South Lebanon. Al-Solh's formal political achievement at the national level meant little in the traditional heartland of South Lebanon where Ahmad al-As'ad dominated. Prior to the 1947 election, United States' diplomats noted that 'Riad Al Solh...has found it impossible to dominate Assad [*sic*]'.[75] This inability to dominate the traditional *za'im* was in many ways a result of the electoral law that served to formalise the power of a *za'im* of al-As'ad's standing. South Lebanon was treated as a single electoral district, and with Shi'a constituting 55% of the district, non-Shi'a candidates (even of the standing of Riad al-Solh) could not afford to ignore al-As'ad's electoral influence.

This was the era of the 'grand list', when a large electoral district such as the South would have the prominent candidates agree on a single electoral ticket, inclusion on which virtually guaranteed election. Riad al-Solh, aware of this (as well as the fact that South Lebanon only elected one Sunni candidate), had attempted to weaken al-As'ad's influence by cultivating rival Shi'a families (including 'Adil 'Usayran, Kazim al-Khalil and Rashid Baydoun) with the aim of running an opposing ticket.[76] This approach was not ultimately successful. Al-Solh was eventually included on al-As'ad's electoral ticket and elected to parliament, although his reliance on al-As'ad diminished his power. It is interesting to note that, during the negotiations with al-Solh to form a joint ticket, al-As'ad vetoed the inclusion of al-Khalil but remained open-minded about the inclusion of al-Solh's two other Shi'a allies. This is further indication of the depth of enmity between al-As'ad and al-Khalil clans. The extent of al-As'ad's influence over the electorate (as well as his stance on political alliances) can be seen in the case of the September 1951 by-election for the seat left vacant by al-Solh's death. Having guaranteed, by his support, al-Solh's election in April, al-As'ad then supported a member of al-Bizri family

against an al-Solh family candidate in September. Salah al-Bizri won the
seat by 17,595 votes to Kazim al-Solh's 4,909. Al-As'ad's home village of
Tayyiba voted in favour of al-Bizri by 354 votes to nil.[77]

The most powerful of the *zu'ama* understood the nature of their
power and the wishes of their constituents, which meant that uncoordinated efforts to change the *status quo* by outsiders were normally unsuccessful in the long term. That is not to say that powerful politicians did
not make the attempt. The rise to the Presidency of Camille Chamun, for
example, was to pose the most serious threat to al-As'ad since he had
entered the Lebanese parliament. Chamun was in many ways the
antithesis of the notables: he was reformist and he was prepared to curb
the political power of the traditional rural *zu'ama* by imposing presidential authority.[78] At the same time, Chamun himself was a *za'im*, hence part
of his motivation for reform was probably to weaken some of his rival
zu'ama. Chamun well understood that the centre of gravity of the *zu'ama*
was their access to parliamentary representation. His first attempt at
curbing their power came in 1952, when he introduced changes to the
electoral laws that divided the existing single electoral districts (North
Lebanon, South Lebanon and the Biqa') into multiple electoral districts.
The South and the Biqa' were divided into seven and four districts respectively. This was designed to dilute the absolute power of the (largely Shi'a)
feudal *zu'ama* by removing the practice of the 'grand list', where the
leading notables held the political fate of all candidates in their hands. The
electoral districts were again modified in time for the 1957 election in an
effort to unseat the long-term incumbents 'by reallocating the electoral
districts in such a way that they cut across the boundaries of the traditional regional and religious territories of certain *zu'ama*.'[79] The effect of
this tactic was felt almost immediately. Ahmad al-As'ad's list had dominated the 1951 elections in South Lebanon, ensuring that Kazim al-Khalil
and Adil 'Usayran were both unsuccessful. By contrast, the 1953 election
saw Kazim al-Khalil elected unopposed in his district of Tyre and 'Adil
'Usayran successful against one other candidate in Zahrani district. Both
Ahmad and his son Kamil al-As'ad were successful in Bint Jbayl and
Marjayoun-Hasbaya districts respectively, although Ahmad faced some
opposition from 'Ali Bazzi, the well-known Shi'a Lebanese nationalist
candidate in the same district. Chamun's tactics were designed to cut the
zu'ama's power through indirect means. By targeting As'ad's supporters
rather than concentrating on the main *za'im* himself, Chamun struck at the

heart of the *za'im's* power: his ability to act as the *wasita*. It was al-As'ad's allies in the other constituencies for whom al-As'ad campaigned, but who were defeated, who felt the impact of the electoral amendment.[80] Indeed, al-As'ads were the only candidates from Ahmad's electoral list that won. In the Biqa' there was less of an immediate impact from Chamun's tactics, because the single district was divided into two districts (Ba'albak-Hermil and West Biqa'-Rashaya). Whilst the 1953 elections did see the defeat of a long-time parliamentary *za'im*, Ibrahim Haydar, this had more to do with internal tribal disputes – his successful rival was his cousin Salim Haydar – than with a centrally-directed campaign.[81] The re-drawing of the electoral district boundaries for the 1957 elections was, however, more successful in achieving what Chamun had set out to do. Traditional leaders such as the Druze, Kamal Jumblatt, suffered from the electoral redistribution in the Shuf, which had created a majority of Christians within his electoral district. Ahmad al-As'ad was forced to run in the district of Tyre, a stronghold of al-Khalil, for one of the two seats available to Shi'a; not surprisingly he was beaten by Kazim al-Khalil and one of his allies, Rida Wahid. Kamil al-As'ad, however, had a close-fought victory in his district.

Although the zu'ama suffered a loss of political prestige through Chamun's actions, national socio-economic conditions had not yet altered sufficiently for it to be anything more than a temporary setback. In fact, the actions of Chamun's government so alienated most Lebanese that it was he, rather than the *zu'ama* whose political hold he had sought to weaken, who ultimately suffered. During the 1958 crisis,[82] for example, al-As'ad family were able to use their traditional influence to ensure that they, rather than the government, controlled the South. This illustrates how, even during the late 1950s, government office was the official imprimatur of power but not its real basis. Indeed Kazim al-Khalil, a minister in the government after his success in the 1957 election, hence a supporter of the now despised Chamun, could not leave the safety of Beirut. When he attempted to return to Tyre from Beirut after the crisis, he came under attack from gunmen several times.[83] There is little doubt that al-As'ad clan had reasserted their authority and would be able to do so for some time yet. In the 1960 elections, Ahmad al-As'ad regained his seat in parliament (this time running in Bint Jbayl district), while his rival, al-Khalil, was unable to gain one of the three seats allotted to the Shi'a in the district of Tyre. Ahmad died in 1961 and his seat was taken by his son

Kamil, who was elected unopposed (having lost his own seat in the 1960 election).

The end of the Chamun era did not, however, represent an end to the threat posed by the non-Shi'a political establishment to the traditional *zu'ama*. Chamun's successor, Fu'ad Shihab, is generally considered to have been one of the best Lebanese presidents. This view is based both on his ability to maintain the neutrality of the Lebanese Army during the 1958 crisis and on his attempts to weaken the political hold of the traditional *zu'ama* – attempts that were more effective, though less confrontational, than those of his predecessor. Shihab well understood the need to reduce the power of the traditional leadership in order to foster the growth of Lebanese democracy, but having seen the divisive impact of Chamun's actions, he also knew the cost of changing the *status quo* by confrontation. To that end, Shihab was more selective in isolating those elements that he felt were an impediment to Lebanese social progress. For example, he supported Ahmad al-As'ad in his attempt to regain his parliamentary seat in the 1960 elections, but he did not support the younger Kamil al-As'ad. The degree to which this popular president's support (or lack of it) determined the electoral result is not known – many factors contribute to electoral outcomes – but Kamil subsequently lost his seat and Ahmad was re-elected to parliament.

The last of the threats faced by the *zu'ama* in the period before the Shi'a population as a whole became politicised, was the emergence of parliamentary candidates from non-notable Shi'a families. These independents were neither *zu'ama* nor members of political parties. Without the benefit of socio-economic factors that would eventually allow for an independent political consciousness to develop amongst the Shi'a, they had little likelihood of success. Faced with the limitations inherent in their status, these independent candidates were unable to build a critical mass of public support. The difficulty they faced is illustrated by the fact that, in the four elections held between 1960 and 1972, only eight of 404 independent candidates (across all communal groups) were elected.[84] Excluded from the electoral lists formulated by the leading candidates, independents stood little chance of making an impact. That they did do so, demonstrates the emergence amongst some elements in the community of a political consciousness and a growing dissatisfaction with the *status quo*. Realistically, these candidates were likely only to provoke the anger of the *zu'ama*, who saw political representation as their hereditary right.

The dangers for independent Shi'a who actively campaigned against the *status quo* are well illustrated by the case of the Beiruti Shi'a lawyer Muhsin Slim. He ran in the 1943 election in the electoral district of Beirut against Hajj Muhammad Baydoun, a member of the rich Shi'a merchant family (Muhammad's brother, Rashid, was an MP for the South). Slim lost the seat, though he did manage to force the election into a second round. He ran again in the 1947 election but was less successful, losing to Rashid Baydoun. Rashid had by this time decided to represent the electoral district of Beirut rather than South Lebanon. This move, aligning Rashid's electoral district with his residential circumstances, also indicates the emergence amongst the Shi'a *zu'ama* of a notion of constituencies rather than of client groups defined merely by communal membership. Later that year, Slim was arrested and imprisoned on suspicion of launching a series of bombings in Beirut. The American Legation believed that his imprisonment was simply 'a reprisal for Slim's energetic efforts to fight the governing clique in the last election in which he was one of the defeated candidates.'[85] It is not clear if his efforts against the ruling clique were directed against *all* communal groups, although the fact that the entire Lebanese Bar went on strike in protest against Slim's arrest would appear to indicate that his electoral campaign targeted all entrenched political authority, not just that of the Shi'a. Nevertheless, it is impossible to separate communal identity from political activism: independents, as well as the *zu'ama*, competed for seats based on their communal identity. The political challenge by Slim, however, was a precursor to future non-*za'im* activism, as the socio-economic transformation of the Shi'a community (outlined in the previous chapter) gained momentum from the 1950s and 1960s, bringing with it internal calls for change in the community's political *status quo*.

Decline of the *Zu'ama*

Threats to the political primacy of the Shi'a *zu'ama* that manifested themselves during the mandatory and early independence periods were largely a product of the Lebanese political system. Shifting alliances within the community, or tactics from the government designed to curb the formal power of the *zu'ama*, temporarily deprived notables of positions of authority within the established political system. They did not represent any fundamental re-ordering of the established power system within the Shi'a community. Rivalries between the notable families had been a feature of traditional Lebanese society. That the prize being sought during this period was political representation in a confessionally-diverse parliament, meant that political alliances were by necessity established with other (often non-Shiʿa) members of parliament. In many ways then, it was a continuation of the types of challenges that the *zuʿama* had faced prior to the mandate.

During the Ottoman era, the Shiʿa *zuʿama* had periodically been attacked by Sunni *walis*; but even when a *zaʿim* did not survive the onslaught, he was soon replaced by another. The end of Ottoman rule and the beginning of the mandatory and early independence periods represented a less violent but nevertheless real threat to the *zuʿama*, although at no stage did the leaders lose their bases of support amongst the people. Indeed, during this period some families not only formalised their political power by gaining election to high public office, they also created political dynasties. The al-Zayns, for example, had the brothers Yusuf (elected) and Husayn (appointed) in the 1927 parliament, and three brothers ʿAbdulatif, ʿAbdul-Karim and ʿAbdul-Majid (sons of Yusuf) elected to the 1968 parliament. As long as the *zuʿama* retained their supporter base, they remained the pre-eminent political players in their community, as well as significant players nationally.

Whilst the threats from this period were generally managed, not all of the challenges that followed were handled so adeptly. Even as the political leaders were busy jockeying for parliamentary seats, profound societal changes were taking place within the Shiʿa population that would ultimately lead to the decline of the largely complacent *zuʿama*. It was precisely these types of changes that the *zuʿama* were collectively unable to answer, because they undermined the very foundations of their power base. Their ability to retain effective formal and informal political power for such a long time had always been predicated on their ability to maintain the loyalty of their constituents. The constituents, in return for this loyalty, received the *zaʿim's* protection, as well as benefits such as employment in state institutions and favourable treatment in dealing with government departments. Any weakening of his ability to deliver these benefits could call into question the legitimacy of his leadership, and could introduce the possibility that other groups might attract his constituents by offering them alternative means of satisfying their needs.

A good example of the difficulties the *zuʿama* faced is President Shihab's drive to engender a national identity by strictly allocating administrative posts equally between Christians and Muslims from 1958 onwards. These public service positions required some form of entrance test, and the Shi'a, given their generally poor level of education, stemming in part from their concentration in rural areas, won proportionally less of the positions allotted to Muslims than did their Sunni and Druze counter-parts.[86] The Shi'a *zu'ama's* inability to deliver such opportunities for government employment meant that they came to be seen as incapable of fulfilling properly the social contract they implicitly held with their constituents. Issues such as these were difficult for the *zu'ama* to address, largely because it was not in their power to resolve them.

The political challenge to the *zu'ama's* authority posed by the Shihabist reforms was only the beginning of the difficulties that confronted them. Of more enduring importance were the social forces that impacted on the Lebanese Shi'a from the 1950s onwards, which resulted in the loosening of the grip the *zu'ama* had on the political development of their clients. There was not one single event that led to the *zu'ama's* political decline. It was a combination of several factors: the internal migration of many Shi'a families to the southern suburbs of Beirut (*dahiya*); the external migration of Shi'a to the Gulf and West Africa, along with the financial remittances from these emigrants back to Lebanon that allowed for a degree of self-sufficiency for their families at home; the emergence of leftist political parties that attracted mass Shi'a support by advocating an end to the confessionalism of the republic; internal pressures from Lebanese polit-ical opponents; and the developing political profile of the hitherto quies-cent clerics. All these issues together created an environment the *zu'ama* were ill-equipped to control.

The *za'im's* ability to act as intermediary between his client and the state was relatively straightforward in the traditional environment of the Biqa' and Jabal 'Amil, given the relatively static nature of the population up until the early part of the twentieth century. In this environment the *zu'ama* were the only ones who could instigate formal contact with governmental authorities in Beirut. But from the 1920s, Shi'a began to migrate to Beirut from their traditional homelands. Most of them were poor rural workers, attracted to Beirut by the opportunities it offered unskilled labourers. By the 1960s, this migratory flow had accelerated considerably; increased mechanisation on large agricultural estates, as well as increased rents and low wages, forced many Shi'a to seek work in Beirut.[87] During the 1940s and 1950s, when the numbers of Shi'a moving to Beirut remained relatively small, and alternative political patrons were not available, most of these internal migrants remained on the electoral rolls of their home villages. On election days, the traditional leaders provided them with transport back to their villages to vote, so that the *zaʿim* would be re-elected.[88] In the face of growing political activism, the occasional return by emigrants to their home villages was insufficient to sustain traditional political loyalties. As a result, the support base of the leaders who relied on this loyalty declined.

At the same time, the return of numerous economic *emigrés* from West Africa back to their traditional homes in Jabal ʿAmil, led to a further eroding of the dominance of the traditional leadership. In the first place, many of these *emigrés* returned with substantial savings from their time abroad and formed an economically-active middle class. However, their newly-won economic power was not matched by access to any commensurate form of political power. The traditional families' hold on power was still strong enough to ensure that they continued to monopolise the political representation of the Shiʿa. The systemic inability to accommodate the political aspirations of the emergent Shiʿa middle class was to present another challenge to the *zuʿama*, and one that was to have a long-term impact. The middle class it was who, having no access to political representation themselves, welcomed those who advocated changes to the *status quo*; and they proved in particular to be strong supporters of the reformist cleric Musa Sadr (discussed in more detail in Chapter Four). This new middle class were men who had moved away from the restrictions of traditional Shiʿa Lebanese life and had become successful businessmen abroad. When they returned, they were unwilling to be constrained by the dictates of the traditional Shiʿa political structure.

These factors were ultimately to prove sufficient to undermine the power of the traditional *zuʿama*; the debilitating impact of the civil war completed their decline. Whilst this decline was sharp enough to result in a re-ordering of the traditional Shiʿa model of political activity, not all the traditional Shiʿa notables were dispossessed of their political status. This disparity in the political fortunes of the Shiʿa is an issue that has not been seriously addressed. The factors that contributed to the decline of the Shiʿa *zuʿama* are relatively well understood, but it is the variation in how individual *zaʿim* responded to it, and how this affected their political power, that has not been examined.

To best understand the manner in which many responded to the changed societal circumstances, it is appropriate to look first at the most powerful of the traditional Shi'a *zu'ama* of the 1960s and early 1970s: Kamil al-As'ad. Al-As'ad faced two major threats to his position: governmental policies aimed at subverting the *zu'ama's* traditional powers (these policies were collectively known as *Shihabism*), and the increasing politicisation of his regional support base through the actions of secular political parties and Musa as-Sadr. Given the position of al-As'ad clan in Lebanese politics, it is no surprise that Kamil's initial reaction to the threats was to advocate a return to more traditional forms of allegiance. Within parliament, he sought to do this by establishing cross-communal alliances with other traditional *zu'ama*. In 1969 he formed a triumvirate with a leading Maronite, Sulayman Franjiyyah, and a leading Sunni, Sa'ib Salam. The political alliance was formally known as the Centre Bloc, and was opposed to Shihabism.[89] It achieved short-term success: the 1970 presidential election saw the rise to power of Franjiyyah and, shortly after, the accession of Salam and al-As'ad to the positions of Prime Minister and Speaker respectively. At this stage, it appeared that al-As'ad's determination to roll back the forces of Shihabism by maintaining the traditional reliance on intra-parliamentary conservative alliance-building was a successful method for maintaining the *status quo*. Outside parliament, he was less able to influence the forces that were shaping the Shi'a political landscape, even though he could recognise the threat they posed. This was both a recognition of the limits of his power and a reflection of his philosophical orientation. A statement he made following his re-election to the position of parliamentary Speaker in 1972 illustrates his inability to offer alternatives to the traditional political allegiances from which he had benefitted:

> While there are many who are calling for reform in this country, the leftists are calling for essential changes that dig deep into the country's basic set-up...[T]he people must resist such a change.[90]

This conservatism and inability to identify realistic alternative avenues for political influence would prove critical in the subsequent demise of al-As'ad's political fortunes. These same factors also contributed considerably to the general destruction and instability of the Lebanese body politic from the 1970s.

A similar situation existed in al-As'ad's dealings with Imam Musa as-Sadr, the charismatic Shi'a jurist who acted as a rallying point for many politically-dispossessed Lebanese Shi'a. As-Sadr was a potential threat to the political position of all Shi'a *zu'ama*. The fact that he was based in Tyre and was the driving force behind the creation of the Supreme Islamic Shi'a Council (see Chapter Four) meant that he operated in two spheres that al-As'ad considered to be his own: the region of southern Lebanon, and the political representation of the Shi'a. Al-As'ad, however, resorted to traditional means of dealing with the situation. Fouad Ajami recounts the story of how al-As'ad, as early as 1965, sought to co-opt Musa as-Sadr.[91] Unsuccessful in his bid, al-As'ad consequently viewed as-Sadr as a man unwilling to countenance the primacy of the traditional leadership and therefore to be treated as a political rival. His fears proved to be well-founded. Musa as-Sadr's impact on al-As'ad's supporter base is exemplified by the 1974 by-election in Nabatiyya (caused by the death of the sitting member Fahmi Shahin): Rafiq Shahin, a candidate supported by Musa as-Sadr, defeated al-As'ad's preferred choice by almost two-to-one.[92] At the same time, al-As'ad's inability to accommodate all the Shi'a candidates who wished to appear on his electoral list had repercussions: those who missed out became his political enemies. A case in point was al-As'ad's refusal in the 1968 and 1972 elections to include on his list a young Shi'a lawyer by the name of Nabih Berri. In 1980, Berri became the head of the Shi'a party Amal (discussed in Chapter Three) and was to remain al-As'ad's implacable foe.

It would not be fair to say that the *zu'ama* made no attempt to change their method of political expression in the face of the increasingly politically-active Shi'a population. Rather, their responses to the changes in society around them often illustrate how little they understood, or even acknowledged, them. Al-As'ad formed the Democratic Socialist Party (DSP) largely because the political left was attractive to the Shi'a. The party's name came out of As'ad's trips to Europe, where he saw the success of the social democratic parties there.[93] Given that al-As'ad himself was neither a socialist nor a democrat, the DSP was never taken seriously. Unlike the parties it was intended to challenge, the DSP had no platform other than to support al-As'ad's personal political viewpoints. Its committee comprised close associates of al-As'ad from traditional southern families such as Ja'far Sharaf al-Din, but it did also include two Christians and one Sunni. Nizar Hamzeh recalls that the party's emer-

gence around Tyre during his secondary school days promised young
Shi'a an alternative to the feudal-style politics that the traditional leaders
had always employed in the past. In practice, however, there was no
substance to the party, and the party hierarchy in the towns adopted the
traditional imperious manner in which 'feudal' families had acted for
generations.[94] Being so closely identified with the traditionalist al-As'ad,
and without the benefit of an armed militia, its members were harassed,
in particular by Amalists. As a result, by the late 1970s the DSP had
become largely inactive.

Despite being under pressure externally from the leftist parties and
Musa as-Sadr's followers, the *zu'ama* managed to retain most of their seats
in the 1972 elections (the last election before the outbreak of the civil
war). With many new political players competing for the attention of the
Shi'a masses, individual *za'ims* still had the stature to command the
support of their client bases. For this reason, notables such as Sabri
Himadah, Kamil al-As'ad, 'Abdulatif al-Zayn, Kazim al-Khalil, 'Adil
'Usayran and Muhammad Baydoun continued to be active in parliamentary politics. Whilst at this stage the *zu'ama* still retained their influence, so
fundamental were the changes that had occurred within Lebanon as a
whole, and within the Shi'a community in particular, that any wider
change to the political landscape threatened to spell the end of their
dominance. The difficulty in responding to these changes was exacerbated
by the fact that the *zu'ama* continued to be divided by internal traditional
rivalries which ensured that self-interest dictated each family's response to
the forces of change.

The Civil War and the Traditional *Zu'ama*

Even though the *zu'ama* were able to retain their formal political positions,
if not influence, until the beginning of the civil war, it is fair to say that by
the time the first post-war election was held in 1992, the traditional Shi'a
political leadership no longer survived in any recognisable form. It has
already been noted that one of the reasons for the demise of the *zu'ama's*
political dominance was the impact of pre-civil-war societal changes.
There were three further reasons, all connected to some degree with the
war: the deaths of several *zu'ama* MPs; the increasing influence within
Lebanon of external actors; and the notables' responses to the civil war.

Given the length of tenure of many MPs, the death of a man while
he held office was not an uncommon event, so the death of a number of

zuʿama during the civil war period was not sufficient in itself to cause a realignment of political leadership. When the death occurred, it was generally accepted, prior to the war, that the seat would be assumed by another member of the man's family. But the civil war and the societal changes that preceded it had the effect of making this form of electoral succession less acceptable to the Shiʿa populace. The impact of the deaths that occurred after 1972 on the political structure of the Shiʿa was exacerbated by two things: the popular support enjoyed by the *zaʿim* who died, and the fact that the next election did not take place until nearly twenty years later. In effect, an entire generation was not exposed to the political power the traditional leadership had once possessed, and were therefore reluctant to pay them respect.

Some of the Shiʿa members of parliament in 1972 had themselves benefited from this traditional method of political succession. An example of this is the career of Kamil al-Asʿad. He was a deputy for the Marjayoun-Hasbaya region but lost his seat in the 1960 elections. Meanwhile, in the same elections, his father won the seat of Bint Jbayl, but in 1961 he died. Subsequently Kamil took his father's place in an unopposed by-election. A similar case is that of the venerable Yusuf al-Zayn, who was in parliament on and off from 1927 and died in 1962. Following his death, a by-election was held between two candidates from the same clan: his son ʿAbdulatif and his nephew Izzat al-Zayn. ʿAbdulatif recalled that whilst a formal by-election would still take place, he and Izzat had already reached an understanding that ʿAbdulatif would succeed to the seat. Indeed, Abdulatif said his father had requested that he run with him during the 1957 election; ʿAbdulatif did not, but the request created an understanding amongst the family (Yusuf had 11 sons) that ʿAbdulatif was the designated ʿparliamentary successorʾ.[95] We can find another example as early as 1935: the death of the Shiʿa deputy Fadl al-Fadl led to a run-off between Fadl's cousin, Bahij al-Fadl, and ʿAbdulatif al-Asʿad. Fadl's cousin won by 21,284 votes to 203.[96]

The post-civil war elections provide clear practical evidence that the long-term decline in the *zuʿamaʾs* influence was nearly complete. One sign that a new power structure was upon them was that when a parliamentary *zaʿim* died, he was no longer as a matter of course replaced by someone from his own clan (either by appointment or through a single candidate by-election). Post-Taʾif Lebanon, with its loss of sovereignty to Syrian interests and the politicisation of its Shiʿa masses, saw an end to the perpetuation of parliamentary succession within traditional notable families. In 1976, Sabri Himadah died and was replaced not by another clan member but by an appointed deputy, 'Ali Hamad Ja'far, following the civil war in 1991. Similarly, Kazim al-Khalil (the long-time opponent of the al-As'ad family) died in 1990 and was replaced by an appointed deputy, Muhammad 'Abdul-Hamid Baydoun (from Amal). In 1984, following the death of 'Abdulatif Baydoun, the Ba'thist 'Abdallah al-Amin was appointed in his place. Events such as these leave no doubt that the influence of the secular political parties (including those with external backing) now far exceeded that of the traditional families.

The fact that non-*zu'ama* Shi'a could be appointed to parliament in the place of notables who had died, is indicative of the extent to which the traditional power structure of the Shi'a community had changed. The post-war Shi'a political elite bore little or no resemblance to those they replaced. The militarisation of Lebanese society brought about by the civil war made it possible for the politically ambitious to 'fast-track' to power through militia leadership. The traditional Shi'a *zu'ama*, though they employed groups of strongmen (*qabadayat*) to back up their authority, were not able to turn these groups into dedicated militias and hence were unable to match their newly militarised Shi'a political opponents. Al-As'ad and al-Khalil both developed militias of their own, but they were too small to make them military players. In addition, the *wasta* traditionally practised by the notables was successful only if the organs of government were working properly; when government ceased to operate effectively, so too did the *zu'ama's* source of legitimacy and power. The *wasta* was soon replaced by the largesse distributed by political parties, particularly the wages from the parties' militia.

More important than this transformation of the political elite was the presence in Lebanon of tens of thousands of Syrian troops, which meant that Syria increasingly played the role of kingmaker amongst the local Shi'a communities. If the traditional notables were unable to reach an accommodation with Syrian powerbrokers, then their ability to continue as political players in parliament was largely eroded. At the same time the Shi'a population increasingly sought political representation from secular or religious political parties that provided *wasta* – a practice that has been described as 'party-directed clientilism'.[97] Hizbullah in particular, and Amal before them, offered social services in the absence of those normally provided by the state and were consequently able to establish an implicit social contract with a large part of the Shi'a community.

The terminal decline of a *za'im's* power was in some cases marked by a defining moment. The unopposed confiscation of al-Khalil family estate by the largely Shi'a Socialist Arab Action Party – Lebanon in 1976 (discussed further in Chapter Three) indicates just how powerless the *zu'ama* were in the face of militias. In another case, the decision by Kamil al-As'ad to support the US-brokered Agreement of 17th May 1983 with Israel[98] (signed by Amin Jummayyil) not only delegitimised him in the eyes of the Shi'a, but also earned him the anger of the Syrians. This simple miscalculation was an act from which he was never able to fully recover politically. The most noticeable impact of al-As'ad's actions came in October 1984 when his fourteen-year reign as Speaker came to an end with his defeat by Husayn Husayni in a parliamentary vote. In addition Amal, which had to date made a point of antagonising supporters of the traditional Shi'a leadership in general, made a point, after the Armistice agreement was signed, of targeting al-As'ad's supporters within the Democratic Socialist Party. This meant that both al-As'ad's personal standing and his ability to command collective political action were virtually destroyed.

The Future of the Shi'a *Zu'ama* in Post Civil War Lebanon

A *za'im* is by definition a leader, and in the Lebanese Shi'a context a man's claim to leadership had been strengthened by his genealogy. With the right connections, however, other individuals had been able to force their way into political power. Such 'connections' once meant the support of a traditional *za'im*, but political and societal changes have rendered this old paradigm obsolete. In the new world of Lebanese Shi'a politics, it is the political parties, or the well-connected individuals within those parties, that hold the reigns of power. Whilst events may have overtaken the *zu'ama's* ability to do anything about this change of fortune, rivalries between, but more importantly within, traditional notable families have not helped their cause. A good example of this is the fractiousness within Kazim al-Khalil's family. This family continues to run for parliament in the Tyre district, whose seat was held by Kazim until his death in 1990. 'Ali al-Khalil, an academic and former Ba'thist, and only distantly related to Kazim's branch of the family, also gained a seat in the Tyre district in the 1972 election, alongside Kazim. The fact that, after Kazim's death,

Muhammad Baydoun, a member of Amal, was appointed to the seat meant that the chain of succession was broken. Other family members subsequently stood for election in the hope of regaining the seat they considered the rightful inheritance of al-Khalil family. Kazim's son, Nasir, for example, ran for his father's old seat in 1996, but was not successful. The family's traditional influence in Tyre obviously counted for little any longer. In contrast, 'Ali al-Khalil's success was due to the fact that he represented the politically-moderate Shi'a intellectuals, rather than because he had distant familial links to a noted *za'im*.

This is not to say that a support base for the traditional Shi'a leadership has disappeared completely. There is little doubt that previously dominant figures such as Kamil al-As'ad have been unable to maintain the formal political power that parliamentary representation bestows. He has, after all, been unsuccessful in securing a seat despite contesting the 1992, 1996 and 2000 elections. These results should not disguise the fact that he can still mobilise a degree of support locally. Whilst the dominance of al-As'ad family is now a thing of the past, Kamil is still able to elicit some support from within his region, as was demonstrated by the reception he received when he returned to his home village of Tayyiba following the Israeli withdrawal in July 2000.[99] Similarly, he still had sufficient influence to be able to compile and head an electoral list for the 2000 election. Neither of these activities, however, can disguise the fact that he is no longer part of the formal political power structure.

The main problem that a traditional notable such as Kamil al-As'ad faced was that because the power of the *za'im* has always been generated at the local level, his decision to live in Jabal Lubnan from 1976 onwards weakened his hold on his constituency.[100] A large part of the power held by the 'feudal' *zu'ama* was exercised through the tradition of the 'open house' (*bayt maftuh*), in which the two-way nature of the relationship between *za'im* and *zilm* (follower) was apparent. Clients had the right to have their grievances heard at the house of their *za'im*. Kamil's father, Ahmad, had continued to practise this tradition; Kamil himself was not so observant of it. His lack of attention to its importance is illustrated by the fact that he left his constituency nearly immediately after the civil war broke out. Halim Barakat noted in 1976 that 'the Speaker of the House, Kamil al-As'ad, who supposedly represented the Shi'ites, sought refuge in the Maronite district of Kisrawan.'[101] By removing himself from the region of his client base, Kamil ensured that the 'open house' relationship could never work. In modern Lebanon, it is more often representatives from Amal and Hizbullah who perform this function.

The other factor that contributed to Kamil's political demise was his inherent conservatism, which stopped him from spreading an alternative message that could have attracted some of those who voted for him in the past. Added to this is the fact that the agents of the Shi'a's politicisation to which he was opposed, Amal and Hizbullah, conspired to support combined electoral tickets that exclude him. The extent to which the old families' expectations have been altered is shown, for example, by the fact that Kamil's son Ahmad has also eschewed the traditional political path, instead creating a movement called Lebanon of the Skilful (*Lubnan al-Kafa'at*) which rejects both the current sectarian political system and the influence of the traditional Lebanese leadership.[102] For the reasons given above, it is likely that we have seen the political demise of the once dominant al-As'ad dynasty.

Although al-As'ads and al-Khalils find themselves in this situation, two other traditional *zu'ama* remain part of the formal political scene. 'Ali 'Usayran and 'Abdulatif al-Zayn have been able to carry some of their pre-war influence, particularly at the local level, into the post-war era. They remain popular within their respective electoral districts, which means they can continue to cultivate their a local support bases. More importantly, however, they have reached a *modus vivendi* with the post-war Shi'a political structure that ensures their continued political survival. By so doing, they maintain their influence through the establishment of political alliances with the Shi'a political parties that in turn gives them access to government support programs. This has cost them some of their power, because they are now partly beholden to the newer breed of Shi'a community leader. As far as 'Abdulatif al-Zayn is concerned, the idea of a *traditional* leader implies a person who retains his independence and is not a member of a political party.[103] That having been said, both 'Abdulatif al-Zayn and 'Ali 'Usayran run on Nabih Berri's electoral ticket, and al-Zayn (although not a member of Amal) votes as part of Amal's parliamentary bloc. He maintains his influence, he says, by having input into the bloc's deliberations before voting takes place in parliament.[104]

The 'Usayran family, on the other hand, has maintained its political longevity by establishing charitable institutions such as the Home of the Arab Orphan (*Dar al-Yatim al-'Arabi*). This has also been the practice of Hizbullah and Amal: the political benefits of establishing social and charitable institutions linked to an individual or party are self-evident. By contrast, al-As'ad family eschewed such activities, believing that the responsibility for the provision of such services lay with the government.[105] Although this attitude may have been based on the family's political philosophy, it revealed a lack of political acumen. 'Ali 'Usayran, meanwhile, believes that the leading role of his father, 'Adil, in the formation of the Lebanese republic has helped his family retain political power in the current era. 'Usayran notes that there is a very practical reason why the *zu'ama* have had increasing difficulty maintaining their electoral success of old: to compete within the large South Lebanon electoral district these days requires a significant financial outlay. In his father's day, the family had to finance Adil's electoral campaigns by selling family land; now, in a time when Hizbullah has access to Iranian money and Amal uses state funds to support its campaigns, traditional families are at a serious disadvantage.[106]

When it comes to the political survival of the traditional families, if we compare the influence of the Shi'a *zu'ama* nationally we find an apparent disparity between the Biqa' and Jabal 'Amil. In the south the 'Usayrans and the al-Zayns are still able to maintain their representation in parliament, but this is not the case in the Biqa'. Although members of the Haydar and Himadah families still run for election there, neither family appears to have had any success in the post-war political climate. Of the Himadahs, for so long the dominant force amongst the Biqa' Shi'a, the patriarch Sabri died in 1976 and his immediate family has failed to continue the tradition of political leadership. One of Sabri's sons, 'Ali, did form a political grouping during the civil war period, but it did not enjoy any long-term success. Known as the Eagles of al-Biqa' (*Nusur al-Biqa'*), it failed to compete against the other nationalist and leftist groups vying for Shi'a support.[107] Sabri's other son, Rashid, was also unsuccessful as a candidate in the 1996 election. The reasons for the political demise of the Himadah family are not immediately clear. 'Ali 'Usayran suggests that their lack of electoral success may be due to a combination of two things: the inability of the clans to agree upon a political accommodation with Syria; and the fact that too many members of the family have stood for election, thus dissipating the existing familial support base.[108] The effect has been to reduce the ability of the family name to attract the requisite client base. Hamzeh's faith in the strength of the *'asabiyya* to bind the clans together would appear to be unwarranted, for it has not been sufficient to guarantee them political representation after the civil war.

In contrast to the Shi'a community, other communities have been able to maintain the power structure of the traditional *zu'ama* to a far greater degree. Families such as the Maronite Franjiyya (North Lebanon), the Sunni Karami (Tripoli) and Salam (Beirut), and the Druze Arslan and Jumblatt (the Shuf *qada* within Mount Lebanon) have all retained parliamentary representation that reflects their traditional leadership roles within the non-Shi'a communities. Notables were at the centre of political parties in these non-Shi'a communities, which meant that to some degree the reversion to sectarian identities during the civil war allowed the traditional leadership to maintain its influence in the community. For this reason they were able to remain influential after the war too. This was particularly the case within the Christian community. Halim Barakat, writing of his visit to Beirut in 1976 after a decade studying Lebanese attitudes to political activism, observed that

> while the Christian traditional leaders have been able to perpetuate themselves or even gain more power to the extent of guaranteeing the ascendancy of their children, the Muslim traditional leaders have lost much of their power and the vacuum waits to be filled.[109]

In the case of the Shi'a, that vacuum was filled by the non-*zu'ama* political groups.

The Jumblatt-led Progressive Socialist Party (PSP) has been able to retain the integrity of family leadership within the community both during and after the civil war. This is largely because the Druze are a notoriously close community and were able to turn the PSP into an effective militia during the war. Similarly, the Maronite Jummayil family continued to lead the Phalange until Amin Jummayil lost in a party leadership battle to his rival Karim Pakradouni in October 2001.[110] The continuing support for some traditional leaders must be understood in the context that the civil war also helped create militia leaders from amongst communal groups, and that these leaders, although they did not enjoy the formal political power of the traditional leaders, certainly engendered loyalty in their subordinate militiamen. Shi'a political parties, on the other hand, were largely a reaction against the traditional leadership, and this resulted in a further distancing of clients from their patrons. At the same time, the relative improvement in the socio-economic status of the Shi'a, and the resultant emergence of a growing middle class, had the effect of reducing and in many cases doing away with their reliance on the traditional *zu'ama* for *wasta*. Consequently it was even harder for Shi'a *zu'ama* to retain their former political power.

There is evidence that the newer elements in politics may be seeking to establish a pattern of family political succession, although this does not appear to be a phenomenon that has extended to the Shi'a community. The late Prime Minister Rafiq al-Hariri, for example, supported his sister Bahiya in the South from the time of her success in the 1992 election; but it should be noted that she was a political activist for some time prior to her election and is not really a successor in the same way that former traditional notables' relatives were. Similarly, Khalil Hrawi, the son of the former deputy George and the nephew of former President Elias Hrawi, has continued the family tradition in parliament since 1992. The direct influence that the Prime Minister and/or President can bring to bear to ensure the election of a close family member is readily apparent. By contrast, this familial succession has not been replicated amongst the Shi'a, as neither Nabih Berri nor Hassan Nasrallah has promoted his own family members as candidates for election to the Lebanese parliament.

As we have seen from their experiences since the civil war, the political role of the traditional *zu'ama* within the Shi'a community is now peripheral at best. Whereas the traditional basis of political power amongst the Shi'a had been established through the ownership of land, there is now an alternative path to political influence. The emergence of Shi'a party leaders such as Nabih Berri arguably represents the latest manifestation of the Lebanese Shi'a *za'im*. In his case, his support base has been developed purely as a result of his access to political power (largely through the close relationship he enjoys with the Syrian government), rather than through the traditional methods of land ownership or commercial wealth. Berri's client base has developed through his leadership of the Amal militia and later the political party, and more recently through his role as Speaker. This domestic party-based leadership has also been bolstered by his close alignment with Syria, which has further cemented his ability to influence events outside his own community.

If the *za'im* is defined purely on the grounds of community leadership through diverse patron-client relationships, then Berri could legitimately be considered a modern *za'im*. But in all communities in Lebanon, the defining characteristic of the traditional *za'im* has been his hereditary power. The pathway to formal political power has been kept within families for generations, and newcomers were accepted only when they were able to pass this power along familial lines. On this basis, Berri does not fit the criteria of the traditional *za'im*, as there is currently no evidence that he intends to perpetuate his political power through the Berri family. It is this fact that is likely to set the future of the Shi'a *zu'ama* apart from that of other communities. To succeed in today's national political system, it is necessary to belong to one of the two main Shi'a parties or to have some affiliation with Syrian interests. Yet neither membership of a political party nor alignment with Syrian interests will ensure hereditary accession to political power, because both are subject to national and international pressures that will alter their degree of influence over time. This fact probably makes it less likely that the traditional *zu'ama* system will continue to be represented, let alone be influential, within Shi'a Lebanese politics. It is not that the traditional families have stopped running for political office; rather, due to both internal and external factors, few traditional Shi'a families have adapted appropriately to the changed social and political circumstances of modern Lebanon. In addition, the strength of the *'asabiyya* amongst the Shi'a clans is no longer sufficient to counter the influence of political parties or external actors.

'Abdulatif al-Zayn and 'Ali 'Usayran may well represent the end of a Shi'a political tradition, although 'Abdulatif al-Zayn believes that either his son or nephew will follow the family tradition and run for office once he retires from politics.[111] 'Ali 'Usayran, on the other hand, remarked that he was positively discouraging his son from entering politics, although he cannot rule out the possibility that other family members may stand for election.[112] With the stage now relatively full of alternative, well-organised political players, it is less attractive for traditional families to strive for political office. Competing against wealthy parties such as Amal and Hizbullah, traditional families are forced to dip into their own limited financial reserves. Electoral campaigns can be costly and are therefore less attractive if results cannot be guaranteed. As the field of political players becomes more crowded, as the power of the Shi'a political parties grows stronger, and as the influence of Syria on Lebanese politics continues, it will only be a matter of time before the Shi'a's last link with their traditional political leadership is severed.

3

An Alternative Path

Shi'a Participation in Political Parties

The Place of Political Parties

The most recent of the three strands of Shi'a political development and the one that is most likely to endure is, outwardly at least, largely western in character: the political party. But for political parties in the Lebanese context, unlike their Western progenitors, it is somewhat difficult to establish a coherent view of their ideological direction and motivation. The plethora of parties, many of which have served merely as political vehicles for Lebanese notables with obvious sectarian orientations, as well as an electoral system that supported the establishment of sectarian alliances of convenience, cloud attempts to draw coherent conclusions as to their ideological development. During the 1970s it was said of the Lebanese parliament that it was:

> not composed of competing political parties having different ideologies or professed programs and goals for the society, but of blocs and temporary alliances headed by traditional leaders and revolving around personal, communal, kinship and sectarian interests.[1]

The lack of documentary evidence about party membership, and the speed with which allegiances shifted between political groups during the civil war, are further obstacles to establishing an understanding of the patterns of political development. Despite these difficulties, the fact that so many Shi'a became active in political parties in the 1960s, and that the Shi'a community is now represented by two strong political parties, illustrates that the appearance of sectarian political parties represents a discrete tier of Shi'a political development.

The emergence and development of political parties is a relatively recent phenomenon in Western states, occurring well after the nation-state first appeared. The main role of political parties has been to repre-sent the interests of a particular stratum of society; consequently, parties have often emerged from religious groups, organised labour or the moneyed classes. In the Lebanese context too, parties tend to mirror the society in which they have developed, with the result that the immaturity of the Lebanese state has been reflected in the character of its political parties. Ghassan Salamé pinpointed the challenge for architects of Lebanon when he observed that its creation 'called for the transfer of an individual's loyalty from a family, a sectarian, or a tribal community which provided the security of yesteryear, to an abstract and alienating structure – the State.'[2] In Lebanon's history this challenge has not, by and large, been met; whilst political parties have developed, they have tended to remain tied to a traditional Lebanese powerbroker or to have been unduly influenced by international forces.

Despite the monopoly the traditional powerbrokers had on the formal levers of political power during the mandatory period and for much of the pre-civil-war independence period, there was also some independent Shi'a involvement in politics outside this traditional structure. Some of it took the form of individual political activism, some of it was limited to wealthy individuals wielding their influence behind-the-scenes, and some manifested itself in active participation in political parties. The last of these must be understood in the context of the Lebanese political system, which has seen political 'parties' develop along three general lines. The first has been the bloc, or front, a collective of like-minded traditional notables who joined forces to achieve limited political aims. Indeed, the group may have originated as an informal parliamentary bloc that subse-quently coalesced into something more structured. The second model has involved the formalisation of the client base of a politically powerful indi-vidual. In this case, the influence that others within the group can have on party policy is largely non-existent, and formal party organisational struc-tures are underdeveloped or missing. The final model resembles Western-style political parties. These parties were, in the beginning at least, nomi-nally secular; and at least regional party organisations, if not national ones, couched party policy in secular (and sometimes sectarian) terms. By and large, and with few notable exceptions, these organisations were in reality mainly sectarian, a smattering of people from other communities giving them the appearance of inclusiveness. All these types of political parties have been a feature of Lebanese political history. It is fair to say that the first of these models is now defunct and the latter two are currently dominant. This reflects the political decline of the traditional notables (outlined in the previous chapter) and the changed socio-economic conditions of the Shi'a populace which saw it become politically active prior to the civil war, and increasingly so afterwards.

Outside the paradigm of a dominant *zu'ama*, the political participation of the Shi'a prior to the civil war is best characterised either in terms of alignment with establishment-dominated Christian parties or of active participation in communist and other leftist (including Palestinian) groups. It is worth noting that, whilst they were willing to participate with Christian *zu'ama* and to a lesser degree with Christian- or Druze-dominated parties, the Shi'a were markedly reluctant to do so with any party in which the Sunnis were the driving force, such as the Helpers Party (*Najjada*).[3] There was a number of reasons for this. Firstly, there were the age-old tensions between the mainstream Sunni and the 'heterodox' Shi'a. In addition, there was a widespread suspicion that the Sunni Lebanese were keenly advocating Syrian nationalism because they wished to be part of a Sunni-majority Syria. The Sunnis had dominated the Muslim side of Lebanese politics at the Shi'a's expense; if the Shi'a now sided with them politically, many Shi'a felt that they would remain marginalised. By eschewing cooperation with Sunni political parties, the Shi'a hoped to blunt any moves towards the dissolution of Lebanon and to assert more authoritatively their role as Muslim Lebanese. Thirdly, the French mandatory authority's attempts to co-opt the Shi'a had met with some success, and the practical benefits the Shi'a community had gained may well have been lost in a merger with Syria.

Pre-Independence Political Parties

The concept of *Le Grand Liban*, as has already been mentioned, was generally accepted by the Shi'a. It is therefore understandable that during the late mandatory and early independence years they showed some support for the Christian-led political groupings dominated by the Maronite elite. The loyalties of this elite were divided between two rivals who vied for Maronite leadership: Emile Edde and Bishara al-Khoury.

Al-Khoury was educated in Lebanon and France, and he maintained pro-French sympathies first as a member of the Progressive Party in 1912 (this party advocated a Maronite-dominated greater Lebanon closely linked to France) and later as part of the *'Alliance Libanaise'*.[4] More enduring was his involvement in the 1936 Constitutional Bloc (*al-Kutla al-Dusturiyya*, or simply *Destour*), a grouping that brought together Maronites from the Mountain and non-Maronite Christians from Beirut, and which ostensibly sought a restoration of the Constitution that had been suspended in 1932.[5] Foremost among the Constitutional Bloc's non-Maronite allies was the Greek Catholic, Michel Chiha, who provided the Bloc with both economic guidance and capital. Although it still represented the establishment, and notwithstanding al-Khoury's personal ambitions, the Constitutional Bloc came to be regarded as a grouping that was in opposition to the French mandatory authorities (after independence, the Bloc attempted to enlarge its appeal by reconstituting itself as the Constitutional Union Party). The Constitutional Bloc attracted some support from amongst regional Shi'a groups, although it is likely that local rather than philosophical factors were the driving force in this. For example, the Shi'a *za'im* Sabri Himadah was a founding member (see Chapter Two). Another Shi'a, the radical socialist 'Abdullah al-Hajj, was prominent in the Bloc in the lead-up to the 1943 elections. Al-Hajj had already contested the 1937 elections and been soundly defeated in the Mount Lebanon electorate by Ahmad Husayni (Husayni represented Mount Lebanon as the Shi'a candidate from 1937-1951). The fact that the electoral contest in 1943 was so close would appear to support the contention that al-Hajj ran on a Constitutional Bloc ticket, because the margin of his defeat by Husayni was a tenth of what it was in the 1937 and 1947 elections.[6]

Even the pro-French forces represented by Emile Edde's National Bloc (*al-Kutla al-Wataniyya*) garnered some Shi'a support. It should be remembered, however, that the National Bloc was nearly exclusively a product of the Mountain, and hence attracted some regional allegiance that cut across sectarian boundaries. As a result, prominent Shi'a from the Mountain such as Ahmad Husayni lent the National Bloc their support. Edde believed that France had a continuing role in an independent Lebanon, above all as the guarantor of its dominance by Christians. He saw the French as an appropriate foil for the pan-Arab sentiments amongst the Muslim majority that would, he felt, overwhelm the Christian minority. Such was his fervent support for Christian primacy that he openly advocated a revision of the 1920 borders so that the Muslim-dominated areas of Tripoli, the Biqa', and Jabal 'Amil would be severed from the rump of Lebanon. For entirely different reasons, this position found favour with some Syrian Arab nationalists who were still opposed to the concept of *Le Grand Liban*. The Shi'a's attraction to the ideological underpinnings of the National Bloc may at first appear somewhat unusual, yet a pragmatic allegiance to the organisation would have been essential in order to gain its support on the electoral ticket. Ahmad Asber, a Shi'a member of the National Bloc,[7] was elected to parliament from the district of Jubayl in 1960, 1968 and 1972. Jubayl's Christian majority would no doubt have been the decisive factor in the success of a Shi'a aligned to the National Bloc. After independence in 1943, the National Bloc renamed itself the National Bloc Party and adopted a Lebanese nationalist stance, which ensured its political survival until the civil war. The Edde family's decision not to raise a militia, and to oppose Syrian intervention in Lebanon, has marginalised the party, which refused to participate in elections as long as the Syrians occupied Lebanon.

Independence and Political Parties

The *Destour* and the National Bloc emerged before Lebanon's independence; the main parties (particularly the socialist ones) emerged afterwards. But what is of more interest to this study is the fact that widespread Shi'a activity within political parties also began after independence. Prior to independence there was little outlet for this political activity other than in pan-Arabist societies that were largely the preserve of the traditional *zu'ama*, or as part of political movements headed mainly by Christian *zu'ama*. The lack of political parties that could provide for a mass support base meant that there was little room for the non-*za'im* to make an impact in Lebanese politics. This was particularly the case in the rural areas where the Shi'a largely resided, because the traditional allegiances held by the *zu'ama*, in combination with the electoral list system, made it extremely difficult for political parties to prosper. It has been said of the electoral list system that it 'strengthened the position of the two or three leading notables of the majority sect – thus reducing and consolidating the number of important power groups in the state.'[8] For this reason, early Shi'a participation in political parties was generally restricted to the alignment of traditional *zu'ama* with particular political blocs (as in the case of

Sabri Himadah and the *Destour*), the attraction to the bloc being the number of supporters these *zu'ama* brought with them. This situation remained the case until the 1960 elections, at which point the more orthodox political parties (ideologically-based and structured in a more hierarchical fashion) began to gain ground on the *za'im*-based political blocs.[9] A large part of the reason for this was that the growing political maturity of the electorate forced political groups to articulate a platform – something the parties were better equipped to do than the *zu'ama*.

There was also some Shi'a representation amongst the rank-and-file of the Lebanese Kata'ib Party (sometimes referred to as the *Phalanges Libanaises*, or simply as the *Phalange*). Given its origins as a right-wing quasi-fascist Maronite youth movement established in 1936 under the guidance of Pierre Jummayil, it is somewhat surprising that it attracted any support from Muslims at all. But its extreme form of Lebanese nationalism may not have been a disincentive for most Shi'a, who still did not wish to be part of a majority Sunni state. Similarly, its advocacy of freedom of religion and social justice (including the establishment of a national social security system) would have found support amongst the politically and socially disadvantaged Shi'a. Its role in the so-called 'counterrevolution' phase of the 1958 crisis marked the turning point in its achieving widespread support amongst the population. This was later turned into significant electoral success during the 1960s. John Entelis noted that the party's actions in this period demonstrated its widespread support amongst 'all Maronites, many Christians, and, to a lesser extent, some Muslims mostly of the Shi'ite sect.'[10]

The actual degree of Shi'a support for the Kata'ib is difficult to determine effectively because the party's overall membership varied over time: it declined after Lebanon won independence because its role became less relevant, and it increased after the 1958 crisis because it repositioned itself intellectually and enjoyed greater electoral success. In addition, none of the texts dealing with the party refer to the records of religious affiliation; what data there is indicates that Shi'a did not become members of the Kata'ib until the early 1950s, and that their numbers as a proportion of party membership rose from 1% in 1952 to 6% by 1969 (an increase from 230 party members to 3850).[11] This increase up to 1969 coincides with the Kata'ib's joining forces with Edde's National Bloc and Camille Chamun's National Liberal Party to form the Triple Alliance (*al-Hilf al-Thulathi*), sometimes referred to simply as the *Hilf*. The Hilf was largely an anti-Shihab coalition, although it also served to confirm the Christian population as the major political force within Lebanon. The overtly Christian dominance of the Hilf makes the Shi'a's continued attraction to the Kata'ib seem strange at first glance; but their affiliation with a Christian party is less surprising given that they had no sectarian political parties of their own and that some of them lived in Christian-dominated areas. This view is supported by Michael Johnson, who believed that the influx of Shi'a into some of the largely Christian suburbs of Beirut initially created goodwill between the two communities because the Shi'a provided a counterweight during Sunni-Maronite disputes.[12] This broadening of the Kata'ib's support base evidently did not extend to the executive levels, because none of the 21-member Political Bureau (*al-Maktab as-Siyasi*), the highest executive organ of the party, was Muslim, let alone Shi'a, by the start of the civil war. Similarly the Central Council (*al-Majlis al-Markazi*), the Kata'ib's main consultative body, had just two Shi'a members out of its total of 157.[13] In addition, there was no successful Shi'a Kata'ib electoral candidate. It is evident from these figures that, whilst the Kata'ib was able to garner some support from amongst the Shi'a, the party's leadership allowed them only very limited access to the Kata'ib executive. This would indicate that the acceptance of Shi'a into the party was largely a token gesture designed to provide the Kata'ib with a veneer of cross-communal support. The Kata'ib example was a theme that came to be repeated elsewhere as Shi'a were regarded by many parties as foot soldiers rather than functionaries.

The National Liberal Party (*Hizb al-Wataniyyin al-Ahrar*) provides another example of Shi'a support for a largely Maronite-dominated political organisation. Camille Chamun, a former member of the Constitutional Bloc, established the National Liberal Party (NLP) in 1959. Its political ideology did not extend much beyond allegiance to its president Camille Chamun and support for Lebanese independence. Like many other Lebanese parties, it has been personality-centred, with the Chamun family providing the leadership from the time of its founding to the present day.[14] The party did have a platform of sorts, for it advocated democratic governance and a free enterprise economic system;[15] and this did at least distinguish it from the burgeoning number of socialist parties. But given its rather limited political doctrine, its status as a political party is questionable. On the other hand, it claimed to have tens of thousands of members.[16] Amongst these was a number of Shi'a. Indeed, the NLP's vice-president was Kazim al-Khalil, the Shi'a *za'im* from Tyre.[17] This arrangement was undoubtedly one of mutual political advantage rather than ideological commitment: Chamun, for his part, would have welcomed an alliance with a Shi'a *za'im* from the South because it broadened his party's appeal amongst another communal group and in another geographic region; al-Khalil, meanwhile, would have welcomed an alliance with a powerful Christian parliamentarian because it was a means of gaining political advantage over his rivals in al-As'ad's family.

The degree to which the NLP received widespread support from the Shi'a is open to question; nevertheless, a Shi'a NLP member was elected to parliament. Mahmud 'Ammar was successful in the district of Ba'bda (province of Mount Lebanon) from 1960-1972. 'Ammar was one of only four NLP members elected to parliament in 1960, but his election should not automatically be seen as a sign of popular Shi'a support for the party's doctrine; after all, one Shi'a MP had to be elected from the district, and since there was no dominant Shi'a *za'im* in the region, affiliation with a strong non-Shi'a *za'im* such as Chamun was necessary for political advancement. 'Ammar's election indicates the strength of Chamun's influence in Mount Lebanon, for political office seekers of all religious persuasions sought to enhance their chances of election by being included on a prominent politician's electoral ticket. Just as the appearance of non-Shi'a on al-As'ad's electoral ticket in the South indicates political alliance rather than ideological affinity, so too does Shi'a support for Chamun.

Shi'a were also active in Sunni-dominated political groups. Although few in number, some achieved a measure of political success. 'Ali Bazzi, for example, a politician from a non-traditional family in the South, was able to cultivate associations with leading Maronite and Sunni politicians. He was close to Taqi al-Din al-Solh (a cousin of Riad al-Solh) who was also from the South, and together they founded the National Call Party (*Hizb al-Nida' al-Qawmi*).[18] This was more of a grouping than a party, its support came from working-class Sunnis in Beirut and Sidon, and it functioned largely as a political vehicle of the al-Solh family.[19] Bazzi's lack of affiliation with the traditional Shi'a powerbrokers, or his inability to create a connection, is probably what forced him to establish himself politically through other, non-Shi'a, sources of support; and the National Call Party was an effective way of doing this in South Lebanon. Both his background and his linkage to a political party also meant that he represented the type of community leader that Shihabism sought to promote. Having been the Interior Minister in 1959, Bazzi received the backing of President Shihab in the 1960 elections and was able to defeat Kamil al-As'ad in the district of Marjayoun-Hasbaya.

Syrian and Arab Nationalist Parties

The antithesis of the Lebanese nationalist Kata'ib was the ultra-Syrian nationalist Syrian Social Nationalist Party (SSNP; though it was sometimes referred to as PPS: *Parti Populaire Syrien*). It was established in November 1932 as the Syrian Nationalist Party by Antun Sa'adah,[20] a Lebanese Greek Orthodox. The SSNP under Sa'adah was an autocratic organisation; the party's constitution established Sa'adah as its leader for life and bound its members to give him their absolute obedience.[21] The party's ideological foundations arose out of the deprivations the Lebanese suffered during the First World War; support for the Turkish war effort had led to a widespread famine. Central to Sa'adah's outlook was his belief that Syria was a discrete nation whose national integrity had been weakened, thus leaving the people of the region open to exploitation and defeat by external forces. Consequently, the SSNP's guiding principle was encapsulated in the party motto, 'Syria is for the Syrians, and the Syrians are a complete nation.'[22]

This vision of Syrian nationhood proved difficult to promote. Firstly, widespread agreement could not be reached as to what constituted Syrian territory. In the early 1930s, for example, Sa'adah defined Syria as encompassing the area between 'the Taurus Mountains in the north, the Euphrates in the east, the Suez Canal in the south and the Mediterranean in the west.'[23] At the end of 1947, he offered an expanded version that incorporated the whole of Iraq and Iran and stretched from the Zagros Mountains in the east to Cyprus in the west.[24] The second difficulty was that Sa'adah's version of Syrian nationalism was dismissive of Arab nationalism. In his view, Arabs were culturally distinct from Syrians and inferior to them. Naturally these views earned him the wrath of the mandatory authorities, who arrested and gaoled him in 1935. With the emergence of an independent Lebanon (and with Sa'adah's 'exile' in Brazil between 1938 and 1947), the SSNP's national branches concentrated less on Syrian nationalism and, particularly in the case of Lebanon, more on pragmatic domestic issues. In Lebanon the party renamed itself the National Party (*al-Hizb al-Qawmi*) and was legally recognised by the Lebanese government.[25]

There were several reasons why such a party was able to attract Shi'a to its ranks. In the process of developing its vision of Greater Syrian national unity, the SSNP first developed a policy of doing away with all social differentiations; and in the case of Lebanon, this meant the party was opposed to the confessional provisions of the National Pact as well as to the confessionalism that defined the Lebanese political and governmental systems.[26] This stance was a precursor to later parties' opposition to the National Pact-dictated structure of the Lebanese state, a policy to which the increasingly frustrated Shi'a became attracted.

The same attraction that led the Shi'a to join a secular reformist political organisation such as the SSNP was also what attracted them to Palestinian and pan-Arabist parties. The Palestinians, like the Shi'a, were in search of a political voice; and although the Shi'a did not feel a deeply held allegiance to the Palestinian cause *per se*, they were attracted to the Palestinians' methodology. As As'ad Abu-Khalil observed:

> when Shi'ites were joining Palestinian organisations they were not fighting for the liberation of Palestine...they were opting for a radical approach to declare their grievances and opposition.[27]

The rush to join Palestinian groups must be seen in the context of the late 1950s and 1960s, when the Palestinian cause offered an outlet, particularly in the wake of the 1967 war, for the frustrations of a highly politicised Shi'a population. Later, in the 1970s and 1980s, considerable animosity developed between the Palestinians and the Shi'a when Israeli retaliation to Palestinian attacks, not to mention the invasions of Lebanon in 1978 and 1982, cost the Shi'a dearly in lives and property.

The relatively immature state of Shi'a political development during the 1960s and 1970s meant that allegiances changed as individuals were attracted to different political alternatives. Some of the Palestinian factions, for example, served to expose future Shi'a political activists to radical methods of political expression. This is well illustrated by the case of a prominent Amal activist from Tyre, Dawud Dawud. Originally a member of the Ba'th party, he had been drawn to the Ba'thists because they were the only instrument of change available to him. Later, from the mid-1960s onwards, he was attracted to the radical Palestinian factions (in this case Fatah), with their involvement in armed resistance to both the

Israelis and the government of the day. His increasing frustration at the behaviour of the Palestinians in South Lebanon, in particular the military actions that provoked Israeli retaliations that also hurt the Shi'a, forced Dawud to seek more sectarian methods for changing the political *status quo*. Musa as-Sadr and eventually Amal became the focus of his allegiance.[28] This movement by many Shi'a away from the radical secular political groups, once an alternative became available, will be discussed in more detail later in the chapter. The tendency to seek more avowedly Shi'a sectarian solutions was a key element of Shi'a political development during the late 1970s and early 1980s, as neither the secular parties' methods nor their results did anything to alter the Shi'a's position in society.

The pan-Arab parties, both in their leadership and in the rank and file, were generally dominated by Sunnis. Nevertheless there was one group that was successful in attracting Shi'a to its ranks: the Arab Nationalists' Movement (*Harakat al-Qawmiyyin al-'Arab*). It began life as a protest movement at the American University of Beirut (AUB); young intellectuals, angry at the Arab states' failure to prevent the defeat of the Palestinians in 1948 and disillusioned by the ineffectiveness of contemporary Lebanese political parties, decided to organise themselves, and so the Arab Nationalists' Movement (ANM) was born.[29] Its ideological foundations were never precisely stated beyond a secular form of Arab unity, a desire for the liberation of Palestine and for revenge against Israel (this part of the organisation's charter was played down over time), and a leaning towards a socialist economic system (largely as a protest against the capitalism that symbolised the West) that gradually became apparent during the 1960s. After establishing the movement in Lebanon, its founders left the country to start ANM branches in other parts of the Arab world.

Most of the ANM's founding members were Palestinian, and much of this AUB-based, Palestinian student leadership were expelled following violent protests against the Baghdad Pact in 1955.[30] The new leadership of (largely non-AUB) Lebanese nationals that had been growing over the years then came to the fore. The ANM's relatively simple ideological appeal also meant that a large proportion of its support base came from people who were not tertiary-educated; and this may be a reason why it attracted a sizeable number of Shi'a Muslims, some of whom became key players within the movement. For example, one of the leading ideologues of the ANM was Muhsin Ibrahim, the son of a poor family from South Lebanon. George Habash often deferred to him for ideological direction during the movement's early years. The ANM also ran a working-class Shi'a candidate in the district of Tyre during the 1960 parliamentary elections; Muhammad az-Zayyat, the son of poor farmers, was unsuccessful, but he still attracted over 4,500 votes.[31] Az-Zayyat had proven his credentials in the 1958 civil war as the ANM leader in Tyre as he had successfully defended a large section of the town against Chamun's supporters.[32] Important members of the movement from an earlier stage, Ibrahim and az-Zayyat had been two of the three Lebanese delegates to the ANM's first pan-Arab Conference in 1956.

When the ANM sought to promote its ideas outside Lebanon, it left to the Lebanese branch the task of winning over Christian Lebanese to the concept of Arab nationalism. The difficulties of this task, given the unique societal makeup of Lebanon, were summed up well by an unnamed leading member of the ANM who, in the mid-1960s, remarked: 'Our position in Lebanon is that of an alien Arab community living in complete estrangement from the immediate environment surrounding us.'[33] Despite the difficulties of selling the message of Arab nationalism to the Christians, it was not because the ANM was a sectarian political movement. On the contrary, the ANM was an avowedly anti-sectarian party. Az-Zayyat and Muhsin Ibrahim, for example, though Shi'a by birth, were not attracted to the ANM by virtue of their communal identity. Ibrahim's socialist orientation, in particular, was influenced more by his humble economic background than by his religion. He was strongly of the opinion that socio-economic rather than political structures would determine the progress of Arab society.[34] Consequently, Ibrahim believed that the nationalist movement (including the ANM) represented the interests of the Arab upper-middle classes rather than the majority proletariat, and was therefore not likely to win popular support. The ANM did not survive as a united political organisation in Lebanon after the 1967 war. By the following year, most of the original Palestinian leadership had transferred to the Popular Front for the Liberation of Palestine (PFLP) under the leadership of George Habash.[35] In 1968, the Lebanese branch of the ANM renamed itself the Organisation of Lebanese Socialists[36] (later to become the Communist Action Organisation), reflecting the increasingly leftist orientation of Muhsin Ibrahim.

The Radical Leftist Parties

As already mentioned, the Shiʻa community's parlous socio-economic conditions had increased their disillusionment with traditional forms of political participation and representation. Yet even before Shiʻa-based political parties had emerged, many Shiʻa (particularly the increasingly well-educated minority) gravitated towards socialist political parties. This was especially the case after the Arab nationalist cause had been severely tested by the twin failures of the unsuccessful attempt to unify Egypt and Syria in the United Arab Republic and the Arab defeat in the 1967 war. The attraction of the leftist parties was twofold. Firstly, they were an alternative to the Arab political parties that had been created by, or were dominated by, traditional notables. Secondly, their objectives of undermining the status quo and creating social equality proved enormously attractive to the poorer classes. These explanations are supported by Halim Barakat's study of student political attitudes during the 1960s and early 1970s: of all the university students he surveyed, the Shiʻa consistently expressed the strongest degree of alienation from the political system[37] and, not surprisingly, the greatest degree of support for radical leftist political groups.[38]

This is not to say that Shiʻa support for leftist political groups is merely a phenomenon of the 1960s, for their participation in socialist groups had been in evidence decades earlier. One of the socialist parties that has had continuous Shiʻa involvement since its inception is the Baʻth (Resurrection) Party. It was founded in 1942 as the Arab Revival Movement (*Harakat al-Ihyatu al-ʻArabi*) by two Syrian teachers, Michel ʻAflaq (a Greek Orthodox) and Salah al-Bitar (a Sunni and future Syrian Prime Minister). After merging with Akram Hawrani's (Syrian) Socialist Party in 1953,[39] it became known as the Arab Socialist Baʻth Party (*Hizb al-Baʻth al-ʻArabi al-Ishtiraki*). A well-organised yet fractious proponent of Arab nationalism and socialism (the Baʻthists have traditionally been weaker on socialism than on nationalism), the party gained and then lost power in both Syria and Iraq during the 1950s.

Aflaq, as the party's chief ideologue, set out his vision of the socialist ideal that he believed was necessary if the Arab nation was once again to become strong. He advocated a uniquely Arab form of socialism that was less doctrinaire than its Western counterpart.[40] He advocated state ownership of the main means of production, as well as of public utilities, education and trade, but he also acknowledged that there was a place for limited private business ownership and inheritance rights. Baʻthist socialism differed from Communism in that it did not adhere to the principle of class struggle, nor was it expansionist. 'Aflaq, although he acknowledged that Islam was central to Arab unity, kept the Ba'th Party secular. Above all, he believed that national 'resurrection' was possible only if an Arab unity of spirit could be attained through a revolutionary, rather than an evolutionary, change in mentality. This position, commendable as it was, proved difficult to convey concisely to the masses, so party membership tended to come from the well-educated lower-middle-class. At the lower levels the party was organised into rings, groups, branches and sub-branches. The branches sent their representatives to the regional (*qutri*) congress, which in turn sent members to the pan-Arab (*qawmi*) congress, which then selected the pan-Arab leadership – the highest level of exec-utive authority.

In Lebanon the party began in a formal sense at the end of 1949.[41] Not surprisingly, it concentrated its efforts on attracting support from university students, particularly from the American University of Beirut. The party held its first Lebanese *qutri* congress in 1956, where it elected its first regional command. When fractures became apparent within the Ba'th in the 1950s and 1960s, Lebanese loyalties tended to stay with Michel 'Aflaq, possibly because he had operated from Lebanon after the Syrian branch of the party was suppressed by Colonel Adib Shishakly in the early 1950s. The Lebanese branch had to exist in a type of no-man's-land for years, operating openly but without the official approval of the Interior Ministry, because the Lebanese government looked suspiciously on any pan-Arab or leftist political organisations.

Most party members came from three areas: Tripoli, Ba'albak, and South Lebanon. Accordingly, although Sunni Muslims made up the largest percentage of the party's membership, there was also a large Shi'a representation, as well as some Christian representation. Membership details are difficult to access, but it appears that communal affiliation was not necessarily an impediment to advancement within the party. For example, 'Ali al-Khalil, an academic and distant member of the traditional notable family from Tyre, was elected to the *qutri* command as early as 1962[42] and was subsequently elected as one of the two Lebanese members of the Ba'th's *qawmi* command at the party's seventh pan-Arab congress in February 1964.[43] The Ba'thists were to undergo a series of splits, both internal and external, particularly between pro-Iraqi and pro-Syrian factions of the Lebanese Ba'th party. 'Ali al-Khalil himself was arrested for a time in Lebanon after he denounced the Syrian military government that ousted the Ba'thist government in a coup in 1965. The Ba'thists were not, however, immediately successful in parliamentary elections; al-Khalil was soundly defeated in his 1968 bid for a seat in Tyre. However, he was very successful in 1972, when in the same constituency he recorded a large victory. Another Shi'a, Assim Qansu, also featured prominently in the Ba'th party; by 1967 he was the Secretary-General of the Lebanese branch of the pro-Syrian element of the Ba'th party.[44]

The same social dislocation and suffering that resulted from World War I and that motivated Antun Sa'adah's search for change to the political *status quo*, also proved to be the genesis of the political ideas of the intellectuals who in 1925 founded the Lebanese People's Party (*Hizb ash-Sha'b al-Lubnani*). This party amalgamated in 1930 with the Armenian Communist Spartacus League to become the Communist Party of Syria and Lebanon,[45] which split into separate Syrian and Lebanese Communist Parties in 1944. The Lebanese Communist Party (LCP) has not tasted electoral success since it began fielding candidates in the 1937 elections (these candidates were Greek Orthodox, Armenian and Sunni), but it has often made use of Shi'a candidates, particularly given the strength of its Shi'a membership.

Support for the LCP came from the large urban areas such as Beirut and Tripoli and from the communist-dominated trade union leadership. The LCP was not, however, typical of communist parties elsewhere. For most of its early existence the party concentrated on political rather than economic issues, calling for democratic reform of the political system rather than for state control of the means of production. This pragmatic approach suited the character of the Lebanese capitalist economy, an economy that was unique in the Arab world. The consequent lack of a truly proletarian support base presented the Party with difficulties, summarised by Michael W. Suleiman's observation that

> where agrarian unrest is non-existent because of strong traditions, familial loyalties and mere backwardness, where there is no urban proletarian class, and where religion remains a strong social force in Lebanon, it is not hard to see why the Communist Party has not attracted many workers.[46]

Whilst the Party's support base tended to centre around the Armenian population, there were also strong committees in Ba'albak (particularly amongst the Sunnis there) and Tyre, thus increasing the possibility of Shi'a participation. In the Party's early years, however, the socio-economic background of its membership base meant that it did not impact much on the rural Shi'a population, even though it opposed the traditional *zu'ama's* exploitation of rural workers. For much of the pre-civil-war period it rarely, if ever, ran candidates in the Shi'a-dominated areas of South Lebanon or the Biqa'.

Most of the Party's support, certainly until the late 1960s, continued to come from the educated middle-class. The example of Sa'dlallah Mazra'ani (a Shi'a), a deputy Secretary-General of the LCP, provides a good case study of the means by which supporters were drawn to the Party. Although Mazra'ani had family connections (his father founded the LCP in South Lebanon during the 1950s), his formal participation did not begin until he joined the Party at the Lebanese University in 1968; he later became President of the Communist Students. Mazra'ani believes that this period was the zenith of Marxism's attractiveness, particularly to the politically-radicalised students. The Arab defeat in 1967 meant that many people turned away from Arab nationalism in favour of Marxism; and the Paris student riots of 1968 also gave hope to young socialists keen to change the political *status quo* in both the East and the West. As to why he joined the LCP, Mazra'ani has insisted that it was not due to his sense of communal identity; rather, his reasons were, in order of priority, familial (following in his father's footsteps), socio-economic (his experience of growing up in an economically depressed area), and ideological (the attraction of Marxism as a solution to contemporary problems).[47]

By the end of the 1960s a rural proletariat had emerged, many of them Shi'a, which provided the support base amongst the working class that the LCP had previously lacked. In response to the commercialisation of agriculture, which saw the number of destitute agricultural workers rise from 20,000 to 60,000 between 1950 and 1970, the LCP, by the beginning of 1974, had formulated a comprehensive agrarian reform program,[48] knowing that this would be of great interest to the rural proletariat (and therefore the Shi'a). It has been said of these years – the early 1970s – that the 'Shi'ite phenomenon was best reflected in the deep penetration of Shi'ite areas by radical, and particularly the Marxist, political organizations.'[49] In Nabatiyya during this period, the LCP attracted supporters from amongst agricultural workers and tobacco industry workers as much because it advocated the armed protection of villages against Israeli and Palestinian actions as for its political ideology.[50] As time wore on, however, the LCP became more hostile towards the Israelis than towards the Palestinians. Meanwhile, many of the destitute Shi'a agricultural workers formed an urban proletariat in the southern and eastern suburbs of Beirut where they made up the bulk of the factory workers in both Christian and Muslim areas during the 1970s.[51] The emphasis in Marxist philosophy on the centrality of class struggle as a societal construct must have appealed to many of the Shi'a, who were dislocated from their traditional community patrons and were therefore more likely to be mobilised by radical political alternatives. The LCP took up the issue of class in the traditional patron/client relationship. Michael Johnson has argued that

> their recruits soon came to classify not only the Israelis and
> the Maronites as their enemies, but also the Shi'ite *za'ims*
> who had formerly been their patrons and lords.[52]

This is not to say that enmity against communal groups, or certain parts of them, was the main reason why people joined the LCP. Its attraction for many was its promise of political and social reform.

The LCP became the dominant party in south Lebanese Shi'a villages such as Houla and 'Aytaroun, where it encouraged their allegiance by providing educational assistance programs. In the case of Houla, over 200 people were sent to study in the Eastern Bloc countries on scholarships.[53] It should be noted at the same time that many other Lebanese, both Christian and Sunni Muslim, also received such scholarships. Although the LCP had many Sunni and Christian (largely non-Maronite) members, such was the Shi'a's dominance that a popular saying during the 1960s and 1970s was '*Shi'i Shuyu'i*' (a Shi'a, a Communist).[54]

The LCP was not the only Marxist political party in Lebanon. The withdrawal of the ANM's Palestinian founders to form the PFLP following the 1967 war saw many of the remaining Lebanese ANM members merge with the Organisation of the Lebanese Socialists (OLS) and Socialist Lebanon (a small group of Marxist intellectuals) to form the Communist Labor Organisation.[55] The Communist Labor Organisation evolved shortly after into the Communist Action Organisation (CAO) under the leadership of the ex-ANM ideologue Muhsin Ibrahim. Ibrahim became more closely aligned with the Palestinian cause at about the time that Syrian influence in Lebanon increased (from 1976 onwards), and he was one of the few Lebanese to remain a supporter of Yassar 'Arafat after the Israeli invasion of 1982.[56] By 1987, Ibrahim's opposition to Syrian policy concerning Arafat had forced the CAO to become an underground movement, and Ibrahim himself gradually withdrew from the organisation. Without his practical and intellectual leadership, most members of the CAO left, and to all intents and purposes it no longer exists.[57]

Whilst part of the ANM membership joined the OLS, many of George Habash's Lebanese supporters continued his radical socialist work by forming the Socialist Arab Action Party – Lebanon (SAAP). At the SAAP's first national congress in 1972, the party distanced itself from what it referred to as the 'evolutionary communists' by advocating violence as the best means by which to end class conflict.[58] The vast majority of its members were Shi'a, for the same reasons that revolutionary parties attracted Shi'a elsewhere. Its Secretary-General was Hashim Ali Muhsin, an Iraqi Shi'a residing in Lebanon. The SAAP was a militarily active party that formed part of the leftist-alliance Lebanese National Movement (LNM), whose charter called for the complete abolition of the sectarian political system. It was at times opposed to the Lebanese government and to Syrian forces. Of particular note is the fact that in 1976 the Shi'a-dominated SAAP confiscated the estates of the Shi'a za'im Kazim al-Khalil at Shabriha, near Tyre (al-Khalil was also vice-president of the National Liberal Party at this stage).[59] The purpose of the action was to turn the estates into a collective; but this never occurred, and the SAAP lost control of the estates in 1982 with the Israeli invasion.

The Progressive Socialist Party (PSP), though normally considered one of the confessional parties given its domination by Druze, is another leftist group that has been able to attract some Shi'a support. Formed in 1949 by leftist intellectuals, the PSP sought a secular, socialist democratic method of achieving political change within Lebanon. Given these aims, it seems anomalous that its founder, Kamal Jumblatt, was from one of Lebanon's traditional notable families and a major Druze za'im. Yet this proved to be one of the party's most appealing features during its formative years: it offered the ideologically attractive option of secular socialism with the imprimatur of a traditional community leader, which gave it access to the traditional Lebanese power structures. Jumblatt was himself a socialist advocate; he studied social philosophy at the Sorbonne, and he distributed some of his traditional lands to his tenant farmers as practical evidence of his commitment.[60] During the 1960 elections, the PSP gained 12 seats from the 18 candidates it ran, making it the largest party bloc in parliament. By the mid-1960s, however, the Lebanese elite's continuing resistance to political reform in the face of societal changes meant that the PSP became increasingly radical and less committed to enacting political change through parliamentary means. This radicalism manifested itself in two significant ways: an increase in support for Arab nationalism and, by association, the Palestinian cause; and the creation of an alliance with other leftist parties such as the Communist Party, the Ba'thists, and the ANM. In 1965, Jumblatt was in charge of the short-lived Front of Progressive Parties and National Figures,[61] and by 1975 he was leader of the Lebanese National Movement.

Whilst the PSP has always been considered a largely Druze party under the leadership of a traditional *za'im*, there was, during the pre-civil-war period, a genuine attempt to make it a nationally significant secular, socialist organisation. Its reformist stance meant that it attracted a significant following from amongst the Shi'a, for the same reasons that motivated them to join other political parties offering reformist agendas. However, the Shi'a were not immediate converts to the PSP, largely because for the first few years its support base did not extend much outside Mount Lebanon. But once it broadened its membership drive to reach a wider area, the Shi'a began to join in significant numbers, particularly in the Biqa'. Between 1949 (the party's inception) and 1958, over 2,000 Shi'a joined, which represented over 20% of the PSP's membership.[62] During the 1960s, the role of Shi'a members grew as their proportion of the party membership increased. This increased role came largely at the expense of the Christians who were becoming increasingly alienated by Jumblatt's radical Arabist stance. In 1960, the Shi'a had one representative on the twelve-man Leadership Council; by 1964, they had one representative on a seven-man Council; and by 1975, this had increased to two representatives on a ten-man Council. Also in 1960, a Shi'a PSP candidate, Muhsin Dalloul, was elected to parliament from the Ba'albak district.[63] Dalloul's story illustrates how successful the PSP was in broadening its membership base. Recruited by his Christian teacher whilst attending secondary school in Zahle in the Biqa' in 1952, he became a Shi'a member of the PSP Leadership Council from 1975, an MP, and later the Minister of Defence.[64]

Political Parties during the Civil War

It is not the intent of this chapter to examine the causes of the civil war or to look at its progress. Rather, it is the impact of the war on the existing political allegiances of the Shi'a that will concern us here. The major impact of the war's outbreak was that it closed off many of the political avenues that had been opening up for the Shi'a. The lack of a functioning government meant that increasingly the populace sought refuge within its own communal groups. For the political parties, this meant that much of the religious diversity they had attracted during the pre-war period was lost because the host party closed ranks around its community base. The Lebanese Communist Party (LCP) was by and large an exception to this, mainly because its ideological appeal transcended religious differences, and on the whole, the LCP retained the loyalty of its Shi'a members. The Shi'a were put in a difficult position when communally-based parties closed ranks, for without their own sectarian party to withdraw into, they had little choice but to remain loyal to non-Shi'a or secular parties.

Given the absence of a viable political environment, as well as the need to assert their authority in the only way now available, most of the political parties formed armed militias, which further militated against cross-communal *rapprochement*. The rise of the militias also put an end to whatever organisational allegiances the political parties had engendered. For example, while the Jummayils had dominated the Kata'ib, the civil war accentuated personal allegiance to the family at the expense of allegiance to the party. This was the same for the Jumblatts and the PSP. Meanwhile, some of the party militia leadership were different to the party political leadership (Samir Ja'ja' and Elie Hubayqa of the Kata'ib, for example), creating a division of loyalties within the party itself. The longer the civil war dragged on, the less ideologically committed many of the militias became, their survival under a patron becoming a more important consideration than adherence to party ideology.[65]

It was in the Shi'a community that the greatest change occurred, and by a process that was the reverse of what the other communities experienced. Amongst these other communities it was the norm for political parties to transform into, or raise, militia groups to defend their interests after the breakdown of sectarian consensus. In the Shi'a community, the emergence of Shi'a-dominated militias pre-dated the establishment of sectarian political parties. This was particularly the case with Hizbullah, and to a lesser degree with Amal. This is not to say that either of these groups has transformed itself into an entirely political organisation, despite the Ta'if Accord of 1989 that required militias to disarm. Hizbullah, while developing its political wing, has remained free to conduct military operations. Amal, on the other hand, has been largely disarmed and has acted nearly exclusively as a political organisation although it has some capability to mount an armed response if required.

The Creation of Amal

The emergence of Amal as a movement has been discussed in great detail by writers such as Augustus Richard Norton and Fouad Ajami, and it is not the intention to repeat their work here. What is important for this study is the place of Amal in the overall scheme of Lebanese Shi'a political development. Amal emerged from Musa as-Sadr's creation of the Movement of the Deprived (*Harakat al-Mahrumin*) in March 1974. It was not a political party as such, but a mass protest movement aimed at forcing the government to address the lack of services for the Shi'a. Although the movement's rhetoric was ostensibly non-sectarian, Musa as-Sadr's background and the fact that the movement was launched at a rally in Ba'albak left no doubt that the 'Deprived' referred to the Shi'a. This was in fact the Shi'a's first attempt to organise themselves politically along sectarian lines and independently of the traditional *zu'ama*. As-Sadr, having lived in Lebanon since 1959, must have been aware that this movement would attract many Shi'a who had hitherto been drawn to the leftist or Arab nationalist parties. For example, Amal's future leader, Nabih Berri, had previously been a member of the Ba'th party. Amal's emergence also quickly spelt the end of widespread Shi'a support for, and membership of, the Palestinian cause; somewhat ironic given that the PLO's Fatah faction had trained the nascent Amal militia in the mid-1970s.

The name Amal (*Afwaj al-Muqawama al-Lubnaniyya*) itself originally referred to the militia that was raised some time in 1975 (and was initially trained by the Palestinian Fatah movement) as an adjunct to Harakat al-Mahrumin. But eventually Amal subsumed the Movement of the Deprived as both a military and political organisation. It is worth noting that Amal, even though it was a distinctly Shi'a militia organisation, did not automatically attract the majority of the politicised Shi'a. This was because in the early stages its militia was relatively ineffectual and did not present itself as a viable alternative source of loyalty. Whilst the movement was relatively slow to capture mass support, three events of the late 1970s rapidly increased its legitimacy in the eyes of its own religious community and enabled it to become a significant force both amongst the Shi'a and within Lebanon generally.[66]

The first of these was the Israeli invasion of Southern Lebanon in March 1978. Whilst its objectives were ostensibly limited, the invasion nevertheless dealt a military blow to the Lebanese National Movement and Palestinian militias in the area; and the vacuum created by their defeat was filled by Amal. Amal was able to provide a security umbrella for many of the Shi'a of the South, which won the movement many sympathisers and laid the groundwork for future political recruitment in the area. The second event was the disappearance of Musa as-Sadr in August 1978, while he was en route from Libya to Rome.[67] For many Shi'a, this event resonated with the occultation of the Twelfth Imam; so, paradoxically, Amal, as-Sadr's creation, benefited from his disappearance. The final event, the Iranian revolution in January 1979, gave a further boost to the Shi'a by providing a successful example of a popular Shi'a opposition movement overthrowing an illegitimate political system. All three events, occurring within less than a year of each other, proved vital in giving Amal the opportunity it needed to establish itself as a viable Shi'a polit-ical presence in Lebanon.

As a political grouping, however, Amal, like so many other Lebanese parties, failed to articulate a plan of action; its Charter outlines what it opposes as much as what it stands for, and even then only in general terms. But what is noteworthy about the Charter is that, for the first time, a Shi'a political group had formally enunciated its opposition to the tradi-tional *zu'ama*; previously, the Shi'a had only ever joined political groups where this aim had been articulated by *non-Shi'a* leadership. In the Charter, Amal's position on the *zu'ama* is stark:

> The descendents of the feudal overlords have inherited the political leadership of the Lebanese state, and political feudalism still plays its influential role in appropriating government positions, usurping public profits for private accounts, and maintaining its dominance over the people. The movement shall therefore exert every effort to expose and depose this feudal leadership.[68]

Opposition to the traditional power structure was only one item on the nascent organisation's agenda. The question of sectarian identity was another; but it was, and remains, one that Amal has approached in a rather disjointed manner. In the first instance, Amal rejected political sectarianism and claimed it was not a sectarian movement; yet the reality is that its membership has always been nearly exclusively Shi'a and it was founded by a Shi'a religious leader. This anomaly is not unique to Amal, for the political parties of all confessional persuasions have offered similar denials regarding their membership. Inclusiveness, even if not practised, has always been espoused by formal political groups in pre- and post-civil war Lebanon.

Three other features of the movement's Charter are worth mentioning. The first is that the Charter firmly identifies Amal as a Lebanese nationalist movement, supporting the concept of national sovereignty:

> Our movement is completely devoted to national sover-
> eignty...It rejects any foreign mandate over the motherland
> [and] works towards preserving its territory and borders...[69]

The dominance of Syria in Lebanon's affairs, and the close relations between the Amal leadership and the Syrian government, mean that the party's ability to meet its Charter's aims regarding state sovereignty are questionable.

The second issue is the degree to which the Charter positions Amal on the left of the political spectrum. The party itself has not really been considered an advocate of socialist ideals, however there are certainly indications in its Charter that it aspires to them. In advocating that it should be the state rather than the market that sets the prices for goods and commodities, and in opposing usury as it is practised in the free market system because 'opposing usury means opposing capitalism and exploitation',[70] the party is decidedly socialist. In a country such as Lebanon, however, the ability to realistically oppose the free market system is questionable. The third issue concerns the movement's position on religion, especially in light of the emergence of its rival, Hizbullah. Since Amal advocates secularism, its Charter is careful to reject religious fanaticism of any kind, yet it does claim that the *Qur'an* is a solid basis for the intellectual development of civilisation, and thus it aligns itself with a

Muslim, not just a distinctly Shi'a, worldview. There is no anomaly in this approach, because it sees the *Qur'an* as a guide, rather than a rule, for development. In this, the Charter is consistent with its founder Musa as-Sadr's willingness to actively engage Lebanon's other communal groups. Similar attitudes about tolerance of all communal views and about the role of the *Qur'an* are also reflected in the outlook of other influential Shi'a figures such as Muhammad Husayn Fadlallah (discussed further in Chapter Four).

Once they had organised themselves politically, the Shi'a of Amal sought to establish good working relations with Syria. Historically, not having an external patron had counted against the Shi'a when administrative positions were being apportioned, for example, or seats resulting from the National Pact were being allocated. Musa as-Sadr was aware of this and, conscious of the designs Syria had on Lebanon, was diligent in courting Syria's favour. He gave his imprimatur to the 'Alawite sect's legitimacy as Muslims (a sect to which Hafiz al-Assad belonged). For its part, Syria provided training to the Amal militia – military proficiency was fundamental to having an increased political presence in civil war Lebanon. As-Sadr's policy of aligning Amal with Syrian interests has certainly been continued by Nabih Berri, and this is well illustrated by a speech Berri gave at Ba'albak in August 1985:

> There must be integration with Syria, by means of actual agreements in the economic, security, political, information and educational fields. Let them not be afraid of Lebanon's sovereignty.[71]

Whilst this may appear inconsistent with the principles set out in Amal's Charter, it represents a compromise in the tradition of *realpolitik* that was necessary to advance the party's interests.

This spirit of pragmatism also enabled Amal, in the absence of electoral contests in which it could gauge its real political impact, to exert influence within the Lebanese political system as it existed during the civil war period. The benefits of this approach were demonstrated by the success of Amal members in attaining government positions. Husayn Husayni, the head of Amal following the disappearance of Musa as-Sadr until Nabih Berri replaced him in 1980, was elected in 1984 to the position of parliamentary speaker, at the expense of Kamil al-As'ad –

a symbolic moment in the eclipsing of the official power of the Shi'a *zu'ama*. Berri himself was appointed to parliament in 1991, when an additional Shi'a seat was created for the district of Saida. Both these successes were due in no small part to direct or indirect Syrian pressure. The political benefits of Amal's close relationship with Syria were becoming increasingly apparent.

It would, however, be wrong to assume that the rise of Amal signifies the emergence of a united front of Shi'a political thought and action; Amal was a victim of the localised allegiances and consequent lack of solidarity of Lebanese militia groups as much as any other movement of the time. Scholars such as As'ad Abu-Khalil have claimed that there were class distinctions within the organisation, the political wing allegedly representing the educated upper middle-class Shi'a, and the Executive Committee representing those of peasant origins (who were normally the more religiously inclined).[72] Even such a defining event as the Israeli invasion of Lebanon in 1982 could not elicit a unified response from Amal's regional leadership: the al-Ghaziyyah leader, Muhammad Ghaddar, for example, supported the invasion,[73] whilst the head of Amal in Sidon, Mahmud al-Faqih, denounced it.[74] This state of affairs is indicative of a rather weak central leadership. Adding to the party's difficulties has been the distribution of the major Shi'a populations between the South, the *dahiya* and the Biqa'; this has caused tensions in Amal over the party's leadership positions, because they need to reflect the geographical location of its members.

In March 1987, internal fighting between regional Amal commanders highlighted the fractiousness of the grouping. Hasan Hashim, a former chairman of Amal's Executive Committee, launched an armed uprising against other Amal elements. This action seriously threatened Nabih Berri's leadership because it forced the party's members to decide whether to support Hashim or Berri. As it happened, they remained loyal to Berri; and Hashim's revolt, which had won no support from the other regional commanders, failed. Hashim was subsequently expelled from Amal by the Central Organisational Bureau.[75] Another internal revolt was launched later that same year by 'Aql Hamiyya, Amal's chief military officer. It too was unsuccessful. Hamiyya resigned from Amal in November, but he was also formally expelled from the organisation.

Amal is not unique: internal dissent was a feature of most political groupings in Lebanon at this time. The examples given here are important because they illustrate how complex were the individual and group loyalties in Lebanese politics – complexities which equally affected the Shi'a. Hamiyya's revolt, for example, received little support for two reasons. Firstly, Amal's militia had performed poorly up to this point in the civil war, and Hamiyya, as Amal's military commander, was held responsible. Secondly, Hamiyya's support base was centred in the Biqa', which meant there was animosity from the Amal elements in the South.[76] Even within the same region, support from outside one's own loyalty group was never assured. A major reason for the lack of success of Hashim's earlier revolt for instance, was his inability to elicit support from southern Lebanese Amal members outside his home village of Marwaniyya.[77] The failure of the two internal revolts is evidence that loyalty to the Amal leadership was more widespread at this stage than may at first be apparent.

As well as the issue of localised and regional rivalries, Amal also had to accommodate a range of ideological differences, particularly regarding allegiances to the Iranian model of Shi'a activism. Naturally, the Iranian revolution was an inspiration to many Shi'a in Lebanon, yet both Musa as-Sadr (before the revolution) and Nabih Berri (after it) had aligned Amal with Syrian rather than Iranian interests. This reflected the reality of life on the ground in Lebanon: a large Syrian military presence since 1976 provided a strong incentive to cultivate relations with the Assad regime, and it was in Syria's interests to ensure that it maintained influence with the developing Shi'a political movement. The secularised, conventional approach that Amal adopted in regard to advancing Shi'a interests within the framework of the Lebanese state was not to everyone's liking; and this, combined with Amal's relatively loose organisational structure led many of its members to be influenced by the Iranian model of political activism. At the same time, post-revolutionary Iran also began to urge a more radical approach to advancing what it believed to be Shi'a interests. For example, Hashemi Rafsanjani, the then speaker of the Iranian Majlis, called for Amal to adopt more militant policies.[78]

The combination of these different forces was eventually to split the Amal movement's unity of purpose. Nabih Berri's rejection of the Islamic national model espoused by pro-Iranian Shi'a and his continuing support for the integrity of a multi-confessional Lebanese state, had alienated certain elements in the movement. Berri's participation in the National Salvation Committee in June 1982 alienated many Shi'a, largely because one of the Committee's members was Bashir Jummayyil, founder of the

Christian Lebanese Forces. Husayn Mussawi, a member of the Amal Command Council, opposed Berri's presence on the National Salvation Committee and appealed for Iranian arbitration on the appropriateness of Shi'a membership of the Committee. The Iranian ambassador to Syria deemed Berri's membership of the Committee inappropriate, but Berri refused to step down. Mussawi, who was opposed to Berri's centrist policies, returned with some of his supporters to his home town of Nabi Sheet in the Biqa' and founded Islamic Amal, a group committed to the concept of *wilayat al-faqih* (discussed in Chapter Four). The strictly local support that Islamic Amal engendered is illustrated by the fact that many of Mussawi's supporters were members of his clan. Mussawi represented an extreme pro-Iranian element of the Shi'a (his cousin was appointed the Iranian *charge d'affaires* in Beirut in 1983.) Once again, external forces had influenced internal Shi'a politics. The entry of Iran into the Lebanese political equation showed that the Shi'a were now considered politically important enough to be courted by external powers.

The Development of Hizbullah

The second of the Shi'a political parties to start out as a militia was Hizbullah. While Amal represented the emergence of a pragmatic Shi'a political movement that sought to represent its community more or less within the existing framework of the Lebanese political system, Hizbullah represented the radical path of sectarian development. Little is known of its early history, except that it began as a radical Shi'a Islamist movement whose activities were largely confined to attacking foreign military forces and kidnapping Western hostages. Instead of a single movement, it was, initially at least, more of an umbrella organisation for other radical Shi'a Islamist groups such as Islamic Amal and the Da'wa party (see Chapter Four); according to Hassan Nasrallah, Hizbullah's founding committee comprised nine delegates, three each from Amal, the Da'wa and the independent *'ulama*.[79] In terms of Shi'a political development, this was a radical departure from tradition. Whilst the leftist parties had represented a secular means by which the disaffected Shi'a could express themselves politically, and Amal had shown that a sectarian movement could do something similar, Hizbullah presented an alternative vision of the political form of the Lebanese state. Although Shi'a in pan-Arab movements had also advocated a radical restructuring of the state, they had normally done so using secular terms; this is apparent from the fact that Lebanese and Iraqi Shiʿa, as well as Syrian ʿAlawites, were leading figures in their respective Baʿth parties. The supporters of Hizbullah, on the other hand, were something completely different: a group wanting to be faithful to an exclusively Shiʿa worldview (as defined by Iran) rather than to import concepts from Western Europe or from the Sunni majority.

In its early days, Hizbullah was a movement based largely in the Biqaʿ. Islamic Amal had established themselves there, many Daʿwa members lived there, and Iranian influence was strongest there following the arrival in Baʿalbak of Iranian Revolutionary Guards in response to the Israeli invasion of Lebanon in 1982. The fact that the Israelis had not penetrated into the Biqaʿ during the invasion also gave Hizbullah the freedom to operate and establish itself without external interference. Once the Israelis had withdrawn from Beirut in 1983, Hizbullah started an active recruitment campaign in Beirut's southern suburbs with a view to expanding into Amal's heartland of South Lebanon. Hizbullah advocated Ayatollah Khumayni's concept of *wilayat al-faqih*, so the movement's leadership consisted of jurists, in contrast to the increasingly secular leadership of Amal. Hizbullah itself had its antecedents in the Iranian Hizbullah, an anti-leftist coalition that had emerged after the Shah's departure in January 1979. The Iranian Hizbullah was organised and controlled by Iran's clerical leadership and was used to break up and suppress non-Islamic political groups in the early days of the Iranian revolution.[80] It continues to operate in Iran today, under the auspices of the Iranian Revolutionary Guard Corps (IRGC).

The two Lebanese Shiʿa political movements started out from two enormously different positions. The ideological rationale for Amal's genesis was based on societal issues; a means of making the Lebanese system more responsive to the aspirations of the Shiʿa community. Hizbullah, on the other hand, emerged as a resistance movement against Israeli occupation and against Western (particularly United States) interference. Consequently, in its early days Hizbullah focused on its military role rather than on a coherent political program of any sort. As Shaykh Hassan Nasrallah said in an interview in 1996: 'There was no plan...other than to resist the occupation...We were thinking at first: Let us restore the homeland and then we will think of the political system.'[81] The Israeli invasion thus provided the trigger and the focus for a militant form of Shiʿa expression. Without the invasion, it is debatable whether it could have flourished. Even though the Iranian revolution was an inspiration to the Shi'a of Lebanon, they had no thoughts, prior to the invasion by Israel, of reproducing its political model in their own country. Even if they had, Syria would not have allowed any such movement to develop. But this did not stop some elements in Hizbullah from advancing the case that Lebanon should become an Islamic state. As Iran's and Syria's strategic aims converged – resulting in the IRGC assisting some elements of the Lebanese Shi'a – the issue of an Iranian-inspired model of government became an important point for discussion in Hizbullah.

In 1985, Hizbullah enunciated some of its views on the Lebanese political system, as well as its own role in Lebanon, in a treatise called 'Hizbullah's Open Letter to the Downtrodden of Lebanon and the World', a political manifesto that formally declared the existence of the movement. The manifesto sets out a number of points regarding Hizbullah's view of foreign and domestic political issues. It states the movement's belief in Ayatollah Khumayni's position as the 'single wise and just leader', in line with Khumayni's own vision of *wilayat al-faqih*. It outlines Hizbullah's rejection of the state of Israel, on the grounds that it occupies appropriated Muslim land and has an expansionist, Zionist philosophy. It also expresses Hizbullah's opposition to the colonial Western nations, particularly the United States for its support of Israel. Importantly, the manifesto is vague in enunciating Hizbullah's preferred political system, although it is specific in identifying the current system's ills. According to the manifesto, the existing political system and its 'sectarian privileges' are the root cause of Lebanon's problems, particularly in respect to the Phalange and those Muslim deputies who supported them in parliament. But rather than advocate a general overhaul of the sectarian political system, as Amal did, Hizbullah saw this system as 'a fundamentally oppressive structure that no reform or patchwork improvement would do any good and that must be changed from the roots'.[82] Until it is changed, the manifesto continues,

> [we] are not at all interested in any projection for political reform within the framework of the rotten sectarian system, just exactly as we are not interested in the formation of any cabinet or the participation of any figure in any ministry representing a part of the oppressive regime.[83]

In place of the existing system, Hizbullah advocated an Islamic form of government, the exact nature of which was never explained, but the implication was that it would be heavily influenced by the Khumayni view of Islamic governance, given the party's acceptance of his juristic opinions. Well aware of the concerns many other Lebanese might have about the implications of this Islamic model, the movement has been particularly careful to allay their fears about the means it may use to achieve its goal. The manifesto is careful to stress that such a transition would be voluntary: 'we urge adoption of the Islamic system on the basis of free and direct selection by the people, not the basis of forceful imposition, as some people imagine.'[84] The contradictions in this approach to reform are, however, readily apparent: if Hizbullah did not participate in the political system, it was unlikely to be able to reform it; and unless there was political reform, the present system of government would remain, thereby blocking any possibility of an Islamic government being directly chosen by the people.

In the absence of a functioning political system during the civil war, Hizbullah was able to content itself with building a support base amongst the Shiʿa to achieve the critical mass it needed to influence events within Lebanon. Shiʿa joined the party for several reasons. In the wake of the Israeli invasion, Hizbullah's militant stance became popular. Internal dissent in Amal, and Berri's participation in the National Salvation Committee, had alienated many Shiʿa, who now turned to Hizbullah as an alternative source of empowerment. In addition, Shiʿa who had fought with the Palestinians prior to the expulsion of the PLO from Beirut were, given the history of Amal-Palestinian relations (the two groups had fought each other on a number of occasions), forced by circumstance and conviction into joining the ranks of Hizbullah. The party's unequivocal opposition to both the Israeli invasion and the Lebanese political system also drew supporters away from Amal and into its own sphere of influence.

The existence in Lebanon of two Shiʿa movements, representing opposing methodologies for change and vying for the support of the same community, was bound to lead them into conflict over the community's leadership. This was particularly the case during the civil war when both parties had an external patron and when militias were the principal means by which to gain the upper hand. Amal and Hizbullah fought each other on several occasions; the most serious was in 1988 when they sought to establish their dominance in the southern suburbs of Beirut and in South Lebanon. Such was the seriousness of the fighting that both Syria and Iran were forced to broker a peace between the warring parties and to establish a *modus vivendi* between the two states regarding each other's relative influence over the Lebanese Shi'a.

The emergence of the two Shi'a-based political groupings, together with other events during the civil war, impacted significantly on Shi'a who supported the non-Shi'a political and militia groups. There was a decline in support for Palestinian groups, as has been indicated previously. In the case of the independent Nasserites' militia (*al-Murabitun*), large numbers of their Shi'a foot soldiers moved their support to their own communal parties once the Murabitun had suffered heavy losses during the war. In some cases the conduct of militias during the civil war also served to hasten changes of allegiance. For example, in August 1976 the Christian Phalange militia expelled all the Shi'a inhabitants of al-Nab'a, a Shi'a-populated quarter of East Beirut; this destroyed any pretence that the Kata'ib constituted a broadly-based political grouping, and the Shi'a withdrew all their support. The Lebanese Communist Party (LCP), troubled not only by the losses its militia suffered during the war but by the ideological challenge it faced following the dissolution of the Soviet Union in 1991, nevertheless fared better. The question of class struggle, which dominated European communist thought, was for the LCP secondary to the struggle to change the communal political order – a struggle that lay at the heart of its *raison d'être*. As a result, the LCP was still able to justify its existence when other communist parties around the world folded. Regardless of the obstacles placed in its path, the LCP continued to hold party congresses. With the advent of alternative means of political expression, the LCP lost a good portion of its Shi'a base, yet the Shi'a continued to make progress amongst its leadership ranks. Indeed, at the fifth Party Congress held in 1987, a Shi'a member, Karim Muruwwa, was nearly elected head of the LCP in place of George Hawi. Muruwwa, a leading intellectual in the LCP, had articulated an ideological path for the party in 1986 that marked it as a coherent political opposition group. It opposed the triple, and sometimes conflicting, positions of: Lebanese isolationism; Arab unity, which called for the dissolution of states and hence disregarded Lebanon as a sovereign entity; and Islamism, which favoured a greater 'Muslim community' at the expense of non-Muslim Lebanese.[85]

Political Parties in the Post Civil War Environment

For the Shi'a, the decline of the traditional notables as a political force was certainly a significant result of the civil war, but more changes than this resulted from the war. The re-emergence of the Lebanese parliament as a viable institution following the 1989 Ta'if Accord has forced both Amal and Hizbullah to change their focus from militia operations to alliance-making, constituent representation and all the other activities common to political parties in a parliamentary system. Whilst the Accord gave the Shi'a some political advantages, they still remained relatively under-represented in parliament. The powers of the Speaker were enhanced[86] and the number of parliamentary seats for the Shi'a increased from 19 to 27 in an expanded parliament. This still only increased their proportional representation in parliament from 19% to 22%, well short of their proportion of the population which is currently estimated at approximately 40%.

On the face of it, the post civil war period should allow a clearer picture to emerge of the place of political parties in the Shi'a's political development. The power of party militias had been neutralised (or, in the case of Hizbullah, focussed against Israeli forces rather than other militias). National – and in 1998 municipal – elections had been held and parliamentary processes re-started. Yet any examination of political parties from the 1990s onwards must be seen in the context of the realities of the Lebanese political system. The sectarian allocation of seats within electoral districts, the production of voting lists backed by prominent political figures, the imposed electoral alliances between Hizbullah and Amal, and the pervasive Syrian influence in Lebanese political matters – all have combined to preclude the free and unconstrained development of political parties. Drawing lasting conclusions about such an environment is difficult; nevertheless, it would be reasonable to see the end of the civil war as a turning point in the political fortunes of the Shi'a. The community now has two functioning sectarian political parties, the *'ulama* being active in one of them, and the loyalty once given to the traditional families has largely been transferred to these groups.

Amal in the Post Civil War Environment

The two main Shi'a political parties have taken quite separate paths in establishing their political credentials. Amal has relied on its relationship with Syria and on the dominant political position of the Speaker Nabih

Berri to establish itself as a major influence in the Lebanese political system. At the same time its ideological orientation is never clearly defined outside the generalities of its Charter; and many of Amal's supporters are therefore attracted by its ability to dispense patronage rather than by its ideological orientation. Consequently there is little or no pressure on the party to develop its ideological position, and in this regard it has stagnated. This is not unique to Lebanese political parties, although in the case of Amal it represents an intellectual and ideological withdrawal from its radical reformist period following its foundation by Musa as-Sadr. In contrast, some parties such as Kata'ib and PSP have been able to re-orient themselves politically so as to be better equipped for the post Ta'if Accord environment.

As with any political organisation, Amal's modification of its reformist stance can be attributed in part to political maturation. Musa as-Sadr's early fiery speeches to massed crowds, and the development of the Amal militia, are both evidence that the Shi'a community was being mobilised to present itself as a political force in its own right. Once it had successfully gained an independent political voice, much of the provocative rhetoric had to make way for compromise and deal-making – which occurs in parliaments the world over. As well as developing into a more mature political organisation, Amal has also had the accusation levelled against it that the more it has come to operate within the formal political system, the more it has come to represent the very system it was set up to oppose. Critics point to the influence the party wields over the Council of the South, a Lebanese government institution established in 1970 to provide financial assistance to the residents of South Lebanon and the western Biqa', and whose funds have often gone to a project on the basis of its sponsor's affiliation to Amal rather than its urgency. This is an accusation the party strenuously denies. Nevertheless, there are indications that support from the Shi'a rank and file has diminished. As the English language *Daily Star* remarked of the party's relatively poor performance in the 1998 municipal elections, Amal's 'less than overwhelming local election success signals, among other things, popular resentment at the *wasta* gravy train.'[87]

Although Amal was well placed to divert criticism of its poor performance by announcing that no party members had stood for election,[88] the fact that it actively backed lists of Shi'a candidates made it abundantly clear to voters who Amal wished to win. With the exception of Hizbullah's dominance in Beirut's southern suburbs, it is fair to say that

Amal and Hizbullah draw their strength from South Lebanon and the Biqa' respectively. Yet even within the South, Hizbullah was able to dominate Nabatiyyah (due in no small part to the fact that it is the hometown of Shaykh Hassan Nasrallah). Hizbullah was also affected by local issues in the Biqa', however, as its list was defeated in Ba'albak (where locals were concerned about the effect on the tourist trade of a Hizbullah-dominated council).[89]

The municipal election result should not be taken to imply that Amal is a spent force. On the contrary, Nabih Berri is still a powerful figure in Lebanese politics, particularly in the South. He has been parliamentary Speaker for the last decade and during that time has established himself as one of the most influential politicians on the national stage. The emergence of Hizbullah as formidable rivals for the allegiance of the Shi'a community has meant Amal's leaders are acutely aware that their party must continue to be relevant both to the community and to the Republic. Amal's recent electoral performance prompted some introspection and even led to calls for the party to reform itself. Key members of Amal acknowledged that there were structural shortfalls, and MP Muhammad 'Abdul-Hamid Baydoun called for a broadening of the party's membership to include all confessions.[90]

Baydoun's call for a broader party membership is noteworthy because it acknowledged that Amal had failed to establish itself as a party attractive to Lebanese outside the Shi'a community. Today Amal is certainly aware that the diverse makeup of the Lebanese population means that political parties, to be nationally successful, must broaden their aims beyond sectarian considerations. Amal admits that, whilst it actively seeks a broader support base for the party, there are few non-Shi'a members.[91] This is the case not only amongst the senior membership but also amongst Amal student groups which have found it virtually impossible to attract non-Shi'a members from the university population – a traditional recruiting ground for political parties.[92] The party has had some success, however, with Christians: twenty signed the original Amal charter, and in villages around Saida some have enrolled as party members.[93] Amal acknowledges that its failure to attract other communal groups to its ranks is disappointing, especially since it sees itself as representing the deprived in all Lebanese communities – a view that reflects the principles originally enunciated by Musa Sadr. Indeed, Amal's members believe that the guidance Sadr provided during his lifetime is sufficient moral guidance for the party even today, and they claim there is no *mujtahid* to which the party looks in the absence of the Imam.[94] This has allowed them to claim secular status, thereby differentiating themselves from Hizbullah. But the secular/sectarian divide in Lebanese party politics is quite problematic. Amal is well aware – as are all parties – that the nature of the electoral law means that each party has to maintain a sufficiently broad political program to garner electoral support across communal groups, whilst at the same time addressing sectarian issues that maintain its core communal support base.

Whilst Amal may not have a precise political platform outside the broad statements contained in its Charter, there is evidence that the party possesses a broad strategic aim. Like Hizbullah, it knows that the current system discriminates against the numerically superior Lebanese Shi'a. It is also fully aware that the current electoral law discriminates against the party's overwhelmingly Shi'a membership. To alter the electoral law that allows the Shi'a's numerical superiority to be reflected in political power, the party must attain positions that will allow it to initiate the requisite changes. The changes Amal proposes are an end to sectarian representation in parliament, and a public service where promotion is based on merit rather than religious confession; both of these are seen as a necessary next step in Lebanon's political development.[95] Party members have a broad strategic aim to form a government and vie for the Republic's executive positions, such as Prime Minister and President, so that these changes can be enacted.[96] They do not see the changes occurring rapidly; rather they advocate a gradual systemic change through legislative action. Indeed, they have already provided a possible blueprint for the future in a draft electoral bill which they presented to parliament in 1998. The bill was ultimately unsuccessful, but it proposed the amendment that, while Amal fully supports an electoral system with proportional representation, provision should also be made in any future parliamentary system for the continued political representation of the religious minorities. The advocating of changes to the electoral laws has both a short and long term goal. This is reflected in the unsuccessful attempt by Amal and Hizbullah to pass legislation lowering the voting age from 21 to 18. Amal estimates that up to 70% of people in this age-group are Shi'a, hence their inclusion in the electoral process would dramatically increase Shi'a voting power and exert pressure for more Shi'a representation in parliament. Although the motion was defeated, the demographic reality it sought to redress is going to impact heavily in the near future regardless of parliament's position.

Hizbullah in Contemporary Lebanon

Whilst Amal is active in the formal organs of government, Hizbullah has remained within parliament but outside government, and consequently does not benefit from the official largesse that participation in government may bring. Instead, to attract political support the party has relied on its own provision of social services (such as health care and education) and on its leadership of the anti-Israeli resistance movement. External patrons have assisted it with both these functions: Iran has largely funded its activities; and Syria, by allowing Hizbullah's militia to retain their weapons post Ta'if, consequently enabled them to fight the Israelis in the South. Hizbullah has moderated its militant stance in recent years as it has sought to widen its support base and turn its popularity as the leading anti-Israeli resistance group into concrete electoral support. The early history of the party's formation and militancy, however, has meant that it must now work hard to attract supporters from outside the Shi'a community.

The non-Shi'a Lebanese are critical to Hizbullah's ability to achieve broad-based multi-sectarian support, and their concerns about its ultimate aims are well understood by the party. The most obvious manifestation of Hizbullah's Islamist foundations has been the political leadership of the clerics in the party. For the first two parliamentary terms after the civil war, for example, Shaykh Ibrahim Amin as-Sayyid – a cleric and one of the party's founders – was the most popularly elected candidate from the district of Ba'albak-Hirmil. But he did not run for parliament in the subsequent 2000 election, and consequently there are now no Hizbullah MPs who are clerics, even though clerics remain dominant within the party leadership. Officially, Hizbullah claims that as-Sayyid's decision not to run in the 2000 election was not intended to present only non-clerics as candidates but was rather a normal consequence of the party's candidate selection processes.[97] There is no doubt, however, that this move makes the public parliamentary face of Hizbullah more mainstream.

Hizbullah has also balanced the need to remain true to its original belief in non-participation in government with the need to avoid making itself irrelevant. The party has walked a fine line in this regard, participating in the electoral process while at the same time performing the role of parliamentary opposition. It has stayed outside cabinet so that it cannot be accused of corrupting itself by having access to government *wasta* in the same way that Amal has. This does not mean that Hizbullah has not sought to provide its own form of patronage outside the governmental system; indeed it has established its political support base not only by leading the resistance movement but also by providing services such as medical clinics and hospitals in areas where the government has failed to do so. Without having access to the official political power of executive government positions, and unwilling to compromise its independence by joining the current government in cabinet, Hizbullah must wait until the electoral law is changed before it can play a more significant role in the formal political leadership of the country.

Although Hizbullah has maintained a strong degree of unity by avoiding the divisions that plagued Amal in its formative years, it has experienced internal dissent on occasion. A former Secretary-General of Hizbullah, Shaykh Subhi al-Tufayli, was expelled from the party in January 1998 after he opposed the direction Hizbullah was taking. Some years before, in 1991, his reign as Secretary-General had ended with his defeat by the more moderate Shaykh 'Abbas al-Mussawi – due in no small part to the influence on Hizbullah's internal affairs of the more moderate Iranian leadership in Tehran. Al-Tufayli had been critical of Hizbullah's decision to participate in the 1992 elections, believing that by taking part in the political process the organisation would lose its reformist ideals by being coopted by the very system it sought to change.[98] (Amal has been accused of the same.) In 1999, Al-Tufayli launched a new political movement, the Revolution of the Hungry (*Thawrat al-Jiya'*), through which he has attempted to mobilise his local rural support base against government agricultural policies. Al-Tufayli achieved some success in the 1998 municipal elections when his candidates were victorious in the towns of Brital and Tarayya in the Biqa'.[99] Although Hizbullah's insistence on achieving electoral reform through parliamentary means may frustrate some party members, given the amount of time it is likely to take to achieve, the current leadership is confident that the dissent of al-Tufayli's group is nothing more than an isolated incident.

For Amal and Hizbullah, the post civil war environment has made it necessary for both parties to formalise their political activity by taking part in parliamentary elections. This has been, philosophically at least, easier for Amal. Amal was always committed to reforming the Lebanese political landscape from within; hence the active participation of its senior leadership in both the electoral process and the formation of cabinets. Hizbullah, on the other hand, has had to modify its ideological position considerably. Hizbullah did not initially support the Ta'if Accord on the grounds that it failed to address the inadequacies of the political system, yet finally endorsed it because it represented an end to the civil war. So having condemned the Lebanese political system for being corrupt and favouring the Maronite elite, Hizbullah was compelled to join that system as a result of pressure from the Syrian and Iranian governments (Iran being at the time under the moderate President Ali Akbar Hashemi-Rafsanjani). The dynamic tension between Hizbullah's opposition to the system and its subsequent participation in it has best been described in the journal *Shu'n al-Awsat* by a member of Hizbullah itself. The party, he notes, has

> been able to go beyond its former political theses in favour of a *realpolitik* which tries to combine ideological principles and goals with objective possibilities and realities, [and in so doing] it used two principles of Muslim jurisprudence: 'Necessity permits what is otherwise prohibited', and 'When two duties are competing, focus on the most important one.'[100]

In practical terms the party's stated position has since been that its participation in the political system should not be construed as support for it; instead it should be viewed as a pragmatic attempt to modify government – hence the party has assumed the role of parliamentary opposition but refuses to acknowledge the legitimacy of the government by becoming part of cabinet. In their role as parliamentary opposition, members of Hizbullah have actively denounced the culture of corruption and the dominance of authoritarianism (rather than consultation) in the political system. Hizbullah deputies, for example, were vocal in their denunciation of the authoritarianism of Prime Minister Rafiq Hariri; they refused votes of confidence in the Hariri government in 1992 and 1995; they argued vehemently against the 1996 budget; and on occasion they supported strike action by workers. Amin as-Sayyid confirmed Hizbullah's stance vis-à-vis the Prime Minister when he said in 1993:

There [is] a climate and a language, that seem to push the
people to accept to follow one single man, that reduce the
nation to one single individual...The mentality of the kings,
princes and sultans is a threat for Lebanon.[101]

Khodr Tlass has been equally critical of the nepotism surrounding the
allocation of administrative appointments, which has served to perpetuate
the traditional form of Lebanese politics. Speaking after the announce-
ment of a series of administrative appointments in 1993, he claimed that

the last nominations...were dictated by *istizlam* [allegiance
to the chief] and *mahsubiyya* [importance of the client
networks of the individual]...[T]hey don't illustrate the
behaviour of a State governing through its institutions, but
rather tribes thinking of their relatives.[102]

Ultimately, however, the parliament's confessional character militates
against the party's ability to put into effect much of what it advocates.
Regardless, Hizbullah continues to use its participation in parliament as a
means of attracting support for its cause, because this helps dispel the
widely-held view that it is a radical Islamist force. Further evidence of the
party's pragmatic approach to political participation is that it has been
represented on parliamentary committees since 1996, thus giving it the
opportunity to influence policy without becoming a part of the government executive. This reflects Hizbullah's growing desire to address inadequacies from within the system. The party's official position is that parliament is the only appropriate means through which formal political change
can be effected, and so it works towards achieving this.[103]

Hizbullah's Islamist platform and its links with Iran have caused
disquiet amongst many non-Shi'a Lebanese, who remain dubious about
the party's intentions regarding the imposition of Islamic rule in Lebanon.
Hizbullah itself has always remained ambivalent on this question,
acknowledging that its ultimate desire is for a state run according to the
tenets of Islam, while at the same time recognising that such an ideal must
not be imposed by force and must take into account the fact that Lebanon
is multi-confessional. Consequently, Hizbullah has been at pains to
present itself as a pragmatic rather than radical political party and to
convince the wider Lebanese community of the desirability of its goal.

This position has been formally outlined by the Secretary-General Hassan Nasrallah:

> I do not wish [an Islamic State] by force or violence, rather we prefer to wait for the day that we succeed in convincing our countrymen – by means of dialogue and in an open atmosphere – that the only alternative is the founding of an Islamic state.[104]

In keeping with this aim, Hizbullah is very particular about getting the message across that the basis of its existence is social justice. Consequently, it conceives of its constituency in terms of social justice rather than sectarian identity or political orientation, and it claims to represent the deprived in all areas of Lebanon. The use of the term 'deprived' (*mahrumin*) is an often-deliberate evocation of the words of Musa as-Sadr, and by implication a bid against Amal to be the real representatives of these people. In this regard, Hizbullah's parliamentary bloc functions not to oppose the government *per se*, but to oppose the government on issues where deprived people's interests are being threatened by government policy.[105] Central to Hizbullah's political platform, therefore, is practical reform, especially electoral reform to achieve a more representative parliament, for which Hizbullah has already developed its own model.[106] If this reform went ahead, there would in all likelihood be a great increase in Shi'a (and consequently Hizbullah) representation at the expense of the other communities and parties. It is the advancement of this single issue that is therefore likely to consume the party's efforts in the immediate future. Indeed, it was essentially for this purpose that the party supported the bill to lower the voting age from 21 to 18.

There is little doubt that Amal and Hizbullah hold different views about the kind of political representation most appropriate for advancing the interests of the Lebanese Shi'a. It is, however, difficult to determine the degree to which each party is followed because of its political platform. Much of the attraction of each party has to do with non-ideological issues such as the type of practical support it provides. For example, Hizbullah and Amal both operate hospitals; Amal dominates the Council for the South that distributes government largesse to South Lebanon; Hizbullah led the successful armed resistance against the Israeli occupation of Lebanon and provides a range of social services in the areas where it has a political presence. Add to this the regional and family or clan loyalties that operate within districts, and one can see why it is difficult to make definitive comparisons between one party's political success and the other's.

A further complication is that during national elections Amal and Hizbullah have established joint electoral tickets, which masks the true state of electoral support for each party. Whilst this tactic is invariably imposed upon the parties by external players, thus constraining the ability of the parties to gauge their true popularity, Hizbullah for one does not publicly regard such a situation as frustrating. Rather it sees that the current electoral system encourages political alliances of this nature and, whilst it would appreciate greater diversity in its electoral tickets, it requires other parties to be responsive to its overtures. The party also cites the pragmatic reason that such actions are a necessary political compromise, as it is in its best interests for the political situation to be calm, particularly in the South to give it maximum freedom of action against the Israelis.[107] Party sources have indicated that Hizbullah has always considered resistance against Israel to be its primary focus, and its political activity and defence of public rights as secondary. Without an electoral alliance with Amal, the political situation in the South would have been more turbulent and could have compromised the ability of Hizbullah's resistance forces to operate as freely as they would have liked. Thus the alliance, as strange as it may have at first appeared, served Hizbullah's wider strategic aims at the cost, perhaps, of some political influence locally. However, the short notice with which some of these electoral tickets have been established (the joint Amal–Hizbullah electoral ticket in 2000 is a case in point) indicates that despite the parties' protestations to the contrary, they are reluctant to ally themselves with a rival. Such is the historical relationship of the two parties, and the fact that they both vie for support from the same constituency, that future joint tickets are only likely to be formed under pressure from Syria.

Shi'a and Other Political Parties after Ta'if

Despite the emergence of the two Shi'a political parties, not all Shi'a supporters of alternative political parties were killed or gravitated towards their own sectarian political parties during the civil war. There is a coterie of Shi'a whose political allegiances remain with the non-sectarian parties that attracted them and so many of their co-religionists prior to the civil war.

The Syrian Social Nationalist Party (SSNP) maintains one elected Shiʿa member on its twelve-man Higher Council (al-Majlis al-ʿAla) – the party's executive committee[108] – and since 1996 the party's president has been ʿAli Khalil Qansu. More noteworthy still is the fact that ʿAli Qansu was also the Labour Minister in the Hariri government even though he was not a member of parliament – an extra-parliamentary appointment that is not so surprising when one considers his background in the labour movement.

Despite the closing of ranks by the Druze majority during the civil war, and the obvious attractions of the emergent Shiʿa parties, the PSP can still count on the support of some Shiʿa. After the party moved away from autocratic rule and towards a small leadership group structure, the Leadership Council was reconstituted in 1994, this time with four of its 17 members being Shiʿa. Other Shiʿa have also occupied senior roles in both the party and in government. Muhsin Dalloul, then a Shiʿa PSP member, was appointed Minister for Defence in 1992. He was also vice-president of the PSP in 1988. Whilst these are notable achievements, it should be remembered that Dalloul is closely aligned with Syrian interests and was a brother-in-law of the then Prime Minister Rafiq Hariri. It is therefore likely that his cabinet appointment resulted as much from his political connections as from his confessional identity or party affiliation. Dalloul later left the PSP after a falling-out with Walid Jumblatt, and he now runs on the electoral ticket of the Greek Catholic Elias Skaff. Another Shiʿa, Doreid Yaghi, is now the PSP's vice-president; he was also a candidate for the party (though unsuccessful) in the 1992 and 2000 elections. The achievements of these two high-profile Shiʿa members are remarkable when compared to how poorly the Shiʿa were represented in the party's upper echelons before the war. Nevertheless, the role of the Shiʿa must be put into perspective: the small number of prominent Shiʿa in the party cannot mask the fact that the PSP's membership base is now even more pronouncedly Druze than it was prior to the civil war, which is indicative of the party platform's lack of attractiveness to the general Shiʿa population. Nor is the PSP a truly national party, for its strength remains in the Mountain and the Biqaʿ; both Dalloul and Yaghi, for example, contested elections in the Biqaʿ district – in the Baʿalbak/Hirmil and Zahle regions respectively. For the PSP, then, its Shiʿa members are a small group whose presence gives the party the veneer of broad community representation; but the reality is that the party appeals only to a small, regionally-focused group of Shiʿa supporters.

The leftist parties, though their numbers were severely depleted during the civil war, have still been able to maintain the allegiance of some Shi'a. The Ba'thists, due undoubtedly to the support of the Syrians, have been able to return a Shi'a candidate to parliament at each of the post-war elections. This was certainly the case with the well-connected Shi'a, 'Abdullah al-Amin: his pro-Syrian contacts were strong enough for him to become the Secretary-General of the Lebanese Ba'th Party during the 1980s; and he was appointed as a minister in 1990 and then to parliament in 1991, before winning a seat during the first post civil-war election in 1992. The Ba'thists' strength amongst the Shi'a remains centred on the Biqa'; they do not have a widespread membership base amongst the community at large.

The next most popular party after Amal and Hizbullah, as far as a Shi'a communal following is concerned, remains the LCP. The LCP is still largely dependent on the Shi'a for its rank and file, and amongst its higher profile positions the community is also represented. Proof of this is the fact that, during the 1993 Party Congress, 41% of the delegates were Shi'a.[109] As the number of delegates has to proportionately reflect the membership base, this figure is indicative of the degree to which the Shi'a constitute the majority community within the party, a fact confirmed by the LCP's deputy secretary-general Sa'dallah Mazra'ani.[110] What this illustrates is the continuing attraction to the Shi'a in particular of the LCP's secular message about Lebanese political reforms.

In response to the dissolution of the Soviet Union, the LCP has continued to develop its own independent political program. It has set itself two aims: a short-term aim of increasing basic freedoms, particularly by introducing an electoral law based on proportionality rather than on confessional identity; and a longer-term aim of introducing socialism in a form different from the Soviet variety. The LCP has adopted a Fabian approach to this issue, advocating an incremental, peaceful transition to socialism through democratic means. In addition to the capitalist system's focus on production and profit, the LCP would also require that social justice be a feature of the capitalist system. The advocacy of social justice is a refrain common to both Amal and Hizbullah too, but it is a concept notoriously difficult to quantify in policy. The LCP claimed that too many parties used 'social justice' as a slogan only and became corrupted by the system once they became part of it. By and large, however, despite its arguably anachronistic name, the LCP has adopted a pragmatic approach to modern

Lebanon's political situation. In fact so pragmatic is the party leadership
that it sought to change the LCP's name to something that would better
reflect its platform. The proposal was defeated in an internal ballot.[111]

The LCP, according to Mazra'ani, should be considered the third most
significant political organisation amongst the Shi'a after Amal and
Hizbullah, particularly in the south; and there is evidence to support his
claim. During the 2000 parliamentary elections the LCP ran only four
candidates. One was Sa'dallah Mazra'ani, and he was able to attract over
ten per cent of the total vote in the Bint Jbayl district of South
Lebanon;[112] Mazra'ani believes, however, that his electoral support as a
proportion of the Shi'a population is significantly greater than this result
indicates. Another Shi'a LCP member, Ahmad Mrad, also took part in the
elections, in Nabatiyya, as part of the Democratic Choice electoral list of
ex-LCP official Habib Sadiq – although the LCP did not endorse Mrad.[113]
There is anecdotal evidence too that the LCP is finding some favour on
university campuses with its appeal across sectarian divides and its
peaceful anti-establishment message.

Whilst the nature of the electoral system and the dominant Amal-
Hizbullah alliance have denied Shi'a LCP members the opportunity to
have an impact on the national stage, the LCP continues to win local Shi'a
support. The challenge for parties like the LCP is to retain the loyalty of
their core constituency even if they have no electoral success. The LCP's
anti-Syrian stance also presents an informal barrier to its having more
impact on the Lebanese political system. Without access to government
funds, the LCP cannot benefit from the traditional *wasta* system – ideological commitment becomes a luxury the LCP cannot afford when rival
Shi'a political parties are able to offer their constituents practical improve-
ments in local infrastructure. As a Soviet-educated ex-communist in the
South Lebanese Shi'a village of Houla commented before the most recent
municipal elections:

> I am no longer a communist. I believe that Amal-Hizbullah
> would allow many beneficial projects to come to the village
> as it isn't opposed to the government.[114]

The role of the political parties in the development of the Shi'a has
reflected the wider social forces impacting on the community. Until socio-
economic conditions altered sufficiently to make the general Shi'a popu-

lation more politically aware and less accepting of the *status quo*, organised political activity remained the preserve of the *zu'ama*. Notables who did join political groups invariably sided with those dominated by Christians, partly because they felt likely to lose their sectarian identity in a Sunni-dominated group, but also because there were regional affiliations – the Christians operated in areas where there were concentrations of Shi'a. The term 'group' is used advisedly: the early manifestations of political activity were based solely on affiliations with a powerful individual, normally in parliamentary blocs. There was really no party apparatus to speak of, and internal cohesion was dependent on short-term political objectives.

A more orthodox form of political structure – the party – began to emerge during the 1950s. These secular and sectarian political parties attracted Shi'a in increasing numbers from the 1960s, particularly given the Shi'a's increasing dissatisfaction with their traditional pattern of political acquiescence. These parties were keen to win the support of this large group of disaffected people for their own purposes: by absorbing this large Muslim group, who historically had been quite docile politically, they were able to widen their appeal within the Lebanese state. The parties recruited them not to advance the Shi'a's needs but to advance their own; and their Shi'a members gave them legitimacy in the sectarian framework of the Lebanese state. Furthermore, within these secular political parties the Shi'a's ability to promote themselves politically was extremely limited; they were not, for the most part, seen as leadership contenders (the one party in which they probably had some chance of advancement was the LCP). Similarly, few were chosen to run as candidates in the general elections, although some did successfully. This success rested largely on the ability of the individual candidate to run for election on a party ticket, endorsed by the dominant community or individual in the electoral district. The political parties introduced to many Shi'a the notion of organised, mass political activity outside their own traditional paradigm. It cannot be said, however, that the parties were overly sympathetic to, nor sought to advance, the Shi'a community's political cause. It was not until the emergence of Amal under Musa as-Sadr that political movements can be said to have been instrumental in leveraging mass Shi'a support for the community's own benefit. The civil war accentuated the need for communities to draw together for protection, but at the same time it highlighted the inferior position of the Shi'a. In other parties the Shi'a were often used as low-level militia fighters, incurring the heaviest losses and with little opportunity for promotion within the organisation. The civil war, and more specifically the Israeli occupation of the South, also saw the emergence of Hizbullah. By the end of the civil war the Shi'a were, with some exceptions, concentrated into two major communal parties, Amal and Hizbullah, which now represent the two alternative and competing versions of Shi'a political expression. On the one hand, Amal stands for the secular Shi'a view of the future Lebanon. It is a party willing to use governmental powers to advance the communal cause, and willing to play an active part in cabinet. Its view in this regard is antithetical to that of Hizbullah, which has come to represent the more radical aspect of Shi'a political expression. Having started out as a militia organisation and only then transformed itself into an organised political party, Hizbullah has struggled to come to terms with the Lebanese republic. Decrying the legitimacy of the Lebanese governmental system, it has chosen to participate in parliament without participating in government. This has allowed the party to position itself as a legitimate parliamentary opposition and to alleviate the concerns many Lebanese had about its political intentions. But regardless of each party's views about the benefits to Lebanon of being secular or Islamic, both are united on one issue: the need to change the electoral law to reflect the country's demographic realities. It is only by achieving this goal that Shi'a political parties feel they will truly be able to advance their community's cause.

4

The Emergent Leadership

Political Participation of the Clergy

The Role of Shi'a Clerics

The third element that has been a driving force behind the development of a political consciousness amongst the Lebanese Shi'a has been the clergy. Before discussing their role, it is very important to make sure that the function of clerics in the Shi'a community is well understood. They are not clerics in the Christian tradition; that is, they act neither as an ordained priesthood nor as intermediaries between believers and God. Rather, their main function is as scholars of jurisprudence – interpreters of the *shari'a* as found in the *Qur'an* and the *sunna*, the latter as handed down through the teachings of the early Imams. This, along with the communal leadership role carried out by the revered scholars that comprised the Imamate, is the key to understanding their potential as a political leadership group within the community. Jurists with the ability and the desire to guide their community of believers naturally present as possible political leaders; and whilst much of this potentiality was eventually realised in Lebanon, it was by no means universally accepted within the community. This illustrates yet again the complexities of Shi'a politics.

This tradition of clerical leadership had its genesis in the period of the Twelve Imams (see Chapter One). Regarded as infallible interpreters of the religious sources, the Imams provided guidance that was binding on their followers, thus giving them great scope for the advocacy of causes that lay outside the purely spiritual sphere. For approximately seventy years following the occultation of the Twelfth Imam, the guidance hitherto provided by the Imams was now given by four of the Twelfth Imam's deputies who, it was believed, had been directly appointed by him to act as functional Imams in his absence. This period was known as the 'short occultation', or the 'period of special deputyship' (al-niyaba al-khas).[1] After the death of the last of the functional Imams in 941 CE, the period of 'complete occultation' commenced: whilst direct designation was no longer possible, guidance of the community was devolved to highly qualified Shi'a jurists who, it was believed, were able to mediate between the Hidden Imam and his followers. This is also referred to as the period of 'general deputyship' (al-niyaba al-'amma).[2] The jurists who were most highly regarded by their peers and followers were looked upon as sources of emulation (maraji' al-taqlid, plural of marji') and could play a significant role in the Shi'a community amongst both the 'ulama and the non-'ulama.

There has not always been unanimity in the role played by juristic scholars in the absence of the Twelfth Imam, and two different concepts have fought for primacy. Followers of the Akhbari school (from the word akhbar, or traditions) rejected any difference in the legal state of the umma before and after the Occultation.[3] As a result this negated the requirement for independent juristic reasoning (ijtihad) and with it the link between the authority of the Imams and the members of the 'ulama. The opposing school of thought is referred to as the Usuli school (from the term usul al-fiqh, or principles of jurisprudence), and it advocated the use of ijtihad. The Usuli school naturally called for a more functional role for Islamic scholars, because it placed greater reliance on their ability to interpret the sources of law. The quality and comprehensiveness of their education therefore became a strong focal point, and this in turn allowed for the establishment of a hierarchy of juristic education. At the same time, the Usuli school encouraged an active link between the 'ulama and the umma in the absence of the hidden Imam. This manifest itself in activities such as the collection and disbursement of the enjoined alms (zakat) and the fifth (khums),[4] the conduct of Friday prayers, and at least theoretically the administration of justice and the declaration of jihad.[5] The financial authority and societal influence these functions bestowed gave the 'ulama the potential for significant political influence both within the community and, to some extent, with the temporal leadership of the day.

The emphasis on the religious scholarship of individuals within the Usuli school inevitably created a hierarchy of maraji'. This brought with it a parallel development of patron-client relationships amongst the 'ulama, as students owed their allegiance to, and became influenced by the teachings of, particular scholars rather than just the religious schools (madrasa) in which they studied. Besides the pedagogical influence the clerics had on their students, they could also bring influence to bear through the distribution of financial support, either to establish *madrasas* or to provide assistance to enable pupils to study. This ability to influence the intellectual direction of Shi'a development by providing access to financial resources resulted in a geographical discrepancy in scholastic advances in the Shi'a world. Some regions allowed the Shi'a to achieve financial autonomy more readily than others, which made studying in those locations more feasible. In most of Qajar Iran (1794–1925), for example, religious endowments (*waqf*) provided scholars with independent income. This was markedly less common for Shi'a communities in the Sunni Ottoman Empire. In the 'shrine cities' of Najaf and Karbala in Iraq, for example, the *waqf* were virtually non-existent.[6] As a result, it was usually the esteem in which an individual scholar was held that dictated the funds he attracted from former students or from adherents who paid him for religious or juristic functions performed. In addition to these sources of income, there were some salaried government positions in areas of the Ottoman empire to which clerics could be appointed, such as a judge (*qadi*) who ruled nearly exclusively on laws of personal status according to the Ja'fari school of jurisprudence.

The primacy of scholars in providing guidance to the community, resulting from the triumph of the Usuli school, has provided the theoretical basis for the participation of clerics in the political processes of the state. Given the indefinite line in the Islamic tradition between the spiritual and the temporal, it is not difficult to see how the establishment of a hierarchy of Islamic jurisprudence, which the Usuli school encouraged, could lend itself to the emergence of clerical political leadership when there was a power vacuum. As has been noted of the development of the concept of the *maraji' al-taqlid*:

> [It] consolidated the authority of Shi'a jurists by initiating an unprecedented relationship between believers and their religious scholars. This sense of devotion to the religious leaders as the representatives of the Imam made possible...the exercise of powerfully influential religious leadership in the Shi'a community, pending the return of the messianic Hidden Imam.[7]

In theory, then, there is great potential for *maraji‘* to exercise political leadership over their adherents. But in order for the transferral of juristic acumen to the political field to occur in practice, the right conditions would first need to exist.

In practice, however, the adoption of a political role by the *maraji‘* has been haphazard at best. To begin with, the conditions that would be sufficient to allow the leadership of the jurists are ill defined. It was not until the turmoil of the Iranian revolution that a situation arose that allowed jurists to dominate the political scene. Another fundamental difficulty has been the fact that at times there has been no universally-recognised supreme *marji‘*; scholars failed to acknowledge unanimously a single authority. In recent years this happened after the death of Ayatollah Hussein Borujerdi in 1961, when the question of succession was contested between scholars from Najaf and scholars from Qum, the Iranian city that had built a reputation as a centre for juristic study that had begun to rival Najaf's.[8]

This is not to say that the ranks of the *maraji‘* were in disarray. Certainly Ayatollah Khumayni (1902-89 CE) achieved the status of an almost unanimously-acknowledged *marji‘* after, if not before, the Iranian revolution. The lack of a single pre-eminent *marji‘* during the nearly two decades between the death of Borujerdi and the Iranian Islamic revolution of 1979 is critical to a discussion of the role of the clerics in the political development of the Shi‘a. The absence of such an authority figure made it easier for various leading activist scholars to advance their ideas: there was no conservatively-minded supreme authority to oppose dissenting points of view. In this way the activism championed by Khumayni was taken up in one form or another by a number of *maraji‘*, who in turn taught it to a range of more junior scholars. This relative freedom to propagate an activist ideology was to prove crucial to the development of a culture of political activism amongst the clergy.

Early Shi‘a Jurists in Modern-Day Lebanon

Historically, there has been a significant tradition of religious scholarship amongst Lebanese Shi‘a, centred for the most part on Jabal ‘Amil. It is claimed that by the end of the fifteenth century Jabal ‘Amil represented the pre-eminent centre of Shi‘a religious learning,[9] attracting students from throughout the Arabic- and Farsi-speaking worlds. Well-regarded *madrasas* were founded in the fifteenth and sixteenth centuries at ‘Inatha,

Mays al-Jabal, Juba', Nabatiyya (in Jabal 'Amil) and Karak Nuh (in the western Biqa'). Of these, Karak Nuh was the most significant, largely because of its location on one of the major trade routes between Damascus and Ba'albak.[10] Many of the graduates of these *madrasas* were subsequently to be found in Najaf and Safavid Iran (1501–1722 CE). The movement of jurists during this period from *madrasas* in Jabal 'Amil and the Biqa' to areas outside modern-day Lebanon represents a high point in the scholarly reputation of 'Amili and Biqa'i jurists. By the first half of the nineteenth century, however, the process was reversed, as some Najafi scholars were sent to Jabal 'Amil to act as local *'ulama*,[11] indicating that a shortage had developed. One reason for this may have been that both Najaf and Safavid Iran were, by that time, able to offer a more supportive scholastic environment than either Jabal 'Amil or the Biqa'. This would have reflected the greater financial support available in Najaf and Iran, and the reluctance of the Sunni Ottoman rulers to become involved in Najaf. The Ottoman authorities were happy to leave Najaf relatively untouched because they understood that any interference there would have provoked resistance amongst the Shi'a of Iraq. There were no similar constraints in Jabal 'Amil and the Biqa', and the actual degree to which the Ottomans persecuted Shi'a scholars here is not well documented. The very presence of Shi'a centres of learning in these places would indicate a considerable degree of tolerance. On the other hand, episodes such as the arrest and execution of the Shi'a scholar Shaykh Zayn al-Din al-'Amili in 1558 after he was allegedly denounced as a heretic,[12] as well as the infliction of damage on the 'Amili Shi'a by Ahmad al-Jazzar in the late eighteenth century, illustrate that there were occasions when the Shi'a were persecuted for their 'heterodox' beliefs.

The pre-eminence of the 'Amili jurists did not last long; a convergence of events resulted in the *'ulama* of the region being marginalised for many years to come. Early in the sixteenth century the Bishara family, the principal Shi'a patron of the 'Amili jurists and their *madrasas*, suffered a major decline in fortune, and consequently the financial support available to jurists suffered too.[13] Official posts with the Ottoman government also became difficult to obtain and, with the general decline in fortunes, the *waqf* revenues suffered accordingly. The relationship between the Shi'a clergy and the Bishara family was a forerunner to the situation in which many of the religious scholars who remained in Jabal 'Amil would later find themselves. In the absence of other means of financial support,

many of the *'ulama* found themselves at the behest of the notable families who dominated the political scene in Lebanon at the time. The
scholars performed the ritual functions of their religion, and in return the
zu'ama provided them with a source of income. The financial incentives
to pursue independent scholastic learning were no longer there, and
consequently the intellectual development of 'Amili jurists stagnated. The
lack of an independent income stream, as well as the position of the Shi'a
under Ottoman rule in general, were significant practical reasons why the
clerics were incapable of pursuing any form of political activism. The rise
of the Safavid dynasty in Iran at the beginning of the sixteenth century,
with its requirement for religious scholars who could propagate the tenets
of the Shi'a faith there, also drained Jabal 'Amil of many of its finest
scholars, given its reputation for scholarly education in this period. Such
were the cumulative effects of the decline in financial support for Shi'a
scholars in Jabal 'Amil, the transfer of scholarly ability from there to
Safavid Iran, and the ongoing persecution of the 'Amili Shi'a by the
Ottoman authorities that by the nineteenth century Jabal 'Amil was of
only peripheral importance to Shi'a scholarship.[14]

The tradition of scholarly work was usually handed down within
particular families, which meant that in any given region many influential
'ulama came from the same family. The central role of both genealogy
(*nasab*) and honour through accomplishment (*hasab*) is a feature of Shi'a
jurisprudence, so it was readily accepted that the children of a noted
scholar were likely to pursue the same calling. It is fair to say that during
the period of ascendancy of the 'Amili *madrasas* the position of the *'alim*
in Jabal 'Amil was held in high regard, but this regard extended only to
their knowledge of jurisprudence and religion; there is little evidence to
suggest that at this stage they were active, let alone influential, politically.
The clerical community represented high learning amongst a largely traditional agrarian society. To propose an activist role for themselves would
have been to alter the political *status quo*, which in turn would have challenged both the traditional Shi'a leadership group and the local Ottoman
rulers. The costs of adopting such a stance would have outweighed the
gains.

Having no access to any independent political body that represented
the interests of the community, and being mindful of the notable families' political and economic power, the clergy for the most part never challenged the political pre-eminence of the leading traditional *zu'ama*. The

'ulama offered no intellectual encouragement for change, which reflected the quietist approach dominant amongst the 'Amili clergy in the absence of the Twelfth Imam. Fouad Ajami summarises the position of the Shi'a *'ulama* up to the 1960s as one in which the 'clerical community...was on the whole economically depressed and politically quiescent.'[15]

Influences on 'Amili Scholars

Since the relatively early decline of Jabal 'Amil as a prominent centre of religious scholarship within the Shi'a world, much of the scholarly discourse and political activity that has influenced the Lebanese in modern times has originated in, or been heavily influenced by, Shi'a centres outside Lebanon, particularly southern Iraq (Najaf and Karbala) and Iran. Recently, this has been most evident publicly in the close relationship between the clerical leadership of Iran and Hizbullah. Iraqi and Iranian influence is hardly surprising given that Iran's majority Shi'a population and Iraq's scholastic centre of Najaf have provided (and continue to provide) opportunities for the development of Shi'a thought that were not available in Lebanon.

Lebanon's widely recognised inter-communal ties with Iran did not come into being until after the rise of the Safavid dynasty in 1501 CE, yet close links had already existed for a long time with Iraq's scholarly centres. As early as the tenth century, for example, 'Amili and Iraqi Shi'a scholars had agreed that the Ja'fari school of law would be used by the Shi'a community.[16] This tradition of scholarly interaction between the two Shi'a regions continued as the Iraqi cities of Hilla and later Najaf and Karbala grew to become important Shi'a scholastic centres that attracted students from Jabal 'Amil. Lebanese scholars moved to the Iraqi 'shrine cities' of Najaf and Karbala (where 'Ali and Husayn, respectively, were buried) principally to gain advanced scholastic qualifications. The movement of 'Amili and Biqa'i Shi'a to Safavid Iran during the sixteenth century, on the other hand, was carried out at the behest of the Iranian Shi'a. It is unclear from exactly where in modern-day Lebanon these scholars were drawn: they were referred to as 'Amili whether they hailed from Jabal 'Amil or the Biqa'. A number of them rose to great prominence in Iran during the Safavid era. These prominent scholars came from a select few families, the most famous of which was the al-Karaki family. Their presence began with the arrival of Nur al-Din 'Ali ibn Husayn al-Karaki. Al-Karaki had originally studied at Karak Nuh, and his reputation spread as a result of the time he subsequently spent at Najaf and Karbala.[17] He became the most senior jurist in the Safavid Empire; and his son followed in his footsteps. Another prominent scholar from the same region was Baha al-Din al-'Amili;[18] indeed, the most senior jurists in the first 120 years of the Safavid Empire were all 'Amili scholars.[19] There are two points that should be noted about the presence of 'Amili scholars in Iran. Firstly, although they were valued for the quality of their scholarship, they were rarely if ever appointed to the politically more powerful position of *sadr* – a *sadr* allocated religious endowments and stipends.[20] Secondly, their links with the region from which they originated became increasingly distant, and the *nisba* al-'Amili in a name no longer guaranteed a scholar's place of birth but served rather to denote where his forebears had come from.

After the early influx of Safavid-era 'Amili scholars, the Iranian connection receded. The Najafi influence on the 'Amili and Biqa'i *'ulama*, on the other hand, proved extremely significant and enduring. Najaf's strength for most of its history was the quality of its scholarship: whilst clerics could have significant political influence and receive considerable financial remuneration in Iran, it was in Najaf that their professional reputation as scholars was largely forged. Thus, whilst 'Amili links with Iran were significant, it was to Iraqi institutions that the 'Amili and Biqa'i *'ulama* turned for their theoretical grounding. Najaf's reputation as the premier Shi'a centre of learning (*al-hawza al-'ilmiyya*) had grown over the centuries. Other centres such as Isfahan flourished during the Safavid era, but eventually Najaf consolidated its position as the centre of Shi'a learning, attracting the leading *mujtahids* of the day. This occurred shortly after the end of the Safavid empire (1722).[21] To undertake one's studies at Najaf in particular came to be considered an important, if not essential, step along the path of scholastic advancement. This held true for Ja'fari Shi'a from all over the world. However, the fact that Shi'a society in modern-day Lebanon was rural and lacked financial resources meant that it could send fewer candidates to Najaf's prestigious schools, due to the prohibitive cost, and had less capacity to support them in their home villages when they returned.

The 'Amili and Biqa'i Shi'a were attracted to Najaf for its scholastic reputation, but they also went there out of necessity: learning Shi'a jurisprudence in foreign *madrasas* was essential because there was little, if anything, in the way of religious education at home. In Jabal 'Amil in particular, there were few educational establishments; the only education on offer was usually that given by the *shaykhs* in Qur'anic schools (*kuttab*), where basic literacy was taught, or in religious schools (*madrasat ad-din*), where both secular and religious education were available. Usually these institutions were impermanent affairs, often closing down once their founder died or moved away. This tendency to transience is well illustrated by the example of two of the most prominent *madrasat ad-din* of the latter part of the nineteenth century. The Hanawiyya school established by Shaykh Muhammad 'Ali Azzedine at Tyre and the Hamadiyya school established by Sayyid Hassan Yusuf in 1891 at Nabatiyya both closed down on the death of their founders.

In such an environment, not at all conducive to independent *ijtihad*, there is little to indicate that modern-day Lebanon would be fertile ground for Shi'a clerical activism. The quietist stance of earlier centuries was widely accepted within the ranks of scholars throughout the Shi'a world. It was also, for Lebanon, a pragmatic stance given the realities of the distribution of political power. Consequently, the more politically active approach that was to decisively influence Lebanese Shi'a politics was not only a product of communal frustration at the *status quo*; rather it was an ideological orientation that had its genesis outside Lebanon, in Najaf and Qum. Its adoption and practical application within Lebanon came about as a result of the activities of non-Lebanese *'ulama* who moved to Lebanon, or more often of Lebanese *'ulama* who had returned from studying in centres such as Najaf.

Undoubtedly the driving force behind the resurgence of Shi'a intellectual activism came from Najaf, evidenced by the rising tide of activist writings emanating from there in the 1950s and 1960s. The emergence of an activist culture amongst the Najafi clergy was largely in response to a decline in the importance of religion in the centres of Shi'a study: between 1918 and 1957 the number of students at Najaf dropped from 6,000 to less than 2,000.[22] Secular government education arrived to challenge the *'ulama's* monopoly on learning and the Communist movement began to find support amongst Najafis. The decline in the *'ulama's* status brought with it a decline in their income, which further depressed student numbers in the *madrasas*. The decline was reversed by a series of *mujtahids* who advocated a more forthright political role for the *'ulama*, which made them more relevant to Shi'a believers. Their subsequent intellectual efforts were not only to produce results in their own country but were to have a far-reaching impact on Shi'a throughout the region.

The Influence of Non-Lebanese Intellectual Forces

One of the best known of the non-Lebanese activist clerics, and one who was to have a direct influence on the future of Lebanese clerical activism, was Muhammad Baqir as-Sadr (1936–80 CE). As-Sadr was a highly-regarded religious scholar and intellectual who argued that the Western models of capitalism and communism were not the only forms of political organisation and that Islam was an appropriate principle by which society should be organised.[23] Consequently he advocated a social revolution that would lead to the application of Islamic values to every sphere of life.[24] As-Sadr was a unique type of jurist for his time. He was a modern clerical activist skilled in Islamic jurisprudence, yet he was at the same time familiar with Western philosophy, and he was willing to provide an alternative to the secular communist and socialist philosophies that were gaining currency in the Arab world in the 1950s and 1960s. More importantly, and perhaps more enduringly, he eschewed the dry exclusivity of detailed juristic scholarship; his writings were designed to influence an audience much wider than fellow jurists. As Talib Aziz noted:

> He wrote his opinions in modern Arabic, addressing himself not principally to other jurists as is usually done, but to Islamic activists, professionals, college students, and other educated people in society whom he was particularly eager to reach.[25]

As-Sadr is best known for his works *Falsafatuna* (Our Philosophy) and *Iqtisaduna* (Our Economics), both of which sought to counter prevailing Western patterns of thought and economic models. He was also an advocate of a greater formal role for the *'ulama*. His belief in the primacy of the jurists as the arbiters of political power, and in the need for the highest *marji'* to act as the supreme leader, mirrors the essential elements of Khumayni's concept of *wilayat al-faqih*. This is even truer of his advocating the institutionalisation of the *marji'yya*, for it provides a practical example of the way in which an Islamic state may function. Supporting such ideas, given the ideological and potentially practical threat they represented to the Iraqi Ba'thist regime, did not come without personal danger: Muhammad Baqir as-Sadr and others, including his sister, were eventually executed by the Iraqi Ba'th leadership in 1980. Perhaps most importantly, as-Sadr taught or worked with a number of the clerics who went on to have a profound influence on the political development of the Lebanese Shiʻa.

The promotion of clerical activism that was to influence later Shiʻa *ʻulama* (including Lebanese) was not the preserve of Najafi scholars alone. Iranian ideologues also enunciated this approach. Dr Ali Shariati, a graduate of both the University of Mashad and the Sorbonne and a noted Muslim sociologist, encouraged the Shiʻa during the late 1960s and early 1970s to become more activist, particularly in opposing unjust rule – this was largely a reaction against the Pahlahvi regime in Iran. He was especially influential with the youth; and his lectures at the Hussein-e-Ershad Religious Institute in Tehran as well as his writings were extremely popular. His sphere of activity was Iran, so he did not directly influence the Lebanese political consciousness in the way as-Sadr had. Instead, he influenced people indirectly through his writings, which expounded a philosophical approach to a broad Islamic revival through adherence to Islamic principles while at the same time accepting modern Western political thought. One person who was influenced greatly by Shariati was Musa as-Sadr, for Shariati advocated the repudiation of religious dogma that had hindered the Shiʻa from taking a more active role in forging their political destiny. After Shariati's death in 1977, as-Sadr publicly eulogised him for his ideological dynamism.[26]

Shariati's intellectual contribution to Lebanese Shiʻa political development is best summed up by his belief that the *ʻulama* ought to play a central role in guiding the faithful in the face of corrupt rule but had failed to do so because they had become too closely involved with the ruling class. His criticism of the *ʻulama* was not universal but was limited to 'those religious leaders who cooperated with these (post-Safavid) rulers and allowed vacillation and misinterpretation of the original teachings of Shiism.'[27] It was further intellectual ammunition in favour of the path that activist clerics were taking at the time and in opposition to the views of more entrenched, conservative clerics. At the popular level the impact of this line of reasoning was significant, particularly in Iran; and in Lebanon it resonated with the perception that many religious leaders were vacillators who did not support systemic reform because of their relationship with the traditional Shiʻa political leadership. The position Shariati advocated regarding the *ʻulama* was all the more noteworthy because he was not an *ʻalim* himself. But it may also have been that his lack of scholarly credentials prevented his message having a broader influence: although he was able, through his writings and public lectures, to disseminate his activist message to a large audience, including many non-scholars, the fact that he had no religious education meant that it was unlikely his message would be taken up with zeal by the *'ulama* themselves. Nevertheless, Shariati did contribute to the intellectual movement behind the acceptance of a politically active *'ulama.*

Shariati was relatively circumspect in outlining his vision of what constituted just rule, but other Iranian scholars were more forthcoming. The person most readily identified with both the concept of clerical activism and the ability of scholars to organise and lead mass political movements is undoubtedly Ayatollah Ruhollah Khumayni. Whilst as-Sadr and Shariati reflected their Najafi and Tehrani backgrounds respectively, Khumayni was well-versed in both the Iranian and Iraqi scholarly traditions. His years from 1922 until his exile in 1964 were spent learning and teaching in Qum. During this period he was an outspoken critic of the government; and once he was allowed to teach in Najaf in 1965, after being exiled first to Turkey and then to Iraq, he became an even more vehement advocate of clerical activism. His polemic – encapsulated in *Khumayni and the Islamic State* (*Al-Khumayni wa ad-Dawla al-Islamiyya*), a collection of lectures delivered while he was at Najaf – is most notable for propounding the concept of *wilayat al-faqih*, or governance of the religious jurist. This work naturally heavily influenced Iran's post-revolutionary system of government. Its influence has also travelled beyond Iran; for instance, Khumayni's arguments form the basis of Hizbullah's political program in Lebanon as well as that of the Supreme Council for the Islamic Revolution in Iraq.

As much as Khumayni's message was attractive to many Shi'a, the chances of a political theorist successfully disseminating his ideas usually requires propitious timing so that these ideas can be debated in an environment conducive to their being accepted. Fortunately for Khumayni, his work in Najaf coincided with the increasingly activist stance being adopted by a number of other clerics; the intellectual synergies this created should not be underestimated. One of Khumayni's strengths, common to all the successful activist clerics, was his appreciation of the power of language. He was therefore careful to speak in plain language that appealed to the masses rather than in the formal language of the learned scholar with which he was extremely familiar. This practice was also used by advocates such as Musa as-Sadr to good effect in Lebanon, where the Shi'a's generally low level of education meant that orators had to speak plainly to get their message across. Khumayni's vision for creating an Islamic government was descriptive rather than prescriptive, and he saw such a government emerging out of an incremental rather than a revolutionary process. He believed that

> the effort will be a long, slow one, over perhaps two centuries, involving first propagation and teaching of true Islam, utilising communal forms of worship as political forums...[28]

Following the overthrow of the Shah in 1979, an Islamic government was set up extremely quickly, and this has served as the popularly-recognised model for adopting such a system of governance; however, it is the long-term evolutionary method of change, articulated by Khumayni before the revolution, that Hizbullah has adopted in its role in Lebanese politics.

The non-Lebanese activist Shi'a scholars had an indirect as well as a direct influence on the subsequent political development of the Lebanese Shi'a clerics, their written works providing a starting point for certain elements of the *'ulama* to conceptualise an activist role for themselves in Lebanon. In fact, without the non-Lebanese activist *'ulama*, it is unlikely that Shi'a jurists would have played the significant role they have in Lebanese politics. Certainly Lebanon possessed neither institutions nor jurists of the style or ability of Baqir as-Sadr or Khumayni. Consequently, any impetus for the development of communal political leadership had to come from outside the country.

Shi'a scholarship lent itself to disseminating a line of thought amongst its pupils to a depth not possible in secular educational institutions. Central to its pedagogical method was the important role played by the *al-hawza al-'ilmiyya*. Students were schooled in Islamic jurisprudence by a particular *mujtahid* and were heavily influenced by their teacher's views on jurisprudential issues. Once they left, their religious opinions often reflected those of their *mujtahid*. This was certainly the case in Najaf during the 1960s and 1970s when the activist Usuli school of thought was being widely advocated. Baqir as-Sadr in particular had a number of Lebanese students who took the essential elements of his activist discourse back to their own country. In some instances this transmission occurred relatively quickly as external events impacted on the *'ulama*.

When the Iraqi Ba'th party carried out an active campaign of suppressing activist Najafi academies in the late 1960s and early 1970s, many foreign 'ulama studying in Iraq were expelled. Some Lebanese amongst them had learnt the Najafi models of activist education and subsequently replicated them in Lebanon after they were forcibly repatriated.[29] A case in point is the fact that two future secretary-generals of Hizbullah, 'Abbas Mussawi and Subhi al-Tufayli, were both students of Baqir as-Sadr during their time in Najaf and were subsequently expelled by the Ba'thist govern-ment.

One should be careful, however, not to assume that a consistent line of thought was passed unquestioned from teacher to pupil. Whilst the relationship between *mujtahid* and *muqallid* was strong – and in the case of a number of Baqir as-Sadr's pupils, extremely influential – it would not be fair to say that the teacher's ideological orientation was replicated auto-matically by his students. Baqir as-Sadr, for example, was a student of Ayatollah Abu al-Qasim al-Khu'i in Najaf. Khu'i, a highly-regarded and widely-respected scholar, did not agree that Shi'a jurists should be directly involved in politics.[30] (Khumayni's *Islamic Government* was formulated partly in response to al-Khu'i's assertion that no obligation existed for clerics to participate in politics.[31]) Nevertheless, as-Sadr developed an activist line of thought, although he did continue to defer to al-Khu'i in matters of jurisprudence. Similarly, the most highly regarded contempo-rary Lebanese *marji'*, Muhammad Husayn Fadlallah, also studied under al-Khu'i in Najaf; and when Fadlallah returned to Lebanon, he was made al-Khu'i's representative there. In Fadlallah's case, context is very important: he did not become publicly politically active until his experiences in the early stages of the Lebanese civil war. Studying under al-Khu'i would not have imparted an intellectual disposition towards activism, but he was exposed to activist thought during his studies in Najaf given that he devel-oped close connections with the activist Da'wa party (discussed later). Musa as-Sadr (Baqir's cousin), who was to lead the political revival of the Lebanese Shi'a, was also a student of al-Khu'i's in Najaf; and in 1970, on the death of the incumbent *marji' al-taqlid*, Muhsin al-Hakim, Musa as-Sadr pledged his allegiance to al-Khu'i.[32] The cases of Musa as-Sadr and Muhammad Fadlallah, arguably the two most influential clerics in Lebanese political history, show that it was possible to develop an indi-vidual commitment to clerical activism without being the pupil of an activist *marji'*. It is fair to say, then, that what contributed most to the subsequent role played by the *'ulama* in Lebanon was not so much the direct transmission of activist ideas and principles from teacher to pupil as the general tolerance that existed in Najaf in the 1960s and 1970s for a politically active role for clerics.

Care should be taken when examining the influence of Iraqi and Iranian Shi'a developments on Lebanese Shi'a politics. Their impact needs to be understood with respect to the political situation in Lebanon and the limited role the Shi'a played in it. The intellectual activism advanced by clerics in Najaf would have to be modified to suit the Lebanese context. In particular, the multi-confessionalism of Lebanese society, as reflected in its unique political system, differed immeasurably from the kinds of society found in both Iraq and Iran. Lebanon also possessed (in regional terms at least) relatively robust parliamentary institutions. The activist model of clerical participation advocated by certain Najafi scholars could serve as an intellectual foundation for Lebanon's Shi'a rather than something to be copied.

Lebanese Shi'a *Ulama* Activism

The diversity of scholastic endeavour in the Shi'a world is reflected in the multi-faceted clerical activism that has subsequently developed. The leading politically-active Lebanese Shi'a jurists of the twentieth century can be classified, in terms of their impact on Lebanese politics, into one of three categories: ideologues, executive political leaders, and activist members of political organisations. In all three categories can be found evidence of strong connections with either a Najafi or Iranian *hawza*, with the influences of these places modified for local conditions. These conditions were without doubt an impediment to the wholesale import of the activist model of clerical participation sought by some *'ulama*. Prime amongst such conditions was the entrenched system of 'feudal' political loyalties that bred within generations of Lebanese *'ulama* a conservatism that eschewed political action in deed or word.

To be fair, the quietist stance that predated Musa as-Sadr and other Lebanese *'ulama*, though largely a product of domestic circumstances, also reflected contemporary thinking by senior clerics outside Lebanon. The Najafi *marji' al-taqlid* of the 1950s, Muhsin al-Hakim, had advocated that the *'ulama* distance themselves from the political arena;[33] the same position was adopted by his successor, al-Khu'i. There is evidence that many Lebanese clerics followed this line in deference to al-Hakim and al-

Khu'i, but at the same time the dominance of the Shi'a 'feudal' families and the *'ulama's* economic reliance on the *zu'ama* (particularly given the lowly economic status of the majority of Shi'a) meant that political quiescence was necessary mainly for the *'ulama's* personal survival. This attitude was reflected in the stance taken by Shaykh Muhammad Taqi Sadiq of Nabatiyya, the pre-eminent Lebanese Shi'a cleric of the 1950s. With firm political allegiance to al-As'ad clan, he refrained from encouraging any kind of political activity amongst the Shi'a of South Lebanon and instead supported the *status quo*.[34] But there were the rare occasions when clerics took a prominent position on an important political issue. Sayyid 'Abdul-Husayn Sharaf al-Din, a cleric born and educated in Iraq, but of Lebanese lineage, is a case in point. He was an active participant in the Arab nationalist movement opposed to French mandatory rule, and in 1920 he headed a Lebanese Shi'a delegation to Damascus to argue the case for an independent Greater Syria[35] (although Halawi claims[36] that he was forced into exile in Damascus the same year). Al-Din also appeared before the King-Crane Commission to announce publicly that he represented 'the desire and hopes of the ['Amili] nation in Syrian unity…under the leadership of Prince Faysal.'[37] For a Shi'a cleric to have such a public political profile during this period was, however, extremely unusual.

A recurring problem in the Shi'a's development of an independent and influential political voice has been their inability to present a unified front on issues. Poor socio-economic status, and the rivalries that existed between some of the leading families, meant that they could often be played off against one another. The *'ulama's* reliance on the patronage of the *zu'ama* also had the effect of replicating amongst the *'ulama* the same rivalries as their patrons'. This prevented the clerics from developing a unified stance that may have led to the natural formation of a politically activist approach. The level of rivalry between some clerics, even during the late Ottoman period, is apparent in the early twentieth-century confrontations between Shaykh Muhsin al-Amin and the pre-eminent 'Amili Shaykh Ja'far Sadiq over the form of *'ashura* celebrations to be undertaken in the South.[38] This confrontation probably reflected the fact that al-Amin was supported by al-Zayns, and Sadiq by al-As'ads and al-Fadls – the traditional rivals of the 'Amili families. By stopping the annual influx of crowds to Nabatiyya to celebrate *'ashura*, al-Amin's supporters realised that it 'would have humbled his [Sadiq's] political front represented by the al-Fadl clan and their followers, and ultimately weakened the power of their leader, Kamil al-As'ad.'[39]

Issues such as religious observances and educational facilities became significant political matters given the fact that local rivalries – reflecting patronage alignments – continued to affect the clerics' ability to transform any kind of public or clerical association into co-ordinated action. The need to satisfy patrons was so intense at times that group paralysis over-rode the ability to agree on a course of action for the common good. Even when the *'ulama* could form organised groups to address particular issues, they could not dissociate themselves from their culture of political dependence. The fate of the 'Amiliyya 'Ulama Society (*Jam'iyyat al-'Ulama al-'Amiliyya*) is a good example of the lack of clerical independence that encouraged such paralysis. The Society was formed in 1929 largely at the instigation of Shaykh Husayn Mughniyya (discussed later) and brought together 'Amili *'ulama* for discussions and actions on mainly educational issues. The Society's main goal was to establish a school for the 'Amili Shi'a. Despite sufficient money having been collected for the school, a location was never satisfactorily established; Mughniyya wanted it at Tyre, to improve the standing of his patron Kazim al-Khalil, and Shaykh Muhsin al-Amin wanted it at Nabatiyya, due to his links with Yusuf al-Zayn.[40] In the late 1930s, after the death of Shaykh Mughniyya, the Society was disestablished without the school ever having been built.

Not all Lebanese *'ulama* were politically quiescent, lacking independence of action or awaiting intellectual guidance from Najaf or Qum. Even before the rise of the activist stance of the 1960s advocated by Khumayni and various Najafi *'ulama*, there was evidence of activism on the part of a few Lebanese Shi'a scholars, albeit in a rather uncoordinated manner. The earliest example of rebellion against the entrenched conservatism of 'Amili *'ulama* is that of a group of young 'Amili scholars who came together during their studies in Najaf, some time in the late 1920s or early 1930s, to form a literary group known as the 'Amili Literary Club (*'Usbat al-Adab al-'Amili*).[41] There is no evidence to suggest that their subsequent activism was a direct result of their studies in the Najafi *hawza 'ilmiyya*. Although their actions back in Lebanon were not significant enough to earn them recognition as reformers of any note, they definitely constituted a repudi-ation of the learned helplessness of many of their colleagues in the matter of communal leadership. Although their reformist ideals were generally vague and were confined to the publication of manifestos in *al-'Irfan*, a

literary journal established in Tyre by Ahmad 'Arif al-Zayn,[42] they nevertheless represent a body of thought from amongst the scholarly class that
was opposed to the prevailing view that it was not possible to change the
political *status quo*. Indeed, opposition to what the group perceived to be
religious obscurantism was one of the central themes of their writings,
foreshadowing the thoughts of other clerics who would champion the
same cause a generation later. Such was the young 'Amili *'ulama's* disillusionment with the quiescence of their colleagues that a number of them –
some from noted scholarly families such as al-Amin and Sharaf al-Din –
renounced their status as *'ulama*, causing consternation amongst this
conservative class.[43] Apart from publicly challenging the *status quo*, there is
little evidence that their reformist endeavours led to any long-term results.
This was partly due to the fact that the conditions for reform did not
present themselves until decades later, and because the circulation of *al-
'Irfan* was limited. Given the literacy rates amongst Shi'a workers at this
time, reformist writings such as those in *al-'Irfan* were only ever likely to be
read by the educated elite. Without being able to influence the masses, the
group could have only peripheral importance in the community. What
their actions did achieve, however, was to introduce the precedent of an
indigenous call for reform by some elements of the *'ulama*, particularly
those scholars educated in Najaf.

Members of *'Usbat al-Adab al-'Amili* were not the last *'ulama* to
renounce their vocation. Another notable Lebanese *'alim* who later
eschewed a religious career for political activism was Husayn Muruwwa,
one of the chief intellectuals of the Lebanese Communist Party. Husayn's
renunciation of the religious path is further evidence of the *'ulama's* political quiescence: he felt he had to join a secular party to express his political views. Another member of the Muruwwa family, Karim, became
Deputy Secretary-General of the LCP and later the editor of the Party's
magazine, *at-Tariq*.

Groups such as *'Usbat al-Adab al-'Amili* represent the beginnings of
today's ideologically-motivated Lebanese Shi'a *'ulama*. Whilst noteworthy
for their openness in advocating change, they did not have a lasting
impact because they offered neither a well-articulated alternative position
for the scholars to adopt, nor a message and mode of address to influence the Shi'a masses. Their limited opposition to the prevailing *'ulama*
orthodoxy concerning political participation was, however, the precursor
to a series of more influential Shi'a activists. Where today's activist *'ulama*

differ from the early activists is in their understanding of where they see the Shi'a community politically and, more importantly, of a coherent method of achieving it. The Lebanese Shi'a activists discussed in the next section inherited the ideas of these early agents for change. By understanding the different methods these scholar-activists employed to bring about such change, we can gain a valuable insight into the broad range of contemporary clerical activism that Lebanon has experienced.

The Political Ideologues

The first of the Shi'a clerical ideologues who can be considered to have influenced the subsequent political development of the community was a Lebanese scholar, Muhammad Jawad Mughniyya (1904–79 CE). Mughniyya, who came from a rather impoverished background, was noted for his scholarship in the field of comparative Islamic jurisprudence, and he once wrote a unique comparison of the five jurisprudential schools (*madhab*) – the Shi'a Ja'fari and the four Sunni schools.[44] He spent the years 1929–40 studying at Najaf, and on his return to Jabal 'Amil in 1940 – to take over a position in the village of Ma'raka left vacant by the death of his brother – he began to rail against the political situation that left South Lebanon without the public amenities available to the rest of the country. He believed that responsibility for the situation rested with the deputies, who failed to represent the region in parliament, and the Shi'a populace, who accepted the *status quo*. He consequently chided the traditional notables publicly:

> We do not want from the deputies of the South that they blindly serve a community against another community…We want Jabal 'Amil to be an integral part of Lebanon with its rights and its duties.[45]

In contrast to later orators such as Musa as-Sadr, Mughniyya was also critical of the docility of the Shi'a working class in the face of the harsh economic conditions in which they found themselves, chastising them by asking, 'How can you spend the day at loss, and live through the night with hunger! You cannot even find work to buy a loaf of bread.'[46] The expression of such views at this time was not likely to endear Mughniyya either to the *zu'ama*, in whose interest it was to maintain the *status quo*, or to many of the other *'ulama*, who had eschewed participation in the political process.

Mughniyya's scholastic education differed from that of other notable Lebanese clerics in that it predated the activist clique that formed around Muhammad Baqir as-Sadr in Najaf. His development of an activist mentality thus arose largely from his personal experiences in Lebanon itself. Despite his not being exposed to an activist peer group, he was willing to criticise the political orthodoxy of the day. During the late 1940s and early 1950s, a time when the Shiʿa's traditional political system was firmly entrenched, he had urged the populace to challenge a political order that benefited only the *zuʿama*. Adding to his unorthodox reputation, during the 1970s he was also prepared to oppose Khumayni's concept of *wilayat al-faqih*. Mughniyya's opposition to Khumayni should be understood in light of the fact that he was a follower of the prominent Iranian jurist Muhammad Kazim Shariʿat Madari, a potential claimant to the role of supreme *marjiʿ* and hence Khumayni's rival. Whether or not this coloured his subsequent disagreement with Khumayni's view of the political role of jurists is unclear; the scholar Chibli Mallat believes it did.[47] What is clear is that Mughniyya disagreed with Khumayni's notion of the *ʿulama's* supremacy over the Shiʿa community in general – and Lebanon in particular – in the absence of the Imam. Mughniyya did, however, concede that it was the *ʿulama's* responsibility to ensure that the body politic was governed in accordance with the *shariʿa*. This requires the scholars to play a supervisory rather than a participatory role in governance.

The stance Mughniyya took against the political orthodoxy of the day was not without personal cost. He lost his job as president of the Shariʿa court in Beirut in 1956, and he was overlooked as successor to the *mufti* of Tyre (his mentor ʿAbd al-Husayn Sharaf ad-Din) in favour of the much younger Musa as-Sadr – a position that also attracted the kudos of being appointed by Sharaf al-Din personally. Opposition to the established order of things was unusual in the period when he was at his most intellectually active, and consequently societal conditions were not yet ripe for accepting his reformist ideas. Despite this, Mughniyya is noteworthy for contributing to Lebanese Shiʿa political development for two reasons. Firstly, he demonstrated that not all clerical activism emanated directly from the Najafi *hawza*; in his case it was a direct result of experiencing the social and political inequalities in his own community. Secondly, he differed from those who had become politicised in the *al-ʿIrfan* literary societies in that he never renounced his status as an *ʿalim* and was thus willing to enunciate a more reasoned approach to questioning the political orthodoxy of the day.

Perhaps the most enduring of the politically active clerics today is Muhammad Husayn Fadlallah. In contrast to Mughniyya, he has followed a more familiar path of Shi'a political activism, influenced during his time in Najaf by the activist clique of the 1960s and further radicalised by his experiences in Beirut during the civil war. Fadlallah was born in Najaf in 1935 to a noted *'alim* of Lebanese extraction, 'Abdul-Ra'uf Fadlallah. Muhammad Fadlallah studied under some of the most highly regarded jurists of the time, including Abu al-Qasim al-Khu'i and Sayyid Muhsin al-Hakim. Fadlallah's education was also much broader than the traditional juristic one; for instance, he learned philosophy from the same teacher who educated Muhammad Baqir as-Sadr in that subject.[48] His time in Najaf coincided with the development by the Najafi *'ulama* of strategies to counter to the attractions of the Communist Party to Iraqi youth. Foremost in establishing these strategies was Baqir as-Sadr, with whom Fadlallah collaborated in writing for the Najaf-based journal *al-Adab* from 1961.[49] Fadlallah had also collaborated with Sayyid Muhammad Mahdi al-Hakim (the son of the *marji'* Muhsin al-Hakim) in producing earlier handwritten versions of the journal. He has thus been a contemporary of, and worked with, the activist Najafi clerics of the 1960s, and he was obviously in broad agreement with their ideological beliefs. Thus whilst he must have had an inclination to a more active political role for clerics, it cannot be said that he imported this into Lebanon immediately. Rather, his overt activism was the result of experiences in the early years of the civil war. Fadlallah moved to the Nab'a district of Beirut in 1966 at the invitation of a group of Shi'a known as *Usrat Akhwaya* (*Family of Fraternity*). A large part of his work involved him in social justice issues and the development of schools, clinics and a library (Shaykh Raghib Harb, a prominent activist cleric in Hizbullah who was assassinated in 1984, was educated in Fadlallah's school.) Also at this time he was formulating a pan-Islamist position in response to the failures of pan-Arabism to restore Arab fortunes including the resolution of the Palestinian problem.[50] His expulsion from Nab'a by Christian militias, and his subsequent move to the *dahiya* in 1976, proved to be a defining experience in his intellectual development. Shortly after being expelled, he wrote *Islam and the Logic of Power* (*Al-Islam wa Mantiq al-Quwwa*). It is the work for which he is most famous, but it was not considered a defining work until

the combination of the Iranian Islamic Revolution and the rise of militant Islamic resistance movements in Lebanon gave it new relevance. It
outlines one of Fadlallah's central beliefs: the Shi'a heritage emerging
from the death of Husayn at Karbala is one of resistance rather than
submission. This in itself is not an unusual position for an *'alim* to take;
indeed it is considered by many Shi'a the traditional Karbala narrative.[51]
Fadlallah's vision was, however, somewhat more expansive than Musa as-
Sadr's view of Shi'a Islam merely in terms of improving the lot of its
Lebanese adherents. Fadlallah saw the Shi'a as Islam's true protectors,
hence their resistance was part of a wider plan for the defence of the
faith.

Fadlallah's contribution to the Shi'a's political development lies not
only in his ability to provide juristic justification for their right to resist an
unjust system, but also in his ability to provide guidance for the form such
resistance should take without threatening the integrity of the Lebanese
state. He maintained that, as Islam was *Da'wa wa Dawla* (a calling and a
state), it was inappropriate if the *'ulama* 'deviated from their religious
mission when they interfere in politics, or resort to force to change social
and political conditions.'[52] As a result, Fadlallah was to some degree an
advocate of Khumayni's belief that the *umma* should be led by jurists.
Where he differs from Khumayni is that he acknowledges the unique situation in which the Lebanese Shi'a find themselves as a minority community. Consequently he supports the 'Lebanonisation' of the Islamist movement in his country rather than the importation of a culturally and politically inappropriate model of Islamic governance. His aim for the Shi'a
community, then, is subsequently less grandiose than the position adopted
by those who see the Khumayni model of government as a desirable goal
for Lebanon. As Fadlallah said in 1995:

> Lebanon cannot be transformed into an Islamic republic,
> but the Islamists should give free reign to their ideas in
> Lebanon...Lebanon could thus be a pulpit from which to
> spread the word of God, just as it has always been a theatre
> for political action.[53]

This has been the key element of Fadlallah's message and, in many ways,
it echoes Musa as-Sadr's: the prevailing reality of the Lebanese situation
means that accommodation with other religious communities is an essen-

tial precondition of Shi'a political advancement. Similarly, his support of parliamentary participation by Hizbullah is designed with the same aim in mind. Fadlallah has on the one hand stipulated the limitations of secular democracy – 'we are not democrats, in the sense that we would allow the people to legislate in contradiction to God's law'[54] – and on the other, due to his pragmatism, acknowledged that in the case of Lebanon, 'Parliament represents an advanced propaganda podium for the Islamists…In this way, you can pass a law for Islam here, and secure a position for Islam there.'[55] This further confirms Fadlallah's standing as a political thinker of some note – willing to modify his beliefs for the greater good of the community, while at the same time continuing to focus on achieving his strategic objective.

Some have ascribed to Fadlallah the spiritual leadership of Hizbullah, but he himself has continually denied having any formal association with it. He does, however, acknowledge that people are free to follow his guidance in accordance with Shi'a juristic tradition, regardless of the organisation to which they belong. Certainly, Fadlallah prizes his independence of thought and action, so his denial of Hizbullah's spiritual leadership is entirely plausible. Also, there have in the past been limits to his influence with the party, such as his inability to resolve the TWA hijacking in 1985 or to secure the release of the Western hostages in the early 1990s. That having been said, he was instrumental in persuading Hizbullah to contest the 1992 parliamentary elections when many in the party did not wish to do so. Fadlallah's reluctance to be intimately associated with Hizbullah may be for two reasons. The experience of Baqir as-Sadr and the Iraqi Da'wa possibly demonstrated the dangers of becoming too closely aligned with formal Islamist groups; this was certainly reinforced by the attempted assassination of Fadlallah in 1985 in Bir al-'Abd, which killed 85 people. Although the bomb attack was most likely the work of the United States, Israel or the Phalangists (or any combination of them), it was almost certainly a result of Fadlallah's perceived position within Hizbullah. The second reason he is reluctant to be identified with Hizbullah is that any formal association with the group threatens to draw him into open competition with Ayatollah Khamenei for the spiritual allegiance of the party's members.

Fadlallah has been, and continues to be, a central figure in Lebanese Shi'a jurisprudence and political thought. Indeed, he is the pre-eminent Lebanese Shi'a jurist of his time. Fadlallah's reputation for scholarship also extends well beyond Lebanon, and he has influence amongst Shi'a communities in other countries. He is widely considered to be amongst the most highly regarded of contemporary *maraji'*. This standing alone would give Fadlallah the potential to be a political leader amongst all Shi'a although, since the Iranian revolution, the supreme leader of Iran has had the ability to influence events in the Shi'a world politically – if not as a *marji'* then certainly as a consequence of his political position. At the height of Khumayni's power, for example, there were those who ascribed to him extra-territorial authority over Muslims. Ayatollah Khamenei, later to become Khumayni's successor, revealed the extent to which Iranians believed it their right to act as leaders for all Shi'a when he declared in 1982 that the 'policy of *wilayat al-faqih* will be Iraq's future policy, and the leader of the Islamic nation is Imam Khumayni.'[56] This comment should be understood in the context of the Iran-Iraq war that was still in its early phases, for it would have been meant as a sign of the Iranian government's expectation that it would eventually win the war. Fadlallah himself does not subscribe to the view that the supreme leader possesses extra-territorial authority, particularly when that leader is currently Ayatollah Khamenei: 'while Iranians might well follow Khamenei's political and spiritual lead, Shiites outside of Iran...were not bound to emulate Khamenei.'[57]

It appears Fadlallah's attitude is partly due to his firm belief in the uniqueness of the Lebanese state and the fact that consequently it is not possible to transpose scholarly opinions (*fatawa*) wholesale from Tehran to Lebanon. This explanation is supported by a statement made by the senior Hizbullah leader Sayyid Sadiq al-Mussawi in 1993, that Khumayni did not meet Fadlallah for three years because the latter refused to support the creation of an Islamic state in Lebanon.[58] Another reason for Fadlallah's independence from Iran no doubt reflects his refusal to recognise Khamenei's claim to juristic authority. Khamenei, unlike Fadlallah, is not considered to be a *marji'*. Indeed, he did not issue any juristic ruling for the first four years of his leadership.[59] By contrast, both the respect in which Fadlallah is held by the Shi'a community and the quality of his oratory skills and scholarly publications show that he has been able to combine the characteristics of well-loved leader and highly-regarded ideologue.

The third in the so-called 'ideologue' school of clerical political activists is Shaykh Muhammad Mahdi Shams al-Din. He represents a slightly different type of political activist from Mughniyya and Fadlallah in that he combined juristic expertise with formal political activity through his association with Amal, and formal communal leadership with a role in the Higher Islamic Shi'a Council (*al-Majlis al-Islami al-Shi'i al-A'la*). Shams al-Din received his advanced juristic training in Najaf too; in fact he was born there, though his father was a Lebanese *'alim* from Qabrika near Marjayoun. For a time he studied with Muhammad Baqir as-Sadr and believed in a politically active role for the *'ulama*. He was a highly-regarded jurist and a prolific writer, articulating his view of divinely-ordained Islamic governance in his work *System of Governance in Islam* (*Nizam al-Hukm fi al-Islam*). He returned to Lebanon in 1968 and later rose to the position of vice-chairman of the Higher Islamic Shi'a Council. (The Chair of the Council has not been filled since the disappearance of the incumbent Musa as-Sadr). This demonstrates Shams al-Din's belief in the Council's cause as well as his close personal relationship with Musa as-Sadr.

Shams al-Din's approach to the role of clerics in Lebanese politics indicates that, like Fadlallah, he was a realist. Although Shams al-Din did not advocate radically restructuring the political system, he was nonetheless committed to promoting the clergy's role and improving his community's position within it. This meant he was able to argue strongly against secularism but without committing himself to the extreme of Khumayni's *wilayat al-faqih*. Rather, he believed in political pluralism (*al-'adadiyya*), where consultation is the key to tying together the disparate religious communities in the Lebanese state. Whilst his commitment to political pluralism sounds very even-handed, Shams al-Din was at the same time conscious of improving the lot of his own community. One means through which he tried to achieve this was his commitment in the late 1980s to a concept he enunciated of numerical democracy.[60] Quite simply, this meant that the community with the largest population would receive the bulk of the state's political appointments and parliamentary seats. This is nothing more than a system of communal proportional representation, yet such concepts were anything but common in Lebanon. As the Ta'if Accord showed, even if the National Pact could be modified, other communities were never likely to cede this degree of power to the Shi'a. As a result, Shams al-Din supported the continuation of political sectarianism for the sake of national unity.

Shams al-Din may not have advocated *wilayat al-faqih* publicly, but there is evidence that he regarded himself as a leading, if not the leading,

Shi'a spiritual and political figure after the disappearance of Musa as-Sadr. Norton, for instance, refers to claims that Shams al-Din saw himself as a challenger to Nabih Berri for leadership of Amal after Husayn al-Husayni.[61] Berri's success, as we know, consolidated secular leadership within Amal. The fact that Shams al-Din cut all ties with Amal from 1983 provides some circumstantial evidence to support Norton's claim. Shams al-Din may then have believed that being head of the Higher Islamic Shi'a Council would be a better vehicle for community leadership. He was certainly politically influential in this position during the early 1980s. This is evident from the excellent public response to his religious opinion (*fatwa*) authorising Shi'a to conduct 'comprehensive civil opposition' to Israeli forces after the Israeli army's interference in a parade commemorating *'ashura* in Nabatiyya in October 1983, during which three Lebanese were killed. Being leader of the Council was quite influential: it allowed the incumbent to distribute funds amongst the community and to approve the appointment of Shi'a to certain government-funded jobs, both of which helped him to establish a client base. Being head of the Council was not in itself enough to bestow *de facto* leadership of the community, as Fadlallah's lack of Council appointment but strong juristic reputation demonstrates. Just as Shams al-Din's efforts to seek influence within Amal brought him into conflict with Berri, his championing of the Council put him in competition with Fadlallah for juristic leadership of the community. There are accounts of conflict between the two eminent scholars over their respective influence within the community.[62] Even so, there was a bond between the two clerics that allowed them to co-exist. With the exception of Fadlallah, the ideologues contributed to the community's political development by establishing the intellectual conditions for clerical participation in politics through their writings. Notable too is the fact that, although both Fadlallah and Shams al-Din were influenced by Najafi activism, all the ideologues were careful to apply their activist beliefs to the idiosyncrasies of Lebanon – whether through Shams al-Din's 'numerical democracy' or Fadlallah's rejection of the extra-territorial authority of Iranian *'ulama*.

Clerical Political Leaders
Perhaps the clergy's most significant, and certainly most visible, effect on Shi'a political development has been through the actions of practical political leaders. The strength of these men lay not in advancing new

theories of political participation but in being able to mobilise the populace. Good examples of this type are Musa as-Sadr and Hassan Nasrallah.
As-Sadr, indeed, is so important to Shi'a political development that it is
impossible to discuss the issue of clerical leadership in Lebanon without
him; and one must be aware that his role may never be replicated by any
other clerical figure in Lebanon. This is partly due to the man's natural
ability as a leader, and partly to the fact that he was politically active during
a tumultuous period in Lebanese history – from shortly after the 1958
civil war to his disappearance in 1978. So effective was his leadership that
he was able to change completely the Shi'a community's political expectations. Though they are still under-represented, their political and
economic circumstances are dramatically different from the days when
Musa as-Sadr first began urging them to develop a communal political
identity. Subsequent clerical leaders may have been able to advance the
Shi'a's political situation further, but never in as dramatic a fashion as
Musa as-Sadr.

More than twenty years after his disappearance, Musa as-Sadr's picture
still adorns the streets of many Lebanese towns and villages, so great was
his impact on Shi'a political consciousness. His success lay in his keen
understanding of the importance of the spoken word to motivate the
masses, combined with an ability to create an institutional framework that
would give him (and successive clerical leaders) formal influence in the
Lebanese political system. He represents a sea change in clerical activity,
as he well understood the most effective means of communicating his
message to the masses. Musa as-Sadr's use of Shi'a religious symbolism
meant he did not have to rely on building political networks based on
local political issues, which would have put him in direct competition with
the local *zu'ama*. His access to, and willingness to use, media resources was
revolutionary for a Shi'a cleric in Lebanon at this time. Because he had a
broad secular and religious education and was born and brought up in
Iran rather than Lebanon, he was not weighed down with the Lebanese
'ulama's traditional reluctance to become politically engaged.

Musa as-Sadr had a distinguished background in juristic education.
Joseph Olmert describes him as an Iranian-schooled cleric,[63] but while it
is true that his early years were spent in Qum, the fact that he studied
under the Grand *marji'* Muhsin al-Hakim for four years at Najaf[64]
between 1954 and 1958 makes this description not entirely accurate. As-
Sadr also received a secular education, studying law at the University of

Tehran. There are conflicting accounts as to whether or not he finished this study. Fouad Ajami refers to as-Sadr's enrolling at the university, but never states that he completed his degree.[65] On the other hand, Halawi notes that he graduated from the course.[66] To what extent as-Sadr was influenced by his time at the university is not known, yet the very fact that he chose this path indicates he had a keen understanding of the secular world and did not wish to spend all his time in a cloistered juristic environment studying the sources of the *shariʿa*. It also marked him as someone who was not happy merely to follow convention. Although born and raised in Iran, as-Sadr came from the family of a noted *ʿalim* from Jabal ʿAmil who had fled persecution there in the late eighteenth century.[67] In common with the families of Shams al-Din and Fadlallah, as-Sadr's family had roots in the land, to which he was to return at the end of the 1950s. But the history of as-Sadr's family, unlike that of the other two clerics', demonstrates a willingness to defy the *status quo*: they were active in opposing the Shah's anti-clerical policies, and Musa was the cousin and brother-in-law of Muhammad Baqir as-Sadr.[68] How much the cousins conversed or shared ideas with each other is unknown; regardless, their respective political paths indicate that they shared a similar philosophy.

Despite his impressive scholarly pedigree and the fact that he taught Islamic jurisprudence (*fiqh*) at Qum[69] and studied under leading *maraji* at Najaf, Musa as-Sadr could not claim to be a *mujtahid* of note. This may be because his practical activities detracted from his ability to write scholarly treatises on issues of the day, or it may simply show that this was not an area he chose to pursue. Either way, there is no evidence that anyone used his lack of written output to cast doubt upon his leadership abilities – probably because his *nasab* and his personal qualities were proof enough. Although he published very little, his practical legacy has been enduring: he was instrumental in establishing the Higher Islamic Shiʿa Council, he was the founder of Amal, and he was a proponent of a communally-inclusive approach to addressing the issue of the underprivileged in Lebanese society. In achieving these things, he demonstrated aspects of clerical leadership that had not been seen before and that have lasted to this day. Firstly, he was an advocate of the power of plain speech in public forums. He took himself out of the *husayniyyas*, which had been the platform for political discussion to date, and addressed large public gatherings (a 1974 rally at Baʿalbak attracted a reported 100,000 Shiʿa[70]), thereby establishing his political reputation. Secondly, he cultivated a relationship with the media. The two most popular national newspapers of the day – *Al-Hayat*, at that time still owned by the Shi'a Muruwwa family, and *an-Nahar*, owned by the Greek Orthodox Tueni family –gave as-Sadr wide coverage, further enhancing his leadership credentials.[71]

As-Sadr understood well the complexities of the Lebanese political system and consequently chose the most appropriate time to alter the political and social *status quo* that so disadvantaged his fellow Shi'a. As individuals and political parties have done for many years in Lebanon, as-Sadr established charitable organisations through which he could provide services to the Shi'a that the government did not, at the same time establishing himself as a benefactor of his community. He did this by expanding existing charitable organisations and by establishing new institutions such as the Social Institute (*al-Mu'assasa al-Ijtima'iyya*) which catered for Tyre's orphans and destitute. Whilst actions such as these were not unusual amongst the clergy, as-Sadr also displayed an admirable pragmatism regarding both the domestic and regional realities of the political environment in which he operated.

On a local level, he was amongst the first clerics to actively court Lebanese outside his own community. For this purpose he gave sermons in Christian churches, an act that Shi'a clerics before him would never have contemplated. Similarly, by participating in the executive council of the non-confessional regional development Social Movement (*al-Harakat al-Ijtima'iyya*), he was exposed to a much broader audience whom he could influence. By encouraging harmonious relations with the other communities, he made sure they did not see his work for the Shi'a as a threat. His ability to court powerful regional allies is apparent from his recognition in 1973 of the minority Alawi community as Twelver Shi'a.[72] This act concomitantly bestowed religious legitimacy on the Syrian (and Alawi) regime of Hafiz al-Assad at a time when it faced rising opposition from the Syrian Muslim Brotherhood; and since Syria (both directly and through proxies) later provided the nascent Amal with weapons and training, this single act illustrates how politically astute as-Sadr was.

There is little doubt that as-Sadr's populist appeal forever changed the political role of the Shi'a *'ulama* in Lebanon, yet his most enduring legacy is the organisational structures he developed. Both the Higher Islamic Shi'a Council and Harakat Amal have outlasted their creator, and, so it has transpired, have become loci for clerical and secular leadership respectively. The Higher Islamic Shiʿa Council is notable for the fact that its establishment by Law 72/67 in the Lebanese Parliament in 1967[73] was the first time a formal representative body (besides the Jaʿfari Tribunal) had been created exclusively for the Shiʿa. As-Sadr's election as its first chairman in May 1969 signalled his claim to the leadership of the Shiʿa community. In the absence of any community-based political party, and despite its non-political nature, the Council actually served a political purpose as an advocacy group for temporal as well as spiritual Shiʿa issues. As-Sadr's acumen in providing organisational structures for the Shiʿa is further illustrated by his creation of *Harakat al-Mahrumin* (Movement of the Deprived) in 1974. The emergence of Amal, the militia adjunct to Harakat al-Mahrumin, in July 1975 is yet more evidence of as-Sadr's ability to coalesce disparate groups and give the Shiʿa a central focus. He understood that each community had to be prepared to provide for its own physical protection. This indicates that as-Sadr himself (ill-equipped as he was militarily) had forsaken attempting to resolve his community's claims peacefully.

The current Secretary-General of Hizbullah, Shaykh Hassan Nasrallah, is a more contemporary case of the pragmatic clerical leader. Nasrallah differs in many ways from the *ʿulama* already discussed. He was not of a scholarly family, and indeed he was the first member of his family to become a cleric.[74] Nasrallah studied for two years in Najaf, but completed his juristic studies in Baʿalbak. Despite some claims that he learnt jurisprudence at Qum, Nasrallah himself acknowledges that he spent only two months there.[75] In his youth, therefore, he was not exposed directly to the teachings of Muhammad Baqir as-Sadr, so he cannot be considered one of the Najafi activist clerics in the same manner as Fadlallah and Musa as-Sadr. His interest in political activism is evident from the fact that he was a member of Amal at age fourteen and head of his town's party branch by the time he was eighteen, which demonstrates his capacity for leadership from a young age. He was expelled from Amal in 1982 because he urged armed resistance in response to the Israeli invasion of that year.[76] Despite his early training in Najaf he is closely aligned with Iran, a situation stemming from his juristic allegiance to the Tehran-based *maraji'*. This loyalty has been reciprocal, and is now based on close personal ties between Nasrallah and the Iranian leadership. Indeed, shortly after Ayatollah Khamenei succeeded Khumayni as Iran's supreme leader in late 1989, he was visited by a senior delegation from Hizbullah.

During the meeting it is reported that Khamenei advised the delegation that in future 'they should refer to Sayyid Hassan and consider his opinion to be my opinion in all circumstances.'[77] Given that Nasrallah was only twenty-nine at the time, had not been born to a scholarly family, and was not a widely-published scholar himself, one can only assume that Khamenei's confidence in him must have been founded on his leadership qualities as much as his ideological convictions. The strength of these qualities and the respect in which the party itself holds him is illustrated by his rapid rise to power. From his position as Hizbullah's Chief of Military Operations, he was elected Secretary-General in 1992 within hours of the death of the previous leader, 'Abbas Mussawi. Since that time, the rules of incumbency for the Secretary-General have been changed from fixed one-year terms to two-year terms and finally to unlimited successive terms in order to accommodate him. Nasrallah has proven to be an adept political leader, well able to utilise the resources available to him to engender loyalty amongst his communal followers.

Like Fadlallah, Nasrallah has worked to reassure the other Lebanese communities that Hizbullah is not looking to make radical political changes under the direction of clerics. Their fears were no doubt fuelled by the comments of previous leaders such as 'Abbas Mussawi, who was less circumspect in outlining his vision for the country when he reportedly said:

> Our interpretation of Islam could not be reconciled with geographic considerations. We follow the leadership of Ayatollah Khumayni, and this leadership is as compelling in Lebanon as it is in Iran...All boundaries dividing up *Dar al-Islam* are artificial and will soon disappear.[78]

This type of language indicates some political immaturity on the part of the clerics during the mid-1980s when the success of the Iranian revolution and the emergence of Hizbullah were still recent events. Now that the civil war has ended, pro-Iranian clerics such as Nasrallah have had to reconcile their adherence to Khumayni's concept of *wilayat al-faqih* and their loyalty to Iran with the realities of the Lebanese situation in which they find themselves.

No matter how effective a cleric such as Nasrallah may be as a leader, his lack of scholarly credentials will continue to limit his influence. Whilst he is an impressive orator and well regarded for his role in resisting the Israeli occupation of Lebanon,[79] he lacks a wider audience as an *'alim* outside of Hizbullah. This limits the audience for his message largely to pro-Hizbullah Shi'a. An attempt to circumvent Nasrallah's limitated sholastic credentials is evident from the fact that Ayatollah Khamenei has declared Nasrallah to be a *hujjat al-Islam* (indicating an aspiring *mujtahid*) when Nasrallah in fact has no dedicated group of adherents (*muqallid*) and is not renowned for his scholarly output. Given that Ayatollah Khamenei's juristic standing is limited, such a declaration is made in his capacity as the leader of Iran rather than as a highly regarded *marji'*, further indicating Nasrallah's constituency. Musa as-Sadr managed to achieve community leadership without any scholarly appellation, but it was probably unnecessary due to the period in which he lived, the groundbreaking political movement he founded, and the absence of a competing communal political party. Nasrallah's position within a well-organised party, on the other hand, means that he will need a broader message than just that of Hizbullah's political aims if he is to attract a wider group of Shi'a to his political views. For this reason it could be argued that within the community Fadlallah wields much wider political influence, as well as spiritual and intellectual, because he is a *marji'* rather than because of any alignment he has with a political party.

The *Ulama* and Political Groups
In terms of clerical political activity that can be considered formally organised, the most noteworthy example is the Higher Islamic Shi'i Council. Whatever Musa as-Sadr's ultimate intentions may have been, the Council was not constituted as a political body but was set up to admin-ister the religious matters that pertained directly to the Shi'a community. As Article One of its charter states:

> The Muslim Shi'a community...independent in its religious affairs, endowments and institutions, has representatives from within it who speak and act on its behalf according to the prescripts of the honourable *shari'a*, and the jurisprudence of the Ja'fari doctrine within the framework of the *fatwa*, issued by the general *marji'* of the community in the world.[80]

Although not composed exclusively of clerics, the head of the Council is an *'alim*, as are approximately half the Council members. Before the Council was established, the most prestigious Shi'a collective body had been the Ja'fari Tribunal, which ruled on personal status laws. Although this was a clerical institution, its responsibility was limited to matters of *fiqh* only, hence it can not really be considered a representative body.

Despite the limited aims of the charter, the fact that the Council's inception preceded the emergence of both Amal and Hizbullah meant that it was very quickly seen as a political vehicle for advancing Shi'a issues, the enunciation of which had previously been the preserve of the traditional Shi'a *zu'ama*. The Council's mandate became one of articulating the Shi'a community's demands within the political system.[81] From its earliest days under Musa as-Sadr, the Council stridently pronounced its community's demands, attacking the government publicly for its failure to attend to Shi'a needs, which were enunciated in the document 'Shi'a Demands' published in December 1974.[82] The document referred to the deprivations suffered by 'the forgotten planters, the helpless workers, the alienated youth, and the students trying to escape an uncertain future.'[83] The naming of these interest groups is important, because they are essentially the same groups (students and workers particularly) who were attracted to the secular leftist political parties that were espousing similar changes to the *status quo* as those advocated by Musa Sadr. He sought to entice these disenfranchised Shi'a back into the communal fold, and he followed up the release of the document with a series of mass rallies to consolidate the Council's position (as well as his own) as the representative of Shi'a needs. It is little wonder, then, that the establishment of the Council, and particularly Musa as-Sadr's role in it, was opposed by Kamil al-As'ad. As-Sadr, having already proven himself a popular alternative to the traditional leadership, used the Council to institutionalise his position within the community by providing a counter to al-As'ad, who had achieved the same outcome using his domination of parliamentary representation.

The position of chairman of the Council, being the preserve of a cleric, created a state-endorsed outlet for a politically-active religious identity. The Council *per se* represented a final break from Sunni domination of Muslim political expression; whilst recognition of the Shi'a as a separate sect by the French mandatory government had allowed them to set up their own courts in accordance with the Ja'fari school of jurisprudence (*madhab*), there was still no discrete body for the advancement of Shi'a relations with the government. The Council provided Musa as-Sadr with a platform from which he could play a leading institutional role in the political life of the Shi'a prior to his establishing Harakat al-Mahrumin; until his disappearance, in fact, he retained the leadership of both organisations. This connection between the Council's leadership and Amal has continued after his disappearance; his successor, Shaykh Muhammad Shams al-Din, was a member of the Amal command structure as well as Deputy Chairman of the Council, until he formally renounced his association with Amal in 1983.[84] Deputy Chairman, Shaykh 'Abd al-Amir Qabalan, who took over after the death of Shams al-Din in 2002, has also been closely associated with Amal, having previously been head of their *shari'a* department.[85] The emergence of alternate loci for Shi'a political expression, with the establishment of Amal and Hizbullah, has meant that the Council no longer plays as central a role in advancing the political interests of the Shi'a as it once did. Nevertheless, the calibre of its leadership since Musa as-Sadr's disappearance has allowed it to continue playing the role of an independent body capable of influencing Shi'a opinion on political issues. That having been said, some of the Council's responsibilities, whilst they sound impressive, are not indicative of the real distribution of power within the community. An example of this is the Council's ostensible responsibility for administering 'the religious endowments, mosques and the philanthropic institutions of the Shi'i community',[86] when the reality is that organisations such as Hizbullah control their own schools and mosques. We can glean some idea of the relative authority of these organisations from the fact that, whilst the Council controls eight mosques in Beirut and several others outside Beirut, Hizbullah controls over forty mosques throughout Lebanon.[87] As a result, the Council's ability to influence mass opinion is extremely limited, although as an advocacy group it still has a role to play.

Whilst Hizbullah continues to be the largest and most prominent Lebanese political organisation in which Shi'a clerics play a leading role, it was not the first. Formally-organised clerical political activity can be traced back to the juristic experience in Iraq, where it formed the basis for the establishment of a Lebanese branch of the Islamic Call (*Da'wa*) Party. The Da'wa was the organisational manifestation of the activist call enunciated by Khumayni and Baqir as-Sadr, although scholars disagree as to its exact origin. Hanna Batatu claims that it emerged in Najaf in 1968 or 1969 under the tutelage of Sayyid Muhammad Mahdi al-Hakim, the son of the supreme authority (*al-marji' al-a'la*) of the day, Sayyid Muhsin al-Hakim.[88] Amatzia Baram, on the other hand, ascribes its genesis to meetings of young *'ulama* under the tutelage of Muhammad Baqir as-Sadr in Najaf during the late 1950s.[89] Baram does, however, note that as-Sadr distanced himself from the party in 1962 after Muhsin al-Hakim requested that he share his scholarly work amongst the whole community rather than concentrating it within one group.[90] The party became strongly represented amongst the younger ranks of the *'ulama*, who were attracted to its activist message. Whatever the true nature of Baqir as-Sadr's relationship with the party, his intellectual work provided much of the impetus for the movement, and his execution in 1980 by Saddam Hussein's regime robbed the movement of much of its intellectual potency in Iraq.

Lebanese graduates of Najafi *madrasa* set up a branch of the Da'wa party in their own country some time in the early 1970s, where it acted as a framework for the more activist members of the Shi'a clergy. It is fair to say that the Da'wa in Lebanon was more an activist movement than a fully functioning political party – although the same could be said of many Lebanese political entities. What is notable about the members of Da'wa is that many of them were also members of the Amal movement, although this is not surprising given Musa as-Sadr's prominence in Amal's establishment and the lack of any alternative means of distinctly Shi'a political expression at the time.

The schism within Amal caused by Nabih Berri's participation in the 1982 National Salvation Committee also affected those with an allegiance to the Da'wa: many left what they perceived to be an increasingly secular movement for the activism that Hizbullah offered. One of the most prominent clerical members of the Da'wa movement, Shaykh Ibrahim al-Amin, a Najafi graduate who became Amal's representative in post-revolutionary Iran, returned to Lebanon in response to Berri's actions and assisted in the transfer of many Da'wa members into the nascent Hizbullah.[91] Al-Amin was later to become Hizbullah's official spokesman. Not all of the Da'wa's members have been absorbed by Hizbullah; a faction has remained with Shaykh Muhammad Fadlallah and therefore sits outside the Hizbullah party network.[92] It is difficult to determine the Da'wa's role in the development of Shi'a political consciousness other than to acknowledge that it represents a direct organisational connection between the Lebanese Shi'a *'ulama* and the Najafi activist movement.

Several other groupings of religious scholars have occasionally emerged to play a role, albeit minor, in Lebanese politics. Some of them have emerged as a result of, or directly through, post-revolutionary Iranian efforts to export the ideals of the revolution. These include the Islamic Movement (*al-Harakat al-Islamiyya*), under the Lebanese Shi'a cleric Sadiq Mussawi, which was reportedly the creation of Tehran-based Shi'a who sought to build a unified Muslim (as opposed to Shi'a) political grouping[93] in order to attract a wider audience to Khumayni's message. Another was the Association of Muslim 'Ulama in Lebanon (*Tajammu' al-'Ulama al-Muslimin fi Lubnan*), which emerged in Beirut after the 1982 Israeli invasion and maintained strong allegiance to Iran. *Tajammu' al-'Ulama al-Muslimin fi Lubnan* was also committed to making itself a more inclusive Muslim organisation because it contained both Shi'a and Sunni scholars who supported the ideals of the Iranian revolution and it sought to incorporate these ideals into the Lebanese context.[94] The most notable of the clerics to emerge from this group was Shaykh Zuhayr Kanj from the Biqa'; and whilst it is claimed that the group's Shi'a elements later became subsumed under Hizbullah in much the same way that Da'wa members were, there are indications that Zuhayr Kanj has maintained contact with the more radical element of ex-Hizbullah members represented by Subhi al-Tufayli.

Since the emergence of Musa as-Sadr and the rise of Hizbullah, many Shi'a *'ulama* have abandoned their traditional distance from political activity in Lebanon and have been at the forefront of their community's political development. Their success stands in stark contrast to the role of the non-Shi'a political parties and the traditional *zu'ama*: in the leftist parties the Shi'a had served merely as the rank and file; and as far as the traditional *zu'ama* were concerned, the Shi'a populace were their clients on whose behalf they would act but who would not be part of the political process themselves. The *'ulama*, on the other hand, have been able to give expression to a distinctly Shi'a form of political activity. They have been able to do this principally by utilising the Imami concept of communal leadership as a means of alleviating the community's sense of deprivation. Even today Nabih Berri is the only secular Shi'a figure to rival *'ulama* such as Fadlallah and Nasrallah for leadership of the community. It remains difficult, nevertheless, to characterise neatly in terms of a single model the methods the *'ulama* have followed in order to provide this leadership, as the descriptions in this chapter of three different types of clerical activity attest.

There is no doubt that the *'ulama* have been influenced to a great degree by the intellectual activities of Shi'a outside Lebanon, but the manner in which the *'ulama* have conducted their political activities has been different to that of their co-religionists in both Iran and Iraq. Of course, this was always going to be the case because the political and social realities of the Lebanese situation differed markedly from the other countries'. Both Fadlallah and Shams al-Din were careful to ensure that whatever political path the *'ulama* advocated, it had to take into account the history and demographics of the multi-confessional Lebanese state. This does not mean there was no common thread of intellectual development linking the Lebanese Shi'a with Shi'a in other countries; much has been made of the Najafi influence on the Lebanese Shi'a, and it is entirely appropriate to identify the activist clerics of Najaf of the 1960s and 1970s as being critical to subsequent developments amongst Lebanese clerics. Despite the undeniable Lebanon-Najaf connection, simply to explain Lebanese clerical political development as an adjunct to Najafi activism is to ignore both the early activists, such as Mughniyya, and the later ones, such as Nasrallah, neither of whom were graduates of Najafi *hawza*. At the same time, whilst there is evidence that Muhammad Fadlallah was a contemporary of, and collaborated with, Muhammad Baqir as-Sadr in producing a literary journal, his philanthropic activities in Lebanon after his arrival in 1966 indicate that he did not bring the Najafi activist approach with him; rather, his political activism was triggered subsequently by his treatment at the hands of Christian militias in Beirut. Similarly, even though 'Abbas Mussawi and Subhi al-Tufayli studied under Baqir as-Sadr, their ideological allegiances shifted to the Khumayni version of clerical political participation enacted following the Iranian revolution. The Najafi legacy should therefore be regarded more as the environment in which scholars were nurtured, rather than simply the teachings of particular *faqih*.

The strongest evidence for a direct causal connection between Baqir as-Sadr's activist ideology and Lebanese clerical activity, relies largely on the life of his cousin Musa as-Sadr. This is a credible link to draw, not only because of the family connection, but also because of the legacy Musa as-Sadr left to other scholars who were to be inspired by his actions. He created a political role for himself, albeit quietly at first, almost immediately from the time he arrived from Najaf. Naturally, as the first *'alim* to actively cultivate a political role for the clergy in Lebanon, his achievements tend to dwarf those of other activists, hence the view that this activist stance is simply the result of his Najafi connection becomes emphasised.

Lebanon has also been influenced, though to a lesser degree, through its links with Iranian *hawza*, as well as Iraqi. However, the sheer number of clerics prominent in Lebanese politics who studied at Najaf has tended to overshadow the intellectual connections between Lebanese and Iranian *'ulama*; the reputation of Najaf as a centre of juristic excellence (particularly before the execution of Baqir as-Sadr) meant that far fewer Lebanese went to places such as Qum for their juristic education. Consequently, whilst there has been a history of significant political activism by Iran's *'ulama*, it has really only been the implementation of Khumayni's theory of *wilayat al-faqih* that has provided a functional example for some of the Lebanese *'ulama* (most notably Hizbullah) to aspire to. Even so, certain elements of the Lebanese *'ulama* dispute Khumayni's view of Shi'a political activism; furthermore, his notion of *wilayat* faces significant practical limitations in a multi-confessional society such as Lebanon. The Najafi conception of the *'ulama's* political role, being less prescriptive than Khumayni's Iranian model, may also explain why it has had more influence in Lebanon.

To successfully influence Lebanese politics, a model of governance must first be acceptable to Lebanese society. Based on this criterion, the Shi'a *'ulama* have enjoyed considerable political success following the groundbreaking achievements of Musa as-Sadr. Indeed, the *'ulama* have been instrumental in providing a communal voice that allows the clerics to influence national politics. Their success has been due to a combination of factors. Leaders of the stature of Musa as-Sadr, Fadlallah and Nasrallah have created an environment in which the *'ulama* are able to articulate the political demands of their community as well as provide it with practical assistance through charitable institutions. In the cases of as-Sadr and Nasrallah in particular, we find the *'ulama* using their juristic qualifications and oratorical skills to motivate large groups of their co-religionists. At the same time, the freedom of political expression available to Shi'a activists in Lebanon has given the *'ulama* the ability to establish and sustain politically active Shi'a organisations. This relatively liberal atmosphere has meant that Lebanese clerics have had the freedom to modify the more extreme schools of Shi'a activist political thought to accommodate the realities of Lebanese society; even the clerics of

Hizbullah have publicly modified their views about establishing an Islamic state in Lebanon. Nevertheless the *'ulama*, despite their success in establishing themselves politically, remain limited in their ability to advance the political cause of their community any further. All the leading *'ulama* realise that, if the electoral laws are not changed, the community's numerical strength will not translate into political power, hence their capacity to transform the political environment will be negligible. Paradoxically, the higher the *'ulama's* profile is in Shi'a political circles, the more apprehensive the other communal groups are in ceding electoral power to the Shi'a. Musa as-Sadr's communally inclusive approach underlined the fact that he recognised this problem. Despite that, the *'ulama* will continue to act politically in the interests of their community as they have done for the past thirty-five years.

Conclusion

The popular understanding of Shi'a political representation in Lebanon is dominated by images of Hizbullah. This view, which is due largely to the lack of studies into the Shi'a, ignores how diverse the community's political representation is. This book has set out to redress that situation and has sought to broaden the approach taken to examining the Shi'a community's political development. However, any study of this subject can offer only a snapshot of the community's current situation. Such is the nature of Lebanese and regional politics, as well as of the internal and external pressures that continue to influence the community, that the future political direction of the Shi'a remains somewhat unpredictable. Nevertheless, this study should serve to indicate the relative influence that each of the three main threads of Lebanese Shi'a political development will have in the years ahead.

The eighty years since the end of Ottoman rule has been a time of tremendous change for the Shi'a community, and, whilst many of the stimuli that provoked that change affected all Lebanese, some affected the Shi'a alone. Events such as the creation of *Le Grand Liban*, the struggle for independence, the impact of Arab nationalism, the civil war, Syrian intervention, the Israeli invasion, and finally the signing of the Ta'if Accord, have affected all Lebanese and have required of them both national and communal responses. In the case of the Shi'a, however, other issues have also had a heavy impact. The internal and external migrations undertaken by many of the community in response to serious demographic and socio-economic problems, and of course the revolution in Iran, have altered the way many Shi'a view both themselves and their place in the Lebanese polity.

The Shi'a community of today is largely unrecognisable compared to that which was appended to the Mountain to form modern-day Lebanon, yet it would be wrong to describe the changes it underwent as either sudden or incremental. They were instead a combination of the two, reflecting the variety of factors by which the community was affected. For most of the first forty years following the imposition of French mandatory rule, the community functioned politically much as it had done for centuries before. All political activity was the domain of the traditional *zuʿama*. At the same time, socio-economic changes were gradually beginning to have an impact on the community, as remittances from successful *émigré* Shiʿa gave their children access to educational and business opportunities never before available. The attraction of Beirut to agricultural workers from the south seeking higher wages was a manifestation of the same aspirations. The social transformation this caused was more pronounced amongst the Shiʿa than other communities. Historically the poorest group, the Shiʿa populace/community acquired new-found expectations that could not be met by their traditional leaders.

It was this inability to meet the raised expectations of their community that ultimately defeated the traditional *zuʿama*. Defeat, however, has not meant complete political extinction. Vestiges of this traditional form of power still exist, evident from the continued representation of al-Zayn and ʿUsayran families in parliament. These days, however, whilst they remain popular locally, their presence in parliament depends on forming electoral alliances with the major parties in their region. Both families, for example, have reached an accommodation with Amal such that they appear on the party's electoral ticket in return for giving it their support in parliament. Whilst they are still represented politically, it may not be long before they finally disappear off the political map. ʿAli ʿUsayran has even raised the prospect that he may be the last of his line to take a seat in parliament. While they may not survive as a group, the role played by the traditional *zuʿama* has not disappeared entirely. The *wasta* functions they traditionally fulfilled are now performed by others with access to political power, although whether these new centres of power have entirely replaced the traditional *zuʿama* is questionable. Some claim that figures such as Nabih Berri are the *zuʿama* of the twenty-first century, yet there are significant differences between these new political figures and the institution of the *zaʿim*. The most fundamental difference at the moment is that, unlike the traditional *zuʿama*, these new figures do not appear to consider the role hereditary: there is currently no indication that family members are being groomed for political succession.

It is in the emergence of Shiʿa political parties that the community's development is most clearly reflected. The Shiʿa have had a presence in many of Lebanon's political parties from the earliest days; but from the 1960s onwards, parties were attractive to the Shi'a less because they had a particular ideological orientation and more because they served as a focus of Shi'a political discontent with the *status quo*. In the absence of any sectarian alternative, many Shi'a chose to join those parties that proposed the most revolutionary changes to the political system. For this reason many of the radical leftist groups had a large Shi'a membership, yet most of these Shi'a – reflecting their lower socio-economic status within Lebanon – served as party members rather than in key leadership positions.

The emergence of Shi'a political parties has proven to be a watershed in the community's development. Both parties – Amal and Hizbullah – have been electorally successful and they share the same short-term goal of altering the electoral law to better reflect the Shi'a's numerical superiority. Whilst the parties' emergence is in many ways a practical manifestation of the community's movement towards political independence, a dependency of sorts still exists: Amal and Hizbullah both rely on external patrons – Syria and Iran respectively – which restricts their freedom to act. On the national stage, the limitations inherent in the electoral law continue to deny the Shi'a political representation proportional to the size of their community, which consequently constrains their ability to exercise political power. Both Amal and Hizbullah seek to change this peacefully. Yet if this were achieved, the parties might find themselves in serious conflict as they both, for their different purposes, seek the support of the same constituency. The secularist Amal party wants a Shi'a head of state as part of the current political system; Hizbullah on the other hand has never renounced its long-term goal of establishing an Islamic state, even while recognising that Lebanon's multi-confessional character dictates that such a goal must evolve rather than be imposed. Whether this is practicable is debatable; at any rate, the continuing parliamentary and electoral success Hizbullah enjoys indicate that its support within the community is unabated.

Apart from Musa as-Sadr and Muhammad Fadlallah, the role of clerics in the community's political development has not been examined widely. To view this role simply in terms of the founding of the two Shi'a political parties is to miss the extent of the clerics' intellectual and organisational influence. In many ways, they were the harbingers of change for the community. This was certainly the case with Musa as-Sadr. It is also essential when discussing the political influence of the clerics to acknowledge that much of the impetus for their activism came from outside Lebanon and was brought into the country when Lebanese *'ulama* returned from places such as Najaf. The Najafi activist model, as espoused by Muhammad Baqir as-Sadr, certainly found favour with his cousin Musa and with Muhammad Fadlallah; at the same time, Khumayni's concept of *wilayat al-faqih* has been subscribed to by the Hizbullah clerics. There has also been a substantial intellectual contribution from scholars within Lebanon; the likes of Mughniyya, Fadlallah and Shams al-Din have helped to give the community political direction.

Lebanon is also notable for those *'ulama* who have guided the community not through their scholastic achievements but through their oratory and practical leadership qualities. Musa as-Sadr, for instance, understood well his community's frustrated political ambitions and was able to appeal to them; that he is venerated both by Amal and Hizbullah is testimony to this. Hassan Nasrallah, on the other hand, has a more defined constituency and is able to appeal to the followers of Hizbullah whilst still acknowledging his loyalties to Iran. It is this second point, however, that has prevented Nasrallah's message being popular with a wider Lebanese Shi'a audience; someone such as Muhammad Fadlallah, by contrast, with the juristic independence arising from his status as an *'alim*, has not suffered from this problem. Interestingly, *all* the politically-influential scholars discussed in this study have sought to establish a Lebanese-specific, rather than a universal, model to advance their community's interests. They have realised that Lebanon's unique societal make-up precludes the wholesale importation of ideological models from Najaf or Qum.

The region in which the Lebanese Shi'a live, and the diverse range of influences to which they are exposed both from inside and outside the country, will ensure that their future political development reflects that diversity. What is striking about the Shi'a's development from 1920 to 2000 is the degree to which they have undergone a seismic shift both socio-economically and politically. Their traditional way of life, which afforded them little say in the political process, has been replaced by one in which forms of power that had lasted for centuries have been supplanted in the space of forty years. This rate of change reflects the amount of pressure the communal political structure has been under. The result of that pressure – the emergence of two dominant yet distinctly different communal political parties – demonstrates the dynamic tension that exists between those who advocate scholarly, and those who advocate non-scholarly leadership for the community. It is this battle for community support that will determine the immediate political future of Lebanon's Shi'a.

Notes

Notes to Introduction

1   AMAL is Arabic for 'hope' and an acronym of Afwaj al-Muqawama al-Lubnaniyya (Lebanese Resistance Groups).
2   Iliya F. Harik, *Politics and Change in a Traditional Society: Lebanon 1711-1845*, Princeton, Princeton University Press, 1968, p 23.

Notes to Chapter One

1   Sayyid Husain M. Jafri, *The Origins and Early Development of Shi'a Islam*, Beirut, Librarie du Liban, 1979, p 75.
2   Abdulaziz A. Sachedina, *The Just Ruler in Shi'ite Islam*, New York, Oxford University Press, 1988, p 117.
3   Occultation refers to removal from the temporal sphere. The Twelfth Imam, Muhammad al-Mahdi, entered a cave in 874 AD and disappeared, to return in the future to establish the rule of justice just prior to the end of the world.
4   The caliphate had been ceded by 'Ali's eldest son Hassan to Mu'awiya (a cousin of 'Uthman) who had been appointed governor of Syria by the second caliph, 'Umar. It was Mu'awiya's son Yazid who was caliph at the time of Karbala.
5   Jafri, *op cit*, p 211. See also Mahmoud Ayoub, *Redemptive Suffering in Islam: A Study of the Devotional Aspects of Twelver Shi'ism*, The Hague, Mouton Publishers, 1978.
6   Jafri, *op cit*, p 249.
7   Abdulaziz A. Sachedina, 'Activist Shi'ism in Iran, Iraq and Lebanon', in Marty & Appleby (eds) *The Fundamentalism Project* vol 1, Chicago, University of Chicago Press, 1991, p 423.
8   From the followers of the *sunna* (traditions of the Prophet)
9   Sachedina, 'Activist Shi'ism in Iran, Iraq and Lebanon', p 433.
10 Albert Hourani, 'From Jabal 'Amil to Persia', *Bulletin of the School of African and Oriental Studies*, vol 49, 1986, p 133.
11 *Ibid.*
12 Rula Abisaab, 'Shi'ite Beginnings and Scholastic Tradition in Jabal 'Amil in Lebanon', *The Muslim World*, Vol. 89, No. 1, January 1999, p 4.
13 *Ibid*, p 6.
14 Hourani, 'From Jabal 'Amil to Persia', quotes Arab writers of the eleventh and twelfth centuries who note the widespread Shi'a population of Syria.
15 The Fatimid rulers, whilst Shi'a Muslims, were followers of the Isma'ili branch

of the sect, based on their belief that the imamate passed through Ja'far as-Sadiq's son Isma'il and onto his son Muhammad.

16 The Buyids dominated, but retained, the 'Abbasid caliph.
17 Kamal Salibi, *The Modern History of Lebanon*, London, Wiedenfeld and Nicholson, 1965, p xvi.
18 Albert Hourani, *A History of the Arab Peoples*, London, Faber & Faber, 1991, p 41.
19 Abisaab, *op cit*, p 10.
20 Al-Amin, Hassan, *Islamic Shi'ite Encyclopaedia* (vol 1), Beirut, 1968, p 36.
21 G.Wiet, "Ammar", in *Encyclopaedia of Islam*, vol I, Leiden, Netherlands, 1960, p 448.
22 Salibi, *The Modern History of Lebanon*, p xvi.
23 Salibi, *A House of Many Mansions*, London, I.B. Tauris & Co., 1988, p 14.
24 Salibi, *The Modern History of Lebanon*, p xviii.
25 Salibi, *A House of Many Mansions*, p 63.
26 J. Sourdel-Thomine, 'al-Bika", in *Encyclopaedia of Islam*, vol I, Leiden, Netherlands, 1960, p 1214; and M. Lavergne, 'Sur', in *Encyclopaedia of Islam*, vol IX, Leiden, Netherlands, 1995, pp 883-5.
27 Salibi, *A House of Many Mansions*, p 63.
28 *Ibid*, p 65.
29 Engin Deniz Akarli, *The Long Peace: Ottoman Lebanon 1861–1920*, London, I.B.Tauris, 1993, p 10.
30 Michael Hudson, *The Precarious Republic – Political Modernisation in Lebanon*, New York, Random House, 1968, p 19.
31 *Ibid*.
32 Iliya F. Harik 'The Iqta' System in Lebanon: a Comparative Political View', *The Middle East Journal*, vol 19, no 4, p 405.
33 C. Cahen, 'Ikta", in *Encyclopaedia of Islam*, vol III, Leiden, Netherlands, 1971, p 1088.
34 F. Muge-Gocek, 'Multezim', in *Encyclopaedia of Islam*, vol VII, Leiden, Netherlands, 1993, pp 550-1.
35 Harik, *op cit*, p 405.
36 *Ibid*, p 411.
37 *Ibid*, p 408.
38 Akarli, *op cit*, pp. 10-11
39 Albert Hourani, 'Lebanon: the Development of a Political Society' in Binder (ed) *Politics in Lebanon*, New York, John Wiley & Sons, 1966, p 16.
40 Akarli, *op cit*, p 17.
41 The origins of the Harfoush are not known, although they claimed descent from the Arabic Khuza'a tribe.
42 Muhammad Adnan Bakhit, *The Ottoman Province of Damascus in the Sixteenth Century*, Beirut, Librarie du Liban, 1982, p 175.
43 *Ibid*, pp 176-7.
44 *Ibid*, p 113.
45 *Ibid*.
46 Moshe Ma'oz, *Ottoman Reform in Syria and Palestine: 1840–1861*, Oxford, Clarendon Press, 1968, p 112.
47 Samir Khalaf, *Lebanon's Predicament*, New York, Columbia University Press, 1987, p 80.
48 Hourani, in Binder (ed), *op cit*, p 17.

49 Iliya F. Harik, *Politics and Change in a Traditional Society: Lebanon, 1711–1845*, Princeton, Princeton University Press, 1968, pp 31-33.
50 Hourani, in Binder (ed), *op cit*, p 19.
51 William R. Polk, *The Opening of South Lebanon, 1788–1840*, Cambridge Mass., Harvard University Press, 1963, p 40.
52 *Ibid*, p 19.
53 Amnon Cohen, *Palestine in the 18th Century*, Jerusalem, Magnes Press, 1973, p 100.
54 Whilst the reason for the uprising is not given, such rebellions normally resulted from tax disputes.
55 Cohen, *op cit*, p 7.
56 *Ibid*, p 6.
57 Dahir's position was officially that of a *muqata'ji* to the *wali* of Saida (*ibid*, p31), although his political and military power meant that he was reliant on the *wali* only for official sanction for actions that he had already undertaken.
58 *Ibid*, p 17.
59 Fouad Ajami, *The Vanished Imam*, London, I.B. Tauris, 1986, p 53.
60 *Ibid*, p 98.
61 *Ibid*, p 14.
62 Although he does not mention the reason that the 'Amili Shi'a were induced to join Dahir in his dispute with the *wali* of Damacus, Amnon Cohen does note that the *wali's* forces contained his Druze allies (most likely from the Mountain). It should be remembered that it was the Druze who had quelled the Shi'a rebellion against the *wali* of Saida and later been granted control over their areas.
63 Cohen, *op cit*, p 100.
64 *Ibid*, pp 101-2.
65 *Ibid*, pp102-3.
66 Ajami, *op cit*, p 55.
67 *Ibid*, p 56.
68 Cohen, *op cit*, p 102.
69 Clyde G. Hess, Jr. & Herbert L. Bodman, Jr. 'Confessionalism and Feudality in Lebanese Politics', *Middle East Journal*, vol 8, no. 1, Winter 1954, p12.
70 Ussama Makdisi, *The Culture of Sectarianism: Community, History and Violence in 19th Century Ottoman Lebanon*, London, University of California Press, 2000, p 78.
71 Akarli, *op cit*, p 28.
72 The judge would settle disputes amongst his co-religionists, whilst the advisor dealt largely with taxation issues.
73 Abdo Baaklini, *Legislative and Political Development: Lebanon, 1842–1972*, Durham, Duke University Press, 1976, p 45.
74 Aziz Abu-Hamad 'Communal Strife in Lebanon: Ancient Animosities or State Intervention?', *Journal of International Affairs*, vol 49, no 1, Summer 1995, p 235.
75 Makdisi, *op cit*, p 162.
76 *Ibid*.
77 *Ibid*.
78 Akarli, *op cit*, p 83.
79 The sub-district of al-Hirmil did eventually become a *qada'*, and brought with it representation from al-Himadah and al-Husayni families in the Central

Administrative Council.

80 Akarli, *op cit*, p 96.

81 Fuad I. Khuri, 'Sectarian Loyalty Among Rural Migrants in Two Lebanese Suburbs: a Stage Between Family and National Allegiance', Antoun & Harik (eds) *Rural Politics and Social Change in the Middle East*, Bloomington, Indiana University Press, 1972, p 198.

82 *Ibid*, pp 202-3.

83 Hudson, *op cit*, p 37.

84 Elizabeth Picard 'Political Identities and Communal Identities: Shifting Mobilisation Among the Lebanese Shi'a Through Ten Years of War, 1975–1985', in Dennis L.Thompson & Dov Ronen (eds) *Ethnicity, Politics and Development*, Boulder, Lynne Reiner, 1986, p 163.

85 Meir Zamir, *Lebanon's Quest: the Road to Statehood 1926–1939*, London, I.B. Tauris, p 2.

86 Pierre Rondot, *Les Institutions Politiques du Liban: des Communaut'es Traditionelles 'a l'etat Moderne*, Paris, Institut d'etudes de l'Orient Contemporain, 1947, p 66.

87 Helena Cobban, *The Making of Modern Lebanon*, London, Westview Press, 1985, p 65.

88 Rania Maktabi 'The Lebanese Census of 1932 Revisited. Who are the Lebanese?', *British Journal of Middle Eastern Studies*, vol 26, no 2, 1999, p 225.

89 *Ibid*, p 222.

90 *Ibid*, p 236.

91 Farid al-Khazen, *The Communal Pact of National Identities: The Making and Politics of the 1943 National Pact*, Papers on Lebanon no 12, Oxford, Centre for Lebanese Studies, October 1991, p 16.

92 *Ibid*, p 36.

93 *Ibid*, p 59.

94 Didier Bigo, 'The Lebanese Community in the Ivory Coast: a non-Native Network at the Heart of Power', in Hourani & Shehadi (eds) *The Lebanese in the World: a Century of Emigration*, London, I.B.Tauris, 1992, p 511.

95 Neil O.Leighton 'Lebanese Emigration: its Effect on the Political Economy of Sierra Leone', in Hourani & Shehadi (eds), *op cit*, p 581.

96 Augustus Richard Norton, *Amal and the Shi'a: Struggle for the Soul of Lebanon*, Austin, University of Texas Press, 1988, p 23.

97 Barabara C. Aswad 'The Lebanese Muslim Community in Dearborn, Michigan', Hourani & Shehadi (eds), *op cit*, p 177.

98 Samir Khalaf & Per Kongstad 'Urbanization and Urbanism in Beirut: Some Preliminary Results', in L. Carl Brown (ed) *From Madina to Metropolis*, Princeton, Darwin Press, USA, 1973, p 117.

99 Sachedina 'Activist Shi'ism in Iran, Iraq and Lebanon', p 444.

100 Michael Johnson, *Class and Client in Beirut*, London, Ithaca Press, 1986, p 170.

101 Leila Fawaz, *Merchants and Migrants in Nineteenth-Century Beirut*, Cambridge, Mass., Harvard University Press, 1983, p 50.

102 Fuad I.Khuri, 'A Comparative Study of Migration Patterns in Two Lebanese Villages', *Human Organisation*, vol 26, no 4, Winter 1967, p 211.

103 Norton, *op cit*, p 22.

104 This is discussed in detail in Chapter 2.

105 Arnold Hottinger, 'Zu'ama in Historical Perspective', in Binder (ed), *op cit*, p99.

Notes to Chapter Two

1   The origins of the word *za'im* are not clear. One theory is that it comes from the title of a category of Ottoman feudal dignitary who was the holder of a *ziamet*. The historical process, however, shows that it was the other way around. The term *za'im* is known as early as pre-Islamic times in Arabia, in the sense of spokesman/leader, and *zu'ama* is still widely used around the Arab world to mean political leaders in general.

2   Samir Khalaf, *Lebanon's Predicament*, New York, Columbia University Press, 1987, p 80.

3   Albert Hourani, *A History of the Arab Peoples*, London, Faber & Faber, 1991, p 287.

4   Aziz Abu-Hamad, 'Communal Strife in Lebanon: Ancient Animosities or State Intervention?', in *Journal of International Affairs*, vol 49, no 1, Summer, 1995, p 225.

5   Tarif Khalidi 'Shaykh Ahmad 'Arif al-Zayn and *al-'Irfan'*, in Buheiry (ed) *Intellectual Life in the Arab East*, 1890-1939', Beirut, American University of Beirut, 1981, p 121.

6   Majed Halawi, *A Lebanon Defied: Musa al-Sadr and the Shi'a Community*, Boulder, Westview Press, 1992, p 89.

7   Nizar Hamzeh 'Clan Conflicts, Hezbollah and the Lebanese State', *Journal of Social, Political and Economic Studies*, vol 19, no 4, Winter 1994, p 156.

8   I have not been able to find evidence for a similar degree of intricate loyalty arrangements in Jabal 'Amil.

9   Hamzeh, *op cit*, p 155.

10 *Ibid*, p 156.

11 *Ibid*.

12 Cohen, *Palestine in the 18th Century*, Jerusalem, Magnes Press, 1973, p 98.

13 Khalidi, *op cit*, p 119.

14 Albert Hourani, 'From Jabal 'Amil to Persia', *Bulletin of the School of African and Oriental Studies*, vol 49, 1986, p 134.

15 Arnold Hottinger 'Zu'ama' in Historical Perspective', in Binder, Leonard (ed) *Politics in Lebanon*, New York, John Wiley & Sons, 1966, p 88.

16 Khalidi, *op cit*, p 121.

17 Hayat Nabil Osseyran, 'The Shi'ite Leadership of South Lebanon: a Reconsideration', Masters Thesis, American University of Beirut, 1997, p 20.

18 Michael C. Hudson, *The Precarious Republic*, New York, Random House, 1968, p 131.

19 Evelyn Aleene Early, 'The 'Amiliyya Society of Beirut: a Case Study of an Emerging Urban Za'im', Masters Thesis, American University of Beirut, 1971, p 92.

20 R. Hrair Dekmejian, *Patterns of Political Leadership: Egypt, Israel, Lebanon*, New York, State University of New York Press, 1975, p 18.

21 *Ibid*, p 20.

22 Literally 'means', the term in this instance refers to one's ability to financially benefit one's clients by accessing jobs or conducting transactions with the government on their behalf.

23 Meir Zamir, *Lebanon's Quest: the Road to Statehood 1926-1939*, London, I.B.Tauris, 1997, p 47.

24 Hottinger, *op cit*, p 90.

25 *Ibid*, p 93.

26 Michael Johnson, *Class and Client in Beirut*, London, Ithaca Press, 1986, p 65. The other representatives were the Sunni Salim Salam and the Greek Orthodox Michel Sursuq.

27 Zamir, *op cit*, p 4.

28 Fouad Ajami, *op cit*, Ithaca, Cornell University Press, USA, 1987, p 57.

29 Also known organisationally as the Committee of Union and Progress.

30 C. Ernest Dawn, *From Ottomanism to Arabism: Essays on the Origins of Arab Nationalism*, Urbana, University of Illinois Press, 1973, pp 149-50.

31 Antonius names the member as Saleh Haydar, whilst Gelvin states that Yusuf Haydar was a founding member, and that Sa'id Haydar joined later. Gelvin also states that al-Khalil was the architect of the group.

32 George Antonius, *The Arab Awakening*, London, Hamish Hamilton, 1938, p 108.

33 Hottinger, *op cit*, p 92.

34 Bernard Lewis, *The Shaping of the Modern Middle East*, London, Oxford University Press, 1994, p 52.

35 Hottinger, *op cit*, p 93.

36 Osseyran, *op cit*, p 40.

37 Interview with Samir al-Khalil, Sydney, 22 April 2003.

38 Hottinger, *op cit*, p 93.

39 Stephen Hemsley Longrigg, *Syria and Lebanon Under the French Mandate*, London, Oxford University Press, 1958, p 28.

40 James L. Gelvin, *Divided Loyalties: Nationalism and Mass Politics in Syria at the Close of Empire*, London, University of California Press, 1998, p 55.

41 Supported by the British Arab Bureau, such organisations were designed to foster the development of a pro-British Arab nationalism, and support for the Islamic modernists rather than traditionalists.

42 Gelvin, *op cit*, p 71. Gelvin also notes that Sa'id and As'ad Haydar were members who advocated a more heavily politicised Arab Club.

43 Majed Halawi, 'Against the Current: the Political Mobilisation of the Shi'a Community', PhD thesis Columbia University, UMI dissertation services, 1991, p 84.

44 Farid al-Khazen, *The Communal Pact of National Identities: the Making and Politics of the 1943 National Pact*, Papers on Lebanon no. 12, Oxford, Centre for Lebanese Studies, UK, 1991, p 57.

45 Halawi, 'Against the Current: the Political Mobilisation of the Shi'a Community', *loc cit*.

46 Halawi, *A Lebanon Defied*, pp 39-40.

47 Osseyran, *op cit*, p 15.

48 Early, *op cit*, p 23.

49 Gelvin, *op cit*, p 123.

50 *Ibid*, p 124.

51 Raghid Sulh 'Arab Nationalists' Attitudes Towards Greater Lebanon', in Nadim Shehadi & Dana Haffar Mills, *Lebanon: a History of Conflict and Consensus*, London, I.B.Tauris, 1988, p 152.

52 Zamir, *op cit*, p 59.

53 Sulh, *op cit*, p 159.

54 Zamir, *op cit*, p 196.

55 Hani A.Bazzi, 'The Lebanese Executive Between 1943-1963', Masters Thesis, American University of Beirut, p 135.

56 Arnold Hottinger 'Zu'ama and Parties in the Lebanese Crisis of 1958', *The Middle East Journal*, vol 15, no 2, Spring 1961, p 131.

57 United States Consular Dispatch No. 717, June 3, 1922, in Walter L. Browne (ed) *The Political History of Lebanon, 1920-1950*, Salisbury, Documentary Publications, 1976-80.

58 South Lebanon: Fadl al-Fadl, Najib 'Usayran and Yusuf al-Zayn; Biqa': Ahmad Husayni and Ibrahim Haydar.

59 United States Consular Dispatch No. 717.

60 Osseyran, *op cit*, p 21.

61 Zamir, *op cit*, p 134.

62 *Ibid*, p 150.

63 Michael W. Suleiman, *Political Parties in Lebanon: the Challenge of a Fragmented Political Culture*, New York, Ithaca Press, 1967, p 251.

64 *Ibid*, p 257.

65 Halawi, *A Lebanon Defied*, p 85.

66 Osseyran, *op cit*, p 49.

67 Eyal Zisser, *Lebanon: The Challenge of Independence*, London, I.B.Tauris, 2000, p115.

68 Richard Hrair Dekmejian, 'Consociational Democracy in Crisis: the Case of Lebanon', *Comparative Politics*, vol 10, January 1978, p 256.

69 Zisser, *op cit*, p 14.

70 *Ibid*, p 115.

71 The World Today, vol 13, no 6, June 1957, p 263, cited in Zisser, *op cit*.

72 Zisser, *op cit*, p 122.

73 Airgram from American Legation, October 28, 1946, in Browne, *loc cit*.

74 Zisser, *op cit*, p 115.

75 Despatch No 59 from the American Legation at Beirut, April 30, 1947, in Browne, *loc cit*.

76 *Ibid*.

77 Zisser, *op cit*, p 203.

78 Dekmejian, 'Consociational Democracy in Crisis: the Case of Lebanon', p253.

79 Hottinger 'Zu'ama and Parties in the Lebanese Crisis of 1958', p 131.

80 Clyde G.Hess, Jr & Herbert L.Bodman, Jr 'Confessionalism and Feudality in Lebanese Politics', *Middle East Journal*, vol 8, no 1, Winter 1954, p 23.

81 *Ibid*.

82 The origins of the 1958 political crisis are too complex to go into detail here, but need to be viewed in light of the regional pan-Arab issues of the same period, particularly the Egyptian-Syrian merger to form the United Arab Republic in the same year. An expansive examination of the subject, including primary source documentation, is contained in M.S.Agwani's *The Lebanese Crisis, 1958*, New Delhi, Asia Publishing House, 1965.

83 Hottinger, 'Zu'ama and Parties in the National Crisis of 1958', p 130.

84 Baaklini, *Legislative and Political Development: Lebanon, 1842–1972*, Durham, Duke University Press, 1976, p 148.

85 Airgram from American Legation, July 25, 1947, in Browne, *loc cit*.

86 Kamal Salibi, 'Lebanon Under Fuad Chehab 1958-1964', *Middle Eastern Studies*, vol 2, April, 1966, p 219.

87 Johnson, *op cit*, p 32.

88 Michael Johnson, 'Popular Movements and Primordial Loyalties in Beirut', in Talal Asad & Roger Owen (eds) *Sociology of 'Developing Societies': The Middle East*, New York, Monthly Review Press, 1983, p 192.

89 Kamal Salibi, *Crossroads to Civil War: Lebanon 1958-1976*, London, Ithaca Press, 1976, p 49.

90 *Daily Star*, 14 May 1972.

91 Ajami, *op cit*, p 110.

92 Osseyran, *op cit*, p 83.

93 Interview with Professor Nizar Hamzeh, Beirut, 7 June 2002.

94 *Ibid.*

95 Interview with 'Abdulatif al-Zayn, Beirut, 5 June 2002.

96 *Liban Vote* (http://libanvote.com)

97 Hamzeh, 'Clientalism, Roots and Trends', p 173.

98 The Agreement effectively limited some aspects of Lebanese sovereignty such as airspace control, and limited the role of external parties such as the UN to oversee Israeli activities within Lebanon.

99 *Daily Star*, 31 July 2000.

100 Augustus Richard Norton, *Amal and the Shi'a: Struggle for the Soul of Lebanon*, Austin, University of Texas Press, 1988, p 95.

101 Halim Barakat, *Lebanon in Strife: Student Preludes to the Civil War*, Austin, University of Texas Press, 1977, p xi.

102 Osseyran, *op cit*, p 55.

103 Interview with 'Abdulatif al-Zayn, Beirut, 5 June 2002.

104 *Ibid.*

105 Zisser, *op cit*, p 115.

106 Interview with 'Ali 'Usayran, Beirut, 6 June 2002.

107 As'ad Abu-Khalil, *Historical Dictionary of Lebanon*, Lanham, Scarecrow Press, 1998, p 64.

108 Interview with 'Ali 'Usayran, Beirut, 6 June 2002.

109 Barakat, *loc cit.*

110 *The Daily Star*, 4 December 2001. It is noteworthy that the Jummayil clan has refused to accept the legitimacy of the new leadership.

111 Interview with 'Abdulatif al-Zayn, Beirut, 5 June 2002.

112 Interview with 'Ali 'Usayran, Beirut, 6 June 2002.

Notes to Chapter Three

1   Halim Barakat, 'Social and Political Integration in Lebanon: A Case of Social Mosaic', *Middle East Journal*, vol 27, no 3, Summer 1973, p 311.

2   Ghassan Salamé, *Lebanon's Injured Identities: Who Represents Whom During a Civil War?*, Papers on Lebanon No 2, Oxford, Centre for Lebanese Studies, August 1986, p 2.

3   The Helpers Party was formed by the dominant Beiruti Sunni families (assisted by 'Adnan al-Hakim) in 1936 as a counter to the Maronite political groupings.

4   Meir Zamir, *Lebanon's Quest: The Road to Statehood 1926-1939*, London, I.B.Tauris, 1997, p 35.

5   Michael Hudson, *The Precarious Republic: Political Modernisation in Lebanon*, New York, Random House, 1968, p 137. The French High Commissioner, Henri Ponsot, suspended the Constitution on 9 May 1932. This was in reaction both to the inability of the self-serving Lebanese parliament to undertake necessary political and economic reforms, and to the prospect of the election of a Muslim, Muhammad Jisr, to the position of president. This latter prospect was anathema to both the Christian Lebanese and the mandatory authorities.

6   The 1943 electoral result was Husayni 21, 192 votes to Hajj 17, 845. In 1937 this had been 32, 585 : 4, 346 and in 1947 this was 32, 554 : 5, 305.

7   Michael W. Suleiman, *op cit*, Ithaca, Cornell University Press, 1967, p 255.

8   Hudson, 'Democracy and Social Mobilisation in Lebanese Politics', *Comparative Politics*, vol 1, January 1969, p 252.

9   John P. Entelis, *Pluralism and Party Transformation in Lebanon: al-Kata'ib, 1936-1970*, Leiden, Brill, 1974, p 141.

10 *Ibid*, p 65.

11 *Ibid*, p 114.

12 Michael Johnson, *Class and Client in Beirut*, London, Ithaca Press, 1986, p 170.

13 Entelis, *op cit*, p 123.

14 Camille died in 1987 and was replaced by his son Dani. Dani's brother Duri succeeded him when he was assassinated in 1990 by pro-Samir Ja'ja' forces.

15 Suleiman, *op cit*, p 261.

16 *Ibid*.

17 *Ibid*, p 145.

18 Wade R. Goria, *Sovereignty and Leadership in Lebanon*, London, Ithaca Press, 1985, p 74.

19 Eyal Zisser, *op cit*, London, I.B.Tauris, 2000, p12.

20 A good account of the rise and fall of Sa'adeh can be found in Michael Suleiman's *Political Parties in Lebanon*.

21 Suleiman *op cit*, p 93.

22 Labib Zuwiyya Yamak, *The Syrian Social Nationalist Party: an Ideological Analysis*, Cambridge, Mass., Harvard University Press, 1966, p 82.

23 *Ibid*, p 84.

24 *Ibid*.

25 Suleiman *op cit*, p 95.

26 *Ibid*, p 115.

27 As'ad Abu-Khalil 'The Palestinian-Shi'ite War in Lebanon: an Examination of its Origins', *Third World Affairs*, 1988, p 79.

28 *Ibid*, p 85.

29 Suleiman, *op cit*, p 156. One of the founding members was George Habash, a Palestinian Christian who was later to found the Popular Front for the Liberation of Palestine (PFLP).

30 The Baghdad Pact was a common defence and economic pact between Iraq, Turkey, Pakistan, Iran and Britain. The United States worked closely with the signatories.

31 As'ad Abu-Khalil 'Druze, Sunni and Shiite Political Leadership in Present-Day Lebanon', *Arab Studies Quarterly*, vol 7, no 4, Fall, 1985.

32 Walid W. Kazziha, *Revolutionary Transformation in the Arab World*, London, Charles Knight, 1975, p 32.

33 *Ibid*, p 33.

34 *Ibid*, p 67.

35 Further splits occurred later. In 1968 Ahmad Jibril formed the PFLP-GC (General Command), and in 1969 Nayaf Hawatmeh broke away from the PFLP to form the Democratic Front for the Liberation of Palestine (DFLP).

36 Kazziha, *op cit*, p 99.

37 Halim Barakat, *Lebanon in Strife: Student Preludes to the Civil War*, Austin, University of Texas Press, 1977, p 126.

38 *Ibid*, p 62.

39 Gordon H.Torrey & John F.Devlin 'Arab Socialism', *Journal of International Affairs*, vol XIX, no 1, 1965, p 50.

40 Suleiman *op cit*, p 145.

41 John F. Devlin, *The Ba'th Party: a History from its Origins to 1966*, Stanford, Hoover Institution Press, 1976, p 110.

42 *Ibid*, p 341.

43 Suleiman, *op cit*, p 126.

44 Goria, *op cit*, p 179.

45 Walter Z. Laqueur, *Communism and Nationalism in the Middle East*, London, Routledge & Kegan Paul, 1956, p 141.

46 Michael W. Suleiman, 'The Lebanese Communist Party', *Middle Eastern Studies*, no 2, January 1967, p 146.

47 Author's interview with Sa'dlallah Mazra'ani, Deputy Secretary-General of the Lebanese Communist Party, Beirut, 6 June 2002.

48 Tareq Y. & Jacqueline S. Ismael, *The Communist Movement in Syria and Lebanon*, Gainesville, University Press of Florida, 1998, p 87.

49 Augustus Richard Norton, *Amal and the Shi'a: Struggle for the Soul of Lebanon*, Austin, University of Texas Press, 1988, p 35.

50 Johnson, *op cit*, p 172.

51 Salame, *op cit*, p 12.

52 Johnson, *op cit*, p 172.

53 *The Daily Star*, 6 September 2001.

54 Majed Halawi 'Against the Current: the Political Mobilisation of the Shi'a Community in Lebanon', p 157.

55 Kazziha, *op cit*, p 99.

56 Ibrahim was also vice-president of the Lebanese National Movement between 1974 and 1983.

57 Author's interview with Sa'dlallah Mazra'ani.

58 Abu-Khalil, 'Ideology and Practice of a Revolutionary Marxist-Leninist Party: the Socialist Arab Action Party – Lebanon', Masters Thesis, American

University of Beirut, May 1983, p 32.

59 *Ibid*, p 91.
60 Hudson, *op cit*, p 184.
61 Nazih Richani, *Dilemmas of Democracy and Political Parties in Sectarian Societies: the Case of the PSP of Lebanon 1949-1996*, New York, St Martin's Press, 1998, p 80.
62 *Ibid*, p 69.
63 *Ibid*, p 50.
64 *Ibid*, p 71.
65 Kamal A.Beyoghlow 'Lebanon's New Leaders: Militias in Politics', *Journal of South Asian and Middle Eastern Studies*, vol XII, no 3, Spring 1989 p 33.
66 Norton, *op cit*, p 50.
67 The Libyans claim that he collected his luggage in Rome after a flight from Libya, but most observers believe that he disappeared whilst in Libya.
68 *The Charter of the Amal Movement*, Beirut, n.d.
69 *Ibid*.
70 *Ibid*.
71 Norton, *op cit*, p 76. The translation Norton uses is courtesy of the Foreign Broadcast Information Service – it has been argued that the use of the English word 'integration' may be better read as 'complementary', given that Berri is unlikely to have advocated complete political integration with Lebanon's neighbour.
72 Abu-Khalil 'Druze, Sunni and Shiite Political Leadership in Present-Day Lebanon', p 49.
73 Ghaddar was subsequently suspended from Amal for his advocacy of this position.
74 Abu-Khalil, 'Druze, Sunni and Shiite Political Leadership in Present-Day Lebanon', p 48.
75 William W. Harris, 'Lebanon', in *Middle East Contemporary Survey 1988*, vol XII, Boulder, Westview , 1990, p 517.
76 *Ibid*.
77 *Ibid*.
78 Shaul Bakhash, *The Reign of the Ayatollahs: Iran and the Islamic Revolution*, London, Counterpoint, 1986, p 235.
79 Interview with Shaykh Hassan Nasrallah, *Middle East Insight*, May-August 1996, p 38.
80 Ali Rahnema & Farhad Nomani, *The Secular Miracle: Religion, Politics and Economic Policy in Iran*, London, Zed Books Ltd, 1990, p 172.
81 Interview with Shaykh Hassan Nasrallah, *op cit*, pp 38-9.
82 Text of 'Hizbullah's Open Letter to the Downtrodden of Lebanon and the World', translated in Norton, *Amal and the Shi'a*, p 167.
83 *Ibid*.
84 *Ibid*.
85 Tareq Y. & Jacqueline S. Ismael, *op cit*, p 118.
86 His term was extended from three to four years and he was accorded a formal position in determining the new Prime Ministers.
87 *The Daily Star*, 30 June 1998.
88 *The Daily Star*, 22 June 1998.
89 *Ibid*.
90 *The Daily Star*, 29 June 1998.
91 Author's interview with Dr. 'Ali Mosmar, Chairman of the Amal Movement's

Foreign Affairs Office, Beirut, 3 June, 2002.

92 Author's interview with Malik Berri, President of AUB Amal Students Party, Beirut, 4 June 2002.

93 *Ibid.*

94 Author's interview with Dr. 'Ali Mosmar.

95 *Ibid.*

96 *Ibid.*

97 Author's interview with Shaykh Hassan Ezzedine, Director of Hizbullah's Media Relations Department, 30 May 2002

98 Norton, *Hizballah of Lebanon: Extremist Ideals vs. Mundane Politics*, New York, Council on Foreign Relations, 1999, p 22.

99 *Ibid*, p 33.

100 Interview with Haytham Mouzahem, *Shu'n al-Awsat 59*, Jan-Feb 1997 quoted in al-Bizri *Islamistes, Parliamentaires et Libanaise*, Beirut, CERMOC, 1999, p 3.

101 Ibrahim as-Sayyid, Minutes of the Council of Deputies (*mahadir majlis an-nuwwab*) 20 March 1993, quoted in *Ibid.*

102 Khodr Tlass, *Ibid.*

103 Author's interview with Shaykh Hassan Ezzedine.

104 *Al-Ahd*, 10 April 1994.

105 Author's interview with Shaykh Hassan Ezzedine.

106 *Ibid.*

107 *Ibid.*

108 Richani, *op cit*, p 116.

109 *Ibid*, p 160.

110 Author's interview with Sa'dlallah Mazra'ani.

111 *Ibid.*

112 *The Daily Star*, 12 July 2000.

113 *The Daily Star*, 25 August 2000.

114 *The Daily Star*, 6 September 2001.

Notes to Chapter 4

1   Abdulaziz A.Sachedina, *The Just Ruler in Shi'ite Islam*, New York, Oxford University Press, 1988, p 55.

2   *Ibid*, p 56.

3   Meir Litvak, *Shi'i Scholars of Nineteenth-Century Iraq: The 'Ulama of Najaf and Karbala*, Cambridge, Cambridge University Press, 1998, p 14.

4   The fifth represents the portion (20%) of annual income that may be paid by Shi'a to the clergy for their upkeep and for personal spiritual and juristic guidance. Originally, the *khums* had been due to the Imam of the time.

5   Litvak *op cit*, p 12.

6   *Ibid*, p 35.

7   Abdulaziz A.Sachedina, 'Activist Shi'ism in Iran, Iraq and Lebanon', in Marty & Appleby (eds), *op cit*, vol 1, Chicago, University of Chicago Press, 1991, p 424.

8   Fouad Ajami, *op cit*, Ithaca, Cornell University Press, 1986, p 193.

9   Graham E. Fuller & Rend Rahim Francke, *The Arab Shi'a: the Forgotten Muslims*, New York, St Martin's Press, 1999, p 15.

10 Albert Hourani 'From Jabal 'Amil to Persia', *Bulletin of the School of African and Oriental Studies*, vol 49, 1986, p 134.

11 Litvak, *op cit*, p 57.

12 Devin J.Stewart 'Notes on the Migration of 'Amili Scholars to Safavid Iran', *Journal of Near Eastern Studies*, vol 55, no 2, 1996, p 93.

13 Fuller & Franke, *op cit*, p 21.

14 Litvak, *op cit*, p 82.

15 Ajami, *op cit*, p 73.

16 Rula Abisaab 'Shi'ite Beginnings and Scholastic Tradition in Jabal 'Amil in Lebanon', *The Muslim World*, vol 89, no 1, January 1999, p 9. The proof of this claim is tenuous at best, Abisaab cites as evidence an elegy in praise of al-Shaykh al-Mufid by the 11th century CE 'Amili poet Abu Muhammad al-Suri.

17 Hourani, *op cit*, p 133.

18 For more detailed information, see J.Pederson, 'al-'Amili', *Encyclopaedia of Islam*, vol I, Brill, Leiden, 1971, p 436.

19 Stewart, *op cit*, p 85.

20 *Ibid*, p 84.

21 Devin J.Stewart, 'The Portrayal of an Academic Rivalry: Najaf and Qum in the Writings and Speeches of Khumayni, 1964-78', in Walbridge (ed), *The Most Learned of the Shi'a: the Institution of the Marja' Taqlid*, London, Oxford University Press, 2001, p 218.

22 Fadil Jamali, 'The Theological Colleges of Najaf', *The Muslim World*, vol L, no 1, January 1960, p 15.

23 John Walbridge, 'Muhammad Baqir al-Sadr: the Search for New Foundations', in Walbridge (ed), *op cit*, p 137. See also Chibli Mallat's article on as-Sadr in John L. Esposito (ed), *Oxford Encyclopaedia of the Modern Islamic World*, New York, Oxford University Press, 1995, pp 450-3.

24 Hanna Batatu, 'Iraq's Underground Shi'a Movements: Characteristics, Causes and Prospects', *The Middle East Journal*, vol 35, no 4, p 579.

25 Talib Aziz, 'Baqir Sadr's Quest for the Marja'iya', in Walbridge (ed), *op cit*, p142.

26 Majed Halawi, *A Lebanon Defied*, p 176.
27 Sachedina 'Ali Shariati: Ideologue of the Iranian Revolution', in Esposito (ed), *Voices of Resurgent Islam*, New York, Oxford University Press, 1983, p 208.
28 Michael M.J. Fischer, 'Imam Khumayni: Four Levels of Understanding', in Esposito (ed), *op cit*, p 159.
29 Shimon Shapira, 'The Origins of Hizballah', *The Jerusalem Quarterly*, no 46, Spring 1988, p 116.
30 Stewart, 'The Portrayal of an Academic Rivalry: Najaf and Qum in the Writings and Speeches of Khumayni, 1964-78', p 223.
31 Fischer, *op cit*, p 157.
32 Ajami, *op cit*, p 194.
33 *Ibid*, p 81.
34 *Ibid*, p 74.
35 Al-Khazen, Farid, *The Communal Pact of National Identities: The Making and Politics of the 1943 National Pact*, Papers on Lebanon no 12, Oxford, Centre for Lebanese Studies, October 1991, p 43.
36 Halawi, *A Lebanon Defied*, p 122.
37 Majid Halawi, 'Against the Current: the Political Mobilisation of the Shi'a Community in Lebanon', p 86.
38 Evelyn Aleene Early 'The 'Amiliyya Society of Beirut: a Case Study of an Emerging Urban Za'im', Masters Thesis, American University of Beirut, 1971, p 37.
39 Ibrahim Farran, 'Two Different Opinions on the Celebration of 'Ashura', quoted in Halawi, *A Lebanon Defied*, p 91.
40 *Ibid*, p 38.
41 Tarif Khalidi, 'Shaykh Ahmad 'Arif al-Zayn and *al-'Irfan*', p 116.
42 *Al-'Irfan* was started by Shaykh Ahmad 'Arif al-Zayn in 1908 and remained in the hands of the al-Zayn family.
43 Khalidi, *op cit*, p 117.
44 His book is entitled *Jurisprudence According to the Five Schools (al-Fiqh 'ala al-Madhahib al-Khamsa)*.
45 Chibli Mallat, *Aspects of Shi'i Thought from the South of Lebanon: Al 'Irfan, Muhammad Jawad Mughniyya, Muhammad Mahdi Shamseddin, Muhammad Husain Fadlallah*, Papers on Lebanon no. 7, Oxford, Centre for Lebanese Studies, 1988, p 8.
46 *Ibid*.
47 *Ibid*, p 19.
48 Muhammad Fadlallah's homepage (www.bayynat.org/www/english/biography/), p 2.
49 *Ibid*, p 4. This should not be confused with the Beirut-based literary journal of the same name.
50 Martin Kramer, 'The Oracle of Hizbullah', in R. Scott Appleby (ed), *Spokesmen for the Despised: Fundamentalist Leaders of the Middle East*, Chicago, University of Chicago Press, 1997, p 93.
51 Kamran Aghaie 'The Karbala Narrative: Shi'i Political Discourse in Modern Iran in the 1960s and 1970s', *Journal of Islamic Studies*, vol 12, no 2, May 2001, p 151.
52 Ajami, *op cit*, p 215.
53 Interview with Shaykh Muhammad Fadlallah, *Journal of Palestine Studies*, vol 25, no 1, Autumn 1995, p 68.
54 Kramer 'The Oracle of Hizbullah', p 156.

55 *Ibid*, p 158.

56 Shaul Bakhash, 'Iran: the Crisis of Legitimacy', *Middle Eastern Lectures*, no 1, Tel Aviv, Moshe Dayan Centre for Middle Eastern & African Studies, 1995, p101. Bakhash has translated the word *wilayat* to mean *vice-regency* rather than *governance.*

57 Judith Miller, 'The Charismatic Islamists', *Middle Eastern Lectures*, no 2, Tel Aviv, Moshe Dayan Centre for Middle Eastern & African Studies, 1997, p 42.

58 Kramer 'The Oracle of Hizbullah', p 129.

59 Bakhash, *op cit*, 109.

60 As'ad Abu-Khalil, 'The Palestinian-Shi'ite War in Lebanon', p 87.

61 Augustus Richard Norton, *Amal and the Shi'a: Struggle for the Soul of Lebanon*, p 63.

62 Kramer 'The Oracle of Hizbullah', p 135.

63 Joseph Olmert 'The Shi'is and the Lebanese State', in Kramer, *Shi'ism, Resistance and Revolution*, Boulder, Westview Press, p 198.

64 Ajami, *op cit*, p 44.

65 *Ibid*, p 42.

66 Halawi, *A Lebanon Defied*, p 126.

67 Ajami, *op cit*, p 33.

68 *Ibid*, p 25. Baqir as-Sadr was married to Musa as-Sadr's sister, Fatima.

69 Halawi, *A Lebanon Defied*, p 126.

70 Raymond Adams, 'Paradoxes of Religious Leadership Amongst the Shi'ites of Lebanon', *MERA (Middle East Research Group in Anthropology) Forum*, vol 6, no 4, Winter 1983, p 10.

71 Halawi, *A Lebanon Defied*, p 135.

72 Moshe Ma'oz, *Asad: the Sphinx of Damascus*, New York, Grove Weidenfeld, 1988, p 151.

73 Norton, *op cit*, p 44.

74 Interview with Shaykh Hassan Nasrallah, *Al-Ahram Weekly*, 30 Jul-5 August 1998.

75 *Ibid*.

76 *Ibid*.

77 *The Daily Star*, 22 January 2002.

78 Ghassan Salame 'Lebanon's Injured Identities: Who represents Whom During a Civil War?', Papers on Lebanon No. 2, Oxford, Centre for Lebanese Studies, 1986, p 10.

79 One of his sons was killed by the Israelis while he was on operations with Hizbullah.

80 Majed Halawi, 'Against the Current', p 216.

81 Norton, *op cit*, p 44.

82 Halawi, *A Lebanon Defied*, p 154.

83 *Ibid*.

84 Norton, *op cit*, p 92.

85 *Ibid*, p 140.

86 *Civil Society and Governance: a Mapping of Civil Society and Its Connection with Governance*, Beirut, Lebanese Centre for Policy Studies, January 1999, p 5.

87 *Ibid*.

88 Batatu, *op cit*, p 588.

89 Amatzia Baram, 'Two Roads to Revolutionary Shi'ite Fundamentalism in Iraq', *The Fundamentalism Project*, Chicago, University of Chicago Press, 1991,

vol 4 pp 532-3.

90 *Ibid*, p 536.

91 Shapira, *op cit*, p 127.

92 Author's interview with Prof Nizar Hamzeh, American University of Beirut, 7 June 2002.

93 Haleh Vaziri 'Iran's Involvement in Lebanon: Polarisation and Radicalisation of Militant Islamic Movements', *Journal of South Asian and Middle Eastern Studies*, vol XVI, no 2, Winter 1992, p 5.

94 Shapira, *op cit*, p 126.

Index

DATE DUE